"I will get right to the point: this is

psychoanalytic psychotherapy that I have ever read, bar none. There are many

introductory texts, but none that I have read achieves this level of intimacy with the reader in the process of assisting him or her in the difficult work of becoming a psychoanalytic psychotherapist. My scribblings in the margins of the book are a response to the depth of understanding of the ideas Quatman discusses and to the intelligence and compassion reflected in her accounts of her own clinical experience, but I realize only after finishing reading the book that most of all I stand in awe and appreciation of the unpretentious, unselfconscious wisdom that weaves through every page. To quote from Dr. Quatman's book, she is first and foremost concerned with helping the reader acquire a "way of being," "a certain readiness" that is involved in becoming a psychotherapist. She talks about what something means when "we stop to think about"—something that is far more easily said than done. And perhaps most surprising to me, the book is filled with "joy"—a sense of delight in talking about what matters most: how to help someone with what each patient most fundamentally wants and needs: "They want more *of* themselves and *for* themselves in their lives." It is also what each psychotherapist most wants and needs in their lives as therapists, and it is precisely this that Dr. Quatman's book so thoroughly and profoundly succeeds in providing. Another source—a principal source—of the joy of reading this book is in the writing. Again, I have never read an introductory text that is written with the informal, highly personal, but never saccharine, voice that one encounters and comes to look forward to spending time with as one reads and re-reads this extraordinary work."

—*Thomas H. Ogden, M.D.*

ESSENTIAL PSYCHODYNAMIC PSYCHOTHERAPY

Essential Psychodynamic Psychotherapy: An Acquired Art provides an essential, accessible grounding in current psychodynamic theory and practice for a wide range of readers. For trainees, it offers a very useful toolset to help them make the transition from purely theoretical training to the uncharted territory of clinical practice. For more seasoned therapists and those seeking to deepen their understanding of psychodynamic therapy, it provides conceptual clarity, and may also serve as a stepping-stone to more complex and denser psychoanalytic works written for advanced clinicians.

Essential Psychodynamic Psychotherapy: An Acquired Art is an introduction to how to think and work psychodynamically. It is written primarily for those training at a postgraduate level in psychoanalysis and psychodynamic psychotherapy, but reaches well beyond that audience. It is grounded in contemporary psychoanalytic theory, drawing on the work of Winnicott, Bion, and Ogden, all of whom are pivotal in current psychodynamic thought and practice. It also integrates attachment theory and research, and includes fresh contributions from neuropsychological research.

The voice of the book is honest and intimate. The tone is practical. It is written with a clear-minded understanding of contemporary psychodynamic theory that allows the new therapist to access the deepest and richest parts of the therapy itself. It translates many of the key theoretical tenets of psychodynamic psychotherapy, giving the reader a clear (but non-formulaic) guide as to how to handle the contours of any analytic session; how to open one's perceptual and emotional apertures as a clinician; how to work in and understand "the relationship"; and how to work with the most common intra- and interpersonal problems patients present. This publication will be a valuable guide for new analysts and therapists, and also for those seeking to understand what the world of psychodynamic therapy may hold for them, no matter where they are in their clinical careers.

Teri Quatman is an Associate Professor of Counseling Psychology in the Graduate Department of Counseling Psychology at Santa Clara University. She earned her Ph.D. from Stanford University in 1990, and has studied, practiced, and taught psychodynamic psychotherapy to graduate students for the past 25 years.

ESSENTIAL PSYCHODYNAMIC PSYCHOTHERAPY

An Acquired Art

Teri Quatman

Routledge
Taylor & Francis Group

LONDON AND NEW YORK

First published 2015
by Routledge
27 Church Road, Hove, East Sussex, BN3 2FA

and by Routledge
711 Third Avenue, New York, NY 10017

Routledge is an imprint of the Taylor & Francis Group, an informa business

British Library Cataloguing in Publication Data
A catalogue record for this book is available from the British Library

Library of Congress Cataloging in Publication Data
Quatman, Teri.
Essential psychodynamic psychotherapy : an acquired art / Teri Quatman.
pages cm
Includes bibliographical references and index.
1. Psychodynamic psychotherapy. I. Title.
RC489.P72Q83 2015
616.89'14--dc23
2014033803

ISBN: 978-1-138-80872-0 (hbk)
ISBN: 978-1-138-80873-7 (pbk)
ISBN: 978-1-315-75009-5 (ebk)

Typeset in Bembo
by Saxon Graphics Ltd, Derby

CONTENTS

FIGURES

PREFACE

I dedicate this book to my students. It is they who have inspired my thoughts; it is they who have, without their direct knowledge, co-created this work. I think of the two thousand plus masters' students I've encountered in classrooms over time, students embarking upon their program of study in Counseling Psychology, students whose goal it was simply to become the best clinician/therapist they could be. I think of myself as I started the same trek in the late 1970s. Naïve to the field in every possible way, I stepped forward with a desire that I might one day grow to be an effective psychotherapist.

As I pursued my education in the late 1970s and throughout the 1980s—one degree followed by the next, and then the next, and the next—I kept having the nagging feeling that while I was piling up degrees, I felt in no way ready to be a therapist. I didn't feel that I had the wisdom, the life experience, the—I didn't know what it was, the, *the way of being*—to be the kind of therapist I'd wanted to become. Over time, and given the training I had received, I felt that I had to redefine my vision of what being a therapist might be in the direction of brief and targeted inventions. These were the halcyon days of the behavioral and cognitive therapies. I had, after all, learned how to de-condition phobic disorders, to reframe depressive disorders, to structure behavioral interventions for acting-out teens. But for all I knew how to *do*, I still didn't *feel* like a *therapist*.

What I did not know, and what very often my students do not know, was that becoming the kind of therapist I wanted to be would require a personal transformation. It would require that I jettison my certainties, re-visit my biases, retract many of my tightly-held beliefs, and walk forward into a great deal of darkness at first. It would also mean (as a prerequisite) that I engage in the process of therapy for myself. This came as a surprise and shock to me, as I had cultivated the self-perception of being a together and well-integrated human being, having come from a stable and loving-enough family, and having felt no need for personal therapy. What I could not know as a beginner was that these self-perceptions themselves created a kind of psychic impermeability that would stand in the way of my becoming the kind of therapist I truly wanted to be.

One evening as I was teaching a class on theories of psychotherapy, a student came to me at break. She said, "You like this stuff!" (referring to my lecture on behavioral interventions). "Yes!" I said, with enthusiasm, "I like this stuff!" She went further, "Can I ask why?" "Sure," I said, "because it *works!*" She replied thoughtfully, "That's strange, because the person I have come to know as my instructor in this class would need more than that." With that rather cryptic comment the student left, but her comment stayed. It would stay and stay, confronting me with my own well-buried misgivings, and reminding me of my original motivation for wanting to be a therapist. I had wanted to develop a deep understanding of other humans and myself; I had wanted to be able to help others see what was underneath their stuckness, their self-sabotages, their inability to live their lives fully.

Thus began my journey into psychodynamic psychotherapy. Piqued by my student's comment, and placed in my internship under the supervision of a highly intuitive psychodynamic supervisor, I began what has become a very long and arduous trek. I was handed Althea Horner's (1984) *Object Relations and the Developing Ego in Therapy*. I found it both intriguing and inscrutable. The next months and years were to take me onto the formerly vilified territory of Freud (whom I had dismissed without ever having really read) and his past and present-day successors. They were known to me initially as Object Relations therapists, but soon broadened to include the multiple worlds of Psychoanalytic and Psychodynamic Psychotherapies. The ensuing time would also include multiple therapies for myself. It would include months stretching into years of practicing a therapy that I couldn't quite visualize and had no way to judge the effectiveness of. It was, for a very long time, a dimly-lit journey.

I sit at my computer this morning not because of the length of my journey but because of its lighting. I write because of my commitment to education and to the quest to make the first steps of the psychodynamic journey less elusive and less inscrutable to my students than they were to me. I write with a particular gratitude to Tom Ogden, who, through the generosity of his mentoring, the clarity of his thinking and painstakingness of his writing, has deepened my work and brightened my path considerably.

In the following pages, I explain some of the basics of the *practice* of psychodynamic psychotherapy (a term which will proxy for Object Relations, Psychoanalysis, and Psychoanalytic Psychotherapies). Our field is theory-intense, but few authors attempt to explain the basics of practice to the beginning/progressing therapist. I dedicate this work to the now thousands of students who have entered my classroom quarter by quarter, wanting to have the tools of insight and effectiveness without knowing how to name their quest. I write because of the terribly long uptime it took to decipher the beginners' materials of the psychodynamic trade. I write to and for my students. I hope this work serves to make the journey brighter for them, as their questions and queries along the way have made my life brighter for me.

ACKNOWLEDGMENTS

I wish to acknowledge the web of support—the village—it takes for us to live our lives and to contribute what we can. There are my mentors along the path who have allowed me the grace of learning this acquired art. There are my patients who have allowed me to practice, to make mistakes and missteps, and to grow along with them. There are the faculty and students of Santa Clara University, who have honored my passion to be alive to this clinical art, and to render it for students for these past 22 years. There are the members of my family and close friends who helped me through the cancer that came in the midst of this project and threatened to take me and it down two years ago.

There are particular people, of course, who helped midwife this work, who encouraged and listened and read and critiqued along the way, too many to name. But I want to extend special thanks to my consultation group members who listened to the emerging chapters of this work out loud, week by week, and told me the truth when they felt lost in it. I want to thank Dr. Bob Fisher, whose weekly generosity over coffee helped me to think around clinical corners and down new pathways. I want to thank my initial readers—Susan Martin, Connie Swanson, Julie Smith—friends, insightful therapists, writers all, who kept me encouraged enough to keep going. I want to thank Dr. Tom Ogden, whose mentorship and generosity of spirit has shaped me profoundly. I want to thank my artist and borrowed son, Tim Lamb, who brought his own generosity and considerable talent to the finish of this work. Finally, I want to give special thanks to Dr. Mardy Ireland, who was my friend and psychodynamic plumb-line throughout this process, encouraging the project to begin with, and then keeping me true to both concept and practice as it emerged.

I am indebted to so many hands and so many voices. I now share with them the pleasure of completion.

Academic Acknowledgments

Excerpt from *Requiem for a Nun* by William Faulkner appears courtesy of Penguin Random House.

Excerpt from *Mending Wall* from the book THE POETRY OF ROBERT FROST edited by Edward Connery Lathem. Copyright © 1930, 1939, 1969, copyright © 1958, copyright © 1967 by Leslie Frost Ballantine. Reprinted by permission of Henry Holt and Company, LLC. All rights reserved.

Excerpt from "Harlem (2)" from *The Collected Poems Of Langston Hughes* by Langston Hughes, edited by Arnold Rampersad with David Roessel, Associate Editor, copyright © 1994 by the Estate of Langston Hughes. Used by permission of Alfred A. Knopf, an imprint of the Knopf Doubleday Publishing Group, a division of Random House LLC. All rights reserved.

1

AN ACQUIRED ART

When I was assigned my first client in graduate school—my first adult client who had made an appointment and was going to meet with me for an hour of psychotherapy—I was *excited*. This would be *real* therapy; not the *ad hoc* school counseling kind I had done along the way as a high school teacher or middle school/high school counselor, not the kind I had done in graduate school classes when I'd paired up and practiced a counseling skill with a classmate. This was the real deal. I was indeed excited.

But as the *idea* of it crept inexorably toward the *reality* of it, I began to have uncertain feelings in my gut. By the time I had one more hour before our therapy meeting, I was beside myself with anxiety. I remember I was sitting in a graduate Career Development seminar and shot a note to my friend Pat, who was sitting next to me. Pat had been an experienced clinical social worker before he joined our doctoral program. "What do I *do*?" was my anxious question. In that moment I really had no idea, despite having sat with scores of students one-on-one as a counselor-in-training, and having conducted dozens of structured interviews for those seeking to qualify for an anxiety disorders study across campus. My program had somehow certified me at this point as being ready to see this real client for just plain therapy—the 50-minute kind. Pat leaned in and whispered, "You listen to him … Just listen to him. And at the end tell him, 'I think I can help you.' He'll be more nervous than you are." Not possible, I thought privately.

Of course, I did meet with that first client. I did listen to his story about a failed marriage in the distant past and its impact on his current relationship. I did tell him I thought I could help him. I do even think I remember meeting with him for a second appointment. Beyond that, my memory fades, or was it that he did not return? The anxious feelings return as I write the story.

Acquiring the art of psychodynamic therapy is a long, arduous process fraught with scary moments: first times, indecipherable concepts, people who can't seem to change, the gap between how we interact with a client or patient and the way we imagine a more mature therapist would, the wish to steer it down a more meaningful track, the wondering where that would be and how we might get there.

We are certified as ready to start practicing at some point, and most of us hope we'll be good at it because we *thought* we would be, or we *hoped* we would—that's why we went through all the trouble and training in the first place. But then, we get in the room with the patient and it seems at times that everything we think we have studied or known exits out the door.

In this book I will be attempting to speak about an acquired art. *Acquired*, because it's something more than studied or even practiced. It comes upon you gradually as you position yourself to take it in and practice what you know to practice. And then there is the inexorable element of time. An acquired art takes a long time, because the various complexities of it require a readiness within us even to identify them as desired elements.

Rather than a practiced art, an acquired art is more like an internalized state. We are taught, we read, we think, we hear our colleagues present, we identify supervisors who do the thing we want to be able to do, we try to copy them. But until a certain readiness is born within us, all the copying in the world does not seem to budge us forward one bit. It truly takes an act of faith to keep going in the pursuit of an acquired art.

This book addresses itself to the very elusive and hard-to-acquire art called psychodynamic psychotherapy. It especially attempts to address the front end of this acquisition process, because this is the time when we feel most lost, most fraudulent, most discouraged, and most seemingly unable to benefit from anything we hear or read about along the way. We keep going, but if we're honest with ourselves, for most of us, it is with a deep sense of doubt that we will ever become the kind of therapist we see (or can't even imagine) in our mind's eye.

I suppose it is not unlike acquiring a truly fine touch as a musician. The beauty will ultimately reside in the nuance, but one has to live for a long time with garish approximations of that nuance, and keep pressing with what one author called "a long obedience in the same direction" (Peterson, 1980). Our mentors, our fellow students, and ultimately our patients give us just enough encouragement along the way for us to bear with our own not-knowings, and to keep on keeping on. For my part, I have only ever observed my own growth as a therapist in retrospect, and that, probably in five-year chunks. Furthermore, I didn't start to make sense to myself as a therapist for the first ten years. It's a long time to stay at something (and even to be paid for doing something) that one doesn't truly understand. But that is our path.

So I will start as close to the beginning as I possibly can, and move forward only when I feel I've said something clearly. This may mean that I give you some of the dryer stuff first, but do try to stay with it. Foundations are never sexy, but the whole rest of the house depends on them. So let's start at the beginning.

The Art of What?

The art of *what*? What are we supposed to be attempting to do or have happen when we "sit with" or "listen to" a client or patient? In this moment, with this person, in this room, what? What is the goal? What is the process? And most importantly, what is the point?

The answer is: it depends. That's a really unsatisfying answer, but it actually does depend. It depends on where we're headed. While it may be true that as psychotherapists our main tool is to listen to the other, absent some orienting compass to tell us where we're going and what our listening might be accomplishing, it can feel like bobbing in an inner tube in the middle of the ocean: too cold, too directionless, ultimately not getting us anywhere, and most certainly not worth being paid to do!

So for a few minutes, let's stand back and consider what is, or might be, the intended goal of our listening, then we can talk about the process of it (and the point of it).

What's the Goal?

The goal of psychotherapy can be thought about in its broadest terms as being oriented toward one of two outcomes: either toward alleviating human suffering or toward promoting human growth (although most therapies do some of both). In general, it is the first—the suffering part—that brings people to a therapist to begin with. And this—suffering part—comes as a surprise and a shock to many new therapists. It's different from what we may have envisioned when we came to the field.

Perhaps we were the confidants of our friends or mothers or fathers as younger people. People came to us with their problems, with their secrets. We learned that we were good listeners, and that they felt safe with us. They opened up to us. That felt good. We found ourselves giving what we thought was wise advice. That felt good. We were valued for our skill, and enjoyed doing it. We decided we wanted to be paid for this thing we did with such success. Good plan.

But when we begin the professional practice of psychotherapy, most of us encounter human suffering well beyond the scope or severity of our experience with friends and relatives. The range of suffering that presents in a therapist's office is enormous; to a new therapist (and sometimes to an old therapist) it is overwhelming. The suffering has many stripes. It can be circumscribed, such as the inability to finish a school degree or the desire to lose weight. It can be global ("I just feel lost in my life"). It can focus on emotions like sadness, guilt, anger, disgust, fear, shame, grief, etc.; or even positive ones ("I get so full of joy and excitement that I spend piles of money all at once"), or dysregulated ones ("I get set off, and then I have to cut myself in order to feel better"). The suffering can focus on behaviors ("I have to check the locks on my house seven times before I can leave" or "I find myself raging at my second child"). It can be intrapersonal ("I'm depressed," "I'm anxious") or interpersonal ("I've never really trusted anyone" or "I feel hated at work"). It can focus on the past (for example, having lived through traumatizing events) or the present ("My marriage is falling apart") or the future ("I have no hope for my life"). The list is endless.

And the examples I've given here, as you may well know by now, are quite sanitized. Some of what we see and listen to is beyond heartbreaking—young adolescents beginning to devolve into psychoticism—hearing voices and sealing off their bedrooms with layers of tin foil; children whose parent has punished them by killing their beloved pet. If we stop to think about it, the suffering that people bring into our counseling room is far more than we bargained for, and is often deeply traumatizing to us. The expectation that we might be able to help in many moments exceeds our bandwidth entirely.

Some therapies focus exclusively on the alleviation of such suffering. This would certainly seem to be a big enough task! But other therapies (i.e., the psychodynamic spectrum) go a step beyond that goal and focus on the life potential inherent in people beyond and underlying their points of suffering. This focus tends to be shifted slightly toward the *person* carrying the symptom rather than the *symptom* itself. This is not to say that the point of suffering is ignored, but it is contextualized within the personality and history of the person expressing this hurt in this particular way.

Let me give you an example of how this might look. A young man came to me some years back because of his wife's concern that he was "losing it" with his children. While he did not feel that *he* was "suffering" from this, the rest of the family was. And he was at risk of experiencing the loss of his marriage and family over this issue. My task as therapist was to help alleviate the suffering in the system.

But as I listened to this young man for several sessions, what struck me about him was his lostness *in general*. He not only "lost it" in particular moments with his children, he seemed to have "lost it" in his life in general. He seemed mechanized with me—dutiful, pasty, routinized, monotonic, depressed—missing the warm glow of interpersonal spontaneity and vitality that makes us most human.

As I experienced this man's *absence*, the focus of the therapy shifted from the circumscribed symptom of his "losing it" with his children to the more general goal of his more fully inhabiting his own life as a human being. The work included the effort to understand his absence: how and why it came to be, what it felt like (physically and emotionally) to be absent with his children, with his wife, with himself, and in his time with me; what it stirred in him to talk about these things with me, and so on.

Over time, the "losing it" with his children subsided. But, as important as this was, the therapy was about much more than this "presenting" symptom. By the end of it, this young man had became much more able to be present in all these contexts, and to understand the forces that had driven him so far from himself that he had gone missing from his own life. (We will get to the hows and whats of such a therapy in the upcoming chapters.)

Different Goals: Different Looks

To be clear, the range of therapies we learn about in school—behavioral through psychodynamic—do share one theme common to all: the effort to change something about a person. And it's worth noting at this point that whatever your theoretical orientation, changing something about a human is, in and of itself, a rather lofty aspiration. We humans are *junkies* for the emotionally familiar. While in a constant change trajectory related to our own physical growth and aging process, we are profoundly wedded to and soothed by the power of the familiar. So without our willing it, we often resist change (even for the better) with a resoluteness that borders on fanaticism (and wanders into the unconscious).

But beyond what the various therapies share in common, they differ substantially in their look and feel. Some are more oriented toward the symptom, are time-limited and focused, and usually feature a rather active stance on the part of the therapist (think behavioral and cognitive behavioral therapies here). Some therapies are more oriented toward the patient or client's more global personal growth, tend to be longer-term and more multi-focal, and usually feature a more non-directive style from the therapist (think psychodynamic psychotherapies here, as well as Rogerian, Gestalt, Jungian, and Existential, among others).

The process of therapy, at least theoretically, should follow from the goal. This is precisely why we study different "schools" of therapy—because there are legitimately different ways to a) define the problem and b) go about its solution in psychotherapy. (This, of course, presents a problem to the naïve seeker of psychotherapy who just wants to see a therapist. These various theoretical nuances make no difference to and indeed are invisible to someone who is seeking a therapist because they have lost a loved one or find themselves overwhelmed with anxiety or have decided they need help with their obesity or are alarmed with how they find themselves treating their children, or…). But that very obvious flaw in the user-end of clinical practice aside, how we as practitioners orient ourselves theoretically will determine where we swim in our inner tube, at what pace, and toward what shore.

Ultimately, since this is a book about psychodynamic process and technique, we will focus there in the remaining chapters. But understanding the legitimacy of other therapeutic approaches helps us to respect rather than to dismiss other therapies, and to know what might be appropriate for a particular client or patient. So let me talk for just a few minutes about several main points along the spectrum of psychotherapies, because where we position on this spectrum determines what we'll be aiming at and doing as a psychotherapist.

Symptom-Focused Therapies

On one end of the spectrum of therapies are the behavioral therapies. If you've potty trained an infant or rewarded a puppy for the "right" behavior, you've no doubt employed the techniques of behavioral therapy—perhaps unawares.

Behavioral therapies aim to change a targeted behavior, such as stopping smoking or increasing behavioral compliance in some way. Virtually anything visible about a human—or mammals in general (animal lovers do this intuitively)—can be subdivided into discrete behavioral entities. So the art and genius of the behavioral therapies lies in this subdividing and conquering analysis. Necessarily, the more amorphous the complaint, the more a behavioral therapist must use a contraction of the target as a proxy for the larger or more amorphous target.

Behavioral therapies are powerful for what they aim at: discrete behavior change. We experienced their power in a group program we set up in the schools for bullying and picked-on middle-schoolers in Southern California. We gathered the teacher-identified twenty-five "worst" kids in the school for one hour per week. We sat them in a large circle and used a curriculum to teach them about assertive, aggressive (bullying), and passive (doormat) behaviors, with much student participation. We observed the kids during the group time, and circulated among them dispensing white (appropriate), red (aggressive), and blue (passive) poker chips, in response to their identifiable behaviors in the group. The chips had positive and negative values, respectively. We also gave teachers a limited number of white chips (only) with instructions on their use. The chips would be reconciled at each session's end, and could be "cashed in" during the school week for certain valued targets, like being able to cut to the front of the food line at lunch ("butt passes"), or being able to be exchanged for ice creams at the cafeteria. Pretty soon, the teens caught onto the game and began to adopt appropriately assertive behaviors inside and outside the group. By the end of the year, the "Social Behavior Group" had become quite high-status among students, and teachers were blown away at the positive changes wrought in members of the group.

Let me offer a quick digression here on a common misapprehension of behaviorism. It is *not* about punishment. There was a reason we only gave *white* (reward) chips to teachers. Parents and teachers often naïvely orient themselves toward meting out punishments for the crimes of children. Time outs, grounding, loss of internet privileges, loss of dessert, change in curfew, canceling the field trip. It's endless, and all well intentioned. What gets lost in the shuffle is the relative power of *positive* reinforcement (think white chips and butt passes) versus the relative impotence of narrow and stimulus-dependent punishment.

Example: when did you last speed on the freeway? When there was no policeman visible, right? So the threat of getting a ticket didn't really extinguish your speeding behavior. The threat of punishment (police car on the side of the road) had to be present and proximate to get its desired effect. Absent constant monitoring, we all game the system. Even when we are ticketed, we go back to our former-surveillance-driven speeding behaviors quite soon. Why? Because punishment requires that the punisher catch the behavior. So get this! All the moments *of not being caught* function to reinforce *positively* (with the feeling of freedom, our need for speed, and our getting away with it) our entrenched speeding behaviors. That's why we all—well, most of us—speed. The system has taught us to.

Now, consider the power of a positive reinforcer. Suppose your insurance company were to devise a (not yet invented) GPS speed monitor in your car, and to rebate a direct percentage of your car insurance per month based upon the percentage of time you drove at or below the speed limit. Different motivational system entirely. Staying at the speed limit would earn something valuable to you. The research is robust and unequivocal on this point. Rewards change behavior; punishments create surveillance behavior. End of digression.

CBT

OK. One step over from the purely behavioral therapies are the cognitive-behavioral approaches (CBT). These have become the genre of choice in the current managed-care environment. The CBT schools differ from the purely behavioral therapies in that its practitioners marshal the substantial role of the thinking process as their aid in achieving behavioral change. Let's take, for instance, someone who has become phobic and panicky in public places in general, or on bridges or in stadiums or restaurants or airplanes in particular. Isolated instances of panic in these places can and do lead to more generalized and life-constraining avoidance of them, sometimes building to what we call "agoraphobia." This range of anxiety-based disorders can wreak havoc in families, careers, and life pursuits. I once interviewed a very well-heeled and well-spoken woman who had not been out of her own bedroom in eight years (except under the influence of the drugs she took to get to our clinic).

Via cognitive behavioral therapy (CBT), the sufferer/client can be helped by a therapist to gradually engage in the feared behavior by simultaneously moving toward the feared entity (behavior) and attending to the thoughts and feelings generated in their mind and body (cognition). With the support of the therapist, the client can be helped to use their mind to understand and challenge the edifice of thoughts underlying and maintaining the target behavior.

We used this powerful set of techniques in the Stanford Anxiety Disorders Clinic to help formerly house-bound or similarly constrained clients to move gradually, step by step, toward the freedom (quite literally) to walk around inside Nordstrom's without having to flee due to overwhelming anxiety (our clinic abutted the Nordstrom parking lot). It was an incredibly effective therapy, and those patients who were able to gradually reclaim their lost freedom of movement in life found the techniques of cognitive behavioral therapy an inestimable gift to them and their families.

This therapy is very often criticized by practitioners of the more psychodynamic psychotherapies as too short-term and too symptom-focused to do any real good. However, those who have been released from the terrible grip of a particular disorder via CBT techniques are not part of this chorus. What's important to keep in mind is that the goal determines the process. If release from a particular symptom (the alleviating of suffering) is the focal goal, then behavioral and cognitive behavioral therapies can be powerful tools. This is why CBT has enjoyed such popularity with managed care companies: it tends to be symptom-focused, it is short-term, it works, and it can be expressed in terms of therapeutic goals and progress reports that non-professionals can read and understand.

Personal Growth/"Beyond-the-symptom"/ Psychodynamic Therapies

But many people are not particularly symptom-focused when they come to see us as therapists. Their discontents are more diffuse. They seek therapy because, more generally, they have the sense that in some way their lives are not working for them or are certainly not optimized. Or some come with a specific complaint but it is imbedded in a much larger matrix of dissatisfaction and dysfunction. Some have experienced one or more shorter-term therapies but have found themselves wanting and needing something more.

It has been my experience that many people come to the first session of therapy with something specific to start—"I don't know how to handle my teenage daughter," "I am having a lot of conflict with my partner and am not sure whether to stay in the marriage," "I can't seem to have any kind of life worth living beyond the death of my son." But at some level, they are seeking therapy because they have come to the realization that rather than having a symptom, or even being had by a symptom, they *themselves* are the locus of their concern. They want more *for* themselves and *of* themselves in their lives.

This is the province of the psychodynamic or depth-oriented psychotherapies. It is lofty, exciting, and very human. But this territory comes with many more practical and existential questions than its more behavioral "cousins." For instance, how do we as therapists even begin to put our arms around a target that is so broad, so undefined, and in many cases, so deeply imbedded in personality, personal history and interpersonal style? And what does therapeutic success look like? And who defines what is healthy or optimum for this particular human being at this particular time in their life? And what gives us the warrant to believe that we can or should pursue such a lofty goal as human optimization? Is our art and our practice up to the task of profound human change?

It is not uncommon to hear students share with me that they have worked with a therapist for a number of years, but see no appreciable difference in how they feel within themselves or in how they live their lives. They enjoy having a person (a therapist) to talk to for personal support and as an emotional backstop, but they do not feel real shifts in how they experience themselves or their relationships. So beyond these other concerns, what makes the difference between a long-term therapy that effects deep psychological growth and one that does not?

These are huge questions, whose presuppositions and orienting axes are often poorly articulated in the training of therapists, even for those purporting to work in psychodynamic genres. We, on the educational side, often step right into therapeutic technique before considering the *what* of what it is we're trying to do—what are we *really* up to?

Carl Jung was uncommonly straightforward about these huge questions. Jung saw the evolution of the soul as the ultimate goal of therapy—a decidedly larger target than symptom relief. To Jung, this meant the full realization of the potentialities of the human person, with attention to those aspects, conscious and unconscious (or "shadow" sides in Jung's lexicon) that get in the way of that progression. Jung further believed that each person had a pull toward personal growth within him or her, and that it was the therapist's job to follow the lead of that inclination in the patient (Jung, 1955).

Jung is certainly not the only clinical writer to hold these views about the locus of long-term therapeutic work, but he does so with a certain clarity of language that is unflinching, and so enormously helpful. As purveyors of long-term, depth-oriented psychotherapy, we commonly hold certain "truths" to be self-evident. But doing long-term work requires a number of presuppositions that can and should be named.

They are, for starters, that human beings can indeed change, that one person can help another more fully realize his/her potential as a human being, that the medium of "the talking cure" can be instrumental in this pursuit, and that human beings contain a gradient of growth within them that can successfully guide the discourse in psychotherapy. The process that is elegantly elaborated by the stream of writers and thinkers within psychodynamic and related disciplines leans heavily on these presuppositions. In their absence, a psychotherapist, no matter how well intentioned, can drift directionless in a sea of possible "helpful" interventions, and cover very little distance in terms of meaningful psychological change in very much time.

Where We're Headed

Our journey together in the pages to follow will lean on these same presuppositions, but will be explicit about such leanings, and will attempt to make sense of how they facilitate a process that can profoundly re-sculpt—*from within*—the people who engage in it. Just as the short-term therapies, done properly, can and do work, the long-term therapies, done with proper training, discipline and spirit, can bring change and new life at the deepest levels of the human "psyche" (Greek for the word "soul"). In the pages to follow, it will be my joy and privilege to lead us together on the beginnings of that journey, whose pursuit, if you choose it, will extend for years in front of you. I hope to illuminate the first steps for us, which will start in the next chapters with a renovation of what it means to listen. Here we go.

But just a brief clarification of terms before we launch. I'll use the term "psychodynamic" throughout this book. This is meant as the largest umbrella term available to designate the range of therapies—Object Relations, Psychoanalysis, and Psychodynamic therapy—that take as their starting point the existence of the unconscious and the primacy of transference (and resistance) in the work of therapy. Questions such as the frequency of sessions, the length of the therapy, the use of a couch, degrees of "relational-ness" and the requirement of formal institute-based training, etc., are particular aspects of the work that are sometimes used to define the boundaries of these subsets of psychodynamic work. But within this work, the word "psychodynamic" will be inclusive of all of these variants.

2

THE ART AND POWER OF LISTENING—DEEPLY

What is it like to listen to another human being? To really listen? This is an oddly emotional question. Humans talk and listen to one another constantly. We are involved in human commerce all the time. At the store, at the ball game, over the dinner table, in the classroom. We're doing it all the time.

But what is it like to listen deeply? What comes to mind is a scene from my friend Gena's funeral. She was a small, beautiful, dark-haired woman, whose deep brown eyes somehow beckoned you toward an honesty and depth in yourself in her presence. We, her friends, stood together around the grave that was to hold her ashes. We breathed silently together with hearts that all hurt in the same way from the ache of having her leave us so quickly. A brain aneurysm. Here, hospitalized, getting better, and then gone. What strikes me was that when we spoke that day, what little we spoke, we seemed to listen to one another as Gena did, with eyes and soul that were open, that could feel the hurt—even physically—that said "Your hurt is welcome here. It can put down its bags and stay awhile. It won't be jostled. It won't be rushed. It won't be asked to hurt less, or to hurt differently, or to distract itself. It won't even be asked to word itself. It can just be. And we can just be together—you, me, the hurt."

The art of listening deeply. I often pass by classrooms in Loyola Hall with beginning counseling students starting to practice listening to another in the new way a counselor should listen to a client or patient. The students sit in dyads at the tables, attempting to hear someone's story above the din of the rest of their classmates doing the same exercise. They practice reflective listening, which means that they listen to a sentence or two then try to say back to the person something of what they have just heard: "So you really wanted to get to the 10K event on time." "So you're starting to get concerned that you won't have the money to register for courses next quarter." I often think to myself that it's a strange exercise for adults to do with one another; that our cultural orientation toward listening has become so thin that we have to be *taught* to track on even the most accessible layers of content that one person is trying to convey to another. It's troubling just to think about it.

What made Gena's eyes and her being a vehicle of listening deeply? This is very close to the heart of the matter in acquiring the art of it, so we'll slow down a bit here.

Attuning

Listening in psychodynamic therapy is a part of a process we call *attunement.* This is a concept used with most precision in the study of babies and their mothers/caregivers. In the process of attunement, one person (baby) attempts to express something, at first entirely non-verbally, to another. When it goes well, the other picks up the signals and responds in a way that is accurate, or is at least progressively accurate, and the baby feels understood, soothed or met in some way that's congruent with the need/signal sent. Attunement is a three-step process: signal-sending, signal-receiving/deciphering, and signal response. The receiving person must necessarily use him/herself as reference, must scan inside him/herself to make sense of what the signal might be saying, then must respond on that basis. Because of this, the response carries a piece of the responder with it. It's signed. It's personal.

This is a different kind of listening from the listening we do in normal social intercourse. It's where just being a "good listener" to the story another is telling differs from the art of listening deeply. *Attuned* listening takes place outside of the medium of words. It is centered around the wordless communication of an emotion, or a need state, or a state of being from one person to another, often underneath and even apart from the language they are using. It is most identifiable, of course, with mothers and their babies, but some—like Gena, routinely listen at this different level.

Attuned listening is one of the centerpieces of psychodynamic psychotherapy, so let's look closely at what is involved. I'll start in this chapter with the art of it, then move in the next chapter to the science of it.

Preliminaries

To become a psychodynamic psychotherapist is to slowly master the art of listening in an entirely different way. It involves accessing parts and pieces of our human repertoire that we may not fully know are there. In this way, it is perhaps like the process of mastering a musical instrument. It takes time, patience, practice that seems tedious and endless, but over time, at what seem ineffably magical moments, new vistas begin to open to us. We begin to feel the feel of it. We sink down into the soul of it. It begins to be in us, to guide us, to move us, to surprise us, to mystify us. It's no longer something we think about doing; it's something that happens *through* us.

Listening deeply—with the entire "satellite dish" of our minds and bodies— this is an acquired art. But it's built on countless hours of practicing the basics;

the chords and scales. It moves, over time, from simple (and awkward) to complex (and overwhelming), and finally, in moments, back to simple (and sometimes elegant).

But, it's delicate, and many things have to be in place in us for it to be fully operational. So my task, as I'm writing, is to parse this art. I'll be as honest as I can along the way. Many days still, I hit the wrong keys or can't feel the rhythm of it. Sometimes the tune sounds way out of tune. Thankfully, my patients are patient with me.

Quieting Down

So, some preliminaries. First and most fundamentally, in order to listen deeply to another in the attuned way a psychodynamic therapist needs to listen, we have to quiet ourselves down inside. It takes practice to learn how to calm ourselves from the anxiety of what it's like to sit with this person, this day, with the expectation that we will be of help to them.

For a novice therapist or a therapist in training, this is—let's be honest—an *impossible* task. There is no way to quickly get over the anxiety of occupying the role of therapist. It takes "time in the chair"—lots and lots of it. Because at the beginning, we watch ourselves. We wonder whether we're really cut out for it. We wonder whether we're really as good at it as our friends and family members have said. We hear ourselves talking in a session. We watch its impact. We wonder what our supervisor would have said, would have thought about, would have picked up on. We see this session going well (yah!), this one going nowhere (huh?), this one completely tanking (uh-oh…). We judge ourselves, moment by moment, session by session. It's a torturous developmental step, and it can't be avoided.

But, given that we are pain-avoidant by nature, it's natural to try to get around this part. Our job is to *listen*—first and foremost—to *sit with* the feelings being expressed. The *why* of why listening is so powerful is something I'll address as we move forward. But for now, we're talking preliminaries: how to settle into the "role" of therapist, and *listen*. Just listen. As beginners, we are often hungry for something more than just listening. New therapists tend to look for scripted language and sure-fire techniques so they can be sure to "do" something that will be helpful.

Even mature therapists at times use "doing" something as a way to stave off the anxiety (and often helplessness) of "merely" listening to the other, merely being *with*. This anxiety has many faces. It can take the form of asking a question when the emotion in the room just needs time to sit there for a while. It can be making a *valuable* suggestion: "Have you ever thought about trying *this,* or *that*?" It can be the irrepressible urge to point out the bright side, or the humorous side, when things in the room have gotten heavy and hopeless—a commonplace strategy in American culture. But lightening the moment, or problem-solving, or attempting to fix something, or make it better, can effectively drop the patient at their point of greatest despair, leaving them utterly alone in the darkness of it. The capacity to listen and to follow the path of pain with the other is a tolerance and a muscle that must be developed over time.

So, first things first. We have to quiet down inside—as new therapists and veterans—in order to listen. No easy task.

Getting Present

Then, we have to get present for this particular person. This entails being in a receptive state of mind, perhaps having shaken off the assaults of the day that have squeezed our own emotional being en route to this moment. We come from the stresses and hurts of our own lives, of course, before we sit down to be with another. Sometimes, paradoxically, these make us more tender, more accessible inside. I've found in my own experience that at the times of greatest loss in my life, I have been my widest open inside; most able to be with the pain of the other.

But of course, sometimes, our stuff inevitably gets in the way. Some hurts are too tragic to allow us to function. These are times when we need and *have to* step back for a while. Then there are the other times when we hurt deeply, but are ok enough to be present with the other.

The next scene only works for cat-lovers, but I'll risk it. I remember in particular doing therapy the day after I had to put down my treasured 17-year-old cat, Bear. The searing hurt of it was everywhere in me. In many ways it made me more deeply present with each of my patients, throughout the day, throughout the whole week following. Then without warning inside, I found myself in the presence of one of the people in my practice who herself had a particularly special affinity for animals, and had also lost her cat a month earlier. That day, in the moments when we sat together, the hurt of it came pounding back at me, disorganizing me inside. I did my best to straddle my world and hers simultaneously, but ultimately was losing the battle, so I decided I needed to tell her what was so heavy in the air between us, something I virtually never do. She said she knew… (how could she know?). It settled both of us.

Listening—A Point of Departure

OK. So, after having settled ourselves with the assignment of being a therapist, and with the job of being present in spite of, or in the midst of, our own emotion, we move on to the complex business of listening to this other person. We're there to listen, after all.

We are taught by life experience and professional training to pay close attention to the content of what our clients/patients are saying. It's our job to be alert, present, engaged. To remember things. To develop an organized view of their life, their concerns, their significant others, all of it. With some people, because of how they engage with us, this is easy; with some, it's really not. But this is a part we're relatively trained in through our normal non-therapist interactions. Usually, people are drawn to the field precisely because they are good listeners.

But now I want to introduce a point of departure—where ordinary listening becomes *attuned* listening—and where the satellite dish comes in. Here it is. *While we're listening to what the other person is saying to us, an attuned listener is simultaneously listening on an entirely different channel.* Two channels at once. The one our patient is talking to us about, and the one being broadcast *apart from the language they're using*—the one coming to us literally from their emotional brain to ours.

Attuned listening requires that we listen to the story line, and *at the same time* (often preferentially) to what *we're* experiencing while we're in this person's presence. So, even while we're paying close attention to what the other is saying to us, we also need to pay close attention to ourselves, to what's happening inside us in their presence. "Are my muscles tight? Everywhere? Is it just in my arms? Hmmm. Am I anxious? (Did I come in anxious today, related to events in my own life? So is the tightness mine?) Is my stomach a little whirly? Does my heart hurt, or race, or bound? How is my breathing? Normal? Constricted? Constricted, how? Do I feel suffocated? How is it changing as they continue to talk to me? How is it different this hour from the feelings in the room last hour?"

Yesterday, as someone presented a case in consultation group, we took a moment to ask the group members what they were experiencing *in their bodies and emotions* as the presenter talked about the case. In other words, for the moment we were not tracking on the content of the case, but on the experience of the listeners. One member said "stifling, like I can't get enough air to breathe." One said "disequilibrating, like I'm in Pigpen's dust cloud." Two others said "shut out, like something feels impenetrable." The therapist presenting the case revealed to us that she had felt *all these ways* in the presence of this patient and again as she relayed the session's highlights to the group. She had made no mention of these feelings to us, but the group had picked up her un-worded emotional experience as she relived with us what the session had felt like to her.

Stereo

In essence, this kind of listening to our own body and emotions amounts to opening up a "stereo" track inside ourselves with which we scan our own experience as we simultaneously listen to the experience of the other. This is, of course, impossible if our attention is pulled or focused too narrowly toward the verbal (our culturally preferred channel). It's even more impossible if we're busy cueing up our next incredibly wise observation or intervention.

So, how do we go about listening to two things at once? Not an easy job, of course. We're actually not built to multi-task. What's required in these moments is that we loosen up a bit as listeners; that we listen *less* attentively to the words someone is saying or the story they are telling. Not entirely, of course. But we can switch back and forth inside. Story. Internal check. Story. Internal check. How am I doing as I'm with this person, this day? What does it feel like?

It requires that we let go of trying to formulate our next response (in Winnicott's words, that we let go of trying to be too "clever" (Winnicott, 1968)). It means that we widen our aperture in order to take in this other part of the scene—the part where their emotional psyche-soma (as Winnicott (1949) named it) is communicating to our emotional psyche-soma, telling us the non-verbal story of what it feels like to be with them, and, as we will explore later, to *be* them in this moment.

This may be new to you, or it may be how you've come to listen without even thinking about it. But attending to yourself in the presence of the other, as counterintuitive as this may seem, is a critical part of the acquired art of listening deeply. We human monkeys are elegantly equipped to be able to read the experience of the other monkeys in the troop. Our survival depends on it, and as therapists, our attunement depends on it.

Stereo Equipment

One of the ways that I help students get a feel for this kind of listening in our advanced psychodynamic psychotherapy seminar is an exercise that always requires some risk-tolerance from me as instructor. In the class, I ask students to pair up with someone they haven't known before. One is to be the therapist; one is to be the patient. (The word "patient" literally means "the one who suffers"; "client" means "the one who pays." From here I will use the word "patient" because I prefer it, and because it's the common parlance in psychodynamic venues.) Their assignment is to meet for a "therapy" for 50 minutes each week during the course of the ten-week quarter. For the first five weeks, the instructions are that the "therapist" is to listen *in silence* to the "patient" for the entire 50 minutes.

This, as you might guess, is an enormously anxious exercise for both parties. People return to class the next week in various states of low-level trauma, which we process together. The "patients" were anxious because they didn't know how to fill the time with their own words; the therapists were anxious because they had no idea what they were supposed to be *doing*.

Then comes week two, then week three. Then something different begins to happen. I begin to hear from the "patients" that they are starting to enjoy the experience of hearing their own voice. They're finding out what they've been thinking. They're finding out they have something to say. They're finding out what they feel. And I begin to hear from the "therapists" that not having to think of something to say allows them to sink into the experience of really hearing their patients. They begin to report to me in their written process notes that their bodies are picking up the feeling in the room, and that they are even beginning to have scenes and images play on the internal movie screen of their minds that are deeply illustrative of the emotion of the moment (more on this later).

Furthermore, and *wildly* surprising to the dyadic participants, the "patients" are feeling deeply listened to and deeply understood by their silent therapists. In other words, something is being transmitted in the space between them—something beyond and underneath the medium of words. So much so that when, at week six, I give permission for the therapists to speak a bit, most (both "patients" and "therapists") don't want it. They don't want the well-intentioned intrusions of the therapist on the sacred space they've developed in the quietude.

Listening deeply to another—being attuned to what they're saying, feeling, and may not yet be ready to feel—these are parts of an acquired art. But it's a delicate art for sure. And many things can get in the way. Let me see whether I can now help us think about some of them together.

Impediments to Attuned Listening

I'd like to tell you a brief story from a week ago and allow you to listen to the feelings underneath it as I write. The setting is a banjo/brass concert at an old Irish pub in South San Francisco. The 20-piece band was doing a spritely medley in honor of Veteran's Day, and as each part of the medley moved from one branch of the service to another, the band members who had served in that branch—Coast Guard, Air Force, Navy, Marines, Army—stood up in place wearing the cap that was emblematic of their service branch. It was fun and celebrative.

At the first bars of the Navy anthem, a banjo player named Jack stood up in the front with a white navy sailor's cap on, which he quickly swapped out for a blue ball-cap-shaped hat bearing the moniker "U.S.S. Midway". This was *his* ship, it dawned on me. I was instantly transformed inside myself to the bow of the huge ship's deck, awash with ocean spray and sailor sweat, feeling the mix of bridled fear and young-manly bravado that pulsed its way through the foamy waters. I saw in my mind's eye a much younger version of the 70-year-old Jack in front of me, tanned and muscled on the deck of that ship, his present and future owned by the random whims of war.

Several minutes later, the tune had switched to the Army anthem, and in the far corner arose a slight, 90-year-old man named Arnold, donning the spare green hat that marked him as an Army vet. I knew instantly that he had fought—truly fought—in World War II, my parents' war, and that he had really engaged in the terror and violence of war, close up. I couldn't finish the sing-along, because my throat ached with the emotion of the moment. I was touched by their service, their pride, and the invisible personal cost of it to each of these men, then, and even now. I teared, but didn't let the tears stream down my face that night.

We learn this skill along the way—the where, when and how to not let ourselves feel. The when, where and how to close ourselves to what might be erupting from within us. To listen deeply is to open ourselves from the inside to the emotion of the moment. We learn from the time we're little how to close to it. We learn that growing up means getting tough enough inside not to fall into tears when we get overwhelmed. It means finding the pathway *out* of our emotional selves—the practiced discipline of disattending to what hurts.

Our Experience-Dependent Emotional Repertoires

Some of this is inherent in the process of growing up; gaining more and more capacity to regulate our own emotional states, as we are regulated from the outside by attuned and caring parents. But sadly, much of it—for many—comes of being disattended to along the way—having our own emotional states ignored, overridden, unrecognized by the people in charge: our parents or caregivers. If our emotions are disattended to, we learn at a *neurological* level—in a way that is *experience-dependent*—to disattend. It's that simple. We learn to be open to and comfortable with a full range of emotions in ourselves and in the other, or not. We learn to be alert to and curious about emotions, and to know how to follow their trail, or not. We learn—often very early on—that some emotions are ok; some are not. We learn that some emotions or internal states get us left alone, dropped, even attacked; that some are dangerous. We perhaps learn that emotions or internal experiences are safer when they're held in, and perhaps even safer if they are obliterated entirely. We also learn within families that *some people's* emotions are ok and are allowed to be expressed, and some are not.

Developmentalist Stanley Greenspan (1989) has observed that by eight months of age, some infants already exhibit a truncated emotional repertoire. *That early*, they have already learned what parts of them their parents can bear, and what parts make their caregivers nervous, overwhelmed, angry, or just somehow absent. Some of these little ones flatten out their emotionality, engage in dissociative behaviors, become less interactive, less demanding, less playful, less needy, less angry. By *eight months*!

University of Massachusetts-Boston researcher Ed Tronick (Tronick et al., 1975) presented a microscopic view of how this process of emotional flattening might happen in a child over time through a series of experiments he called the "Still Face" experiments. In these, he invited a sample of mother-infant pairs into the lab, and asked the moms to play with their six-month-old child in their carrier for a while. Tronick's cameras recorded the interactions, one of which I'll describe here.

We, as observers, beheld what amounted to a perfectly choreographed dance between infant and mother: mother coming in with her face to tickle the infant; infant squealing with glee. Mother pausing to let the infant catch his breath; infant smiling broadly with his mouth and eyes to re-invite her into the game. Tronick's experimenters then instructed the mom simply to discontinue the game by putting on a still face—not an angry face, not a depressed face, just a still face. What happened next was remarkable. The baby noticed her expression, was visibly disturbed by it, tried to calm himself for a few seconds by fixing his gaze on his own hands, and then made a concerted foray to get her to re-engage. If she continued to present a still face, the baby, seemingly unable to bear the disconnection, began progressively to fall apart—first with small signs of facial bewilderment and physical dysregulation—tonguing, drooling, hiccupping; next with full body dysregulation; agitation across his entire body; and finally with hard, expressive crying.

What we have come to know observationally and experimentally is that parents' own repeated emotional responses to their babies' and little ones' emotions can selectively preserve parts of that child's emotional repertoire and can make other emotions inaccessible or scary. The development of our emotional capacities—even down to our brainstems—is experience-dependent (Panksepp & Biven, 2012). Moreover, decades of attachment research have helped us to understand that a parent's pattern of attunement to the physical and emotional needs of a child sets up predictable emotional response patterns in their babies— "secure," "avoidant," "ambivalent," "disorganized" attachment styles—which carry forward with great consistency into childhood and beyond (Waters et al., 2000). If a parent disattends to, or is toxically reactive to the emotional signals of a child, the child's very pliable mind/brain *learns* about the results of his/her own emotional expression in relation to its caregivers, and makes the needed adjustments. These then become the template a child carries forward into subsequent relationships.

Of course, we grow up generally unaware that this process has happened to and in us, and have a tendency to think of ourselves as always having been "this" way or "that" way; whatever this or that way is. I have, on occasion, asked a class of graduate students how many have had the experience of anger as adults. Of perhaps twenty-five mostly female students, ten or so will raise their hands. When I ask how many think they got angry as an infant or toddler, twenty-five hands go up. The next question—an easy step—stumps the group: "What do you think happened to your anger?"

The Point

Here's the point. Many things can get in the way of our capacity to listen deeply to the emotions of another as therapists. We ourselves can have truncated emotional repertoires. We might have had one or both of our own parents unable to be present with some of our emotions because of their own emotional histories. We may find ourselves strangely unable to be with certain states in our patients. Some states might cause us to freeze inside, momentarily emotionally leaving the patient, as the still-faced mother left her infant. Some states may catapult us into problem-solving mode, such that we leave the feelings of the patient and transit stealthfully into a "why don't you try this?" stance. Some things may trigger a cascade of (what we don't recognize as) anxious questioning from us. It's tricky, because we don't necessarily see in ourselves what we've muted over time, so we can't necessarily know where we are emotionally underdeveloped, and therefore under-attuned to our patients.

I picture our built-in emotional repertoire as a piano keyboard. Certain keys can become taped down within us. Whole octaves can be missing. But we get used to the sound of the music within ourselves and don't even know what the song would sound like (and how beautiful it might be) if, for instance, the base notes were added in.

Expanding the Repertoire

This is why those of us who want to acquire the art of listening deeply as psychotherapists need to have the experience of receiving attuned therapy for ourselves. It is in this setting where another human being can listen for the music within us, and can help us slowly and carefully to untape the muted keys of our own emotional keyboard. This is often a painful process. It hurts to understand that we've lost parts of our emotional birthright (and how this came to be); it hurts to realize how thin our music has sounded all along, to others and to ourselves; it hurts to practice awkwardly as an adult what we might easily have mastered as a child. But we simply can't attune to another in ways that no one has attuned to us. We can't open in another what is closed in ourselves.

Listening deeply. The art of it. Let me take a moment to re-gather us now. In this chapter we've begun to talk about using the registrations in our whole body as resonators to help catch the proto-emotional pieces of emotional and bodily experience in the other. We'll talk more about this later. We've talked about what sets us up to do this piece: calming ourselves from the anxiety of listening, getting present in, and in spite of our own emotional world. We've talked about listening in stereo, scanning our own experience as we simultaneously listen to the experience of the other. And we've touched on the painful reality that we are limited as therapists by our own experience-dependent emotional development, and that we cannot attune to another in ways that no one has attuned to us.

Now as I wind down this chapter, I find myself where I started some pages ago, with my friend Gena in my mind. She listened deeply and unflinchingly to the emotion in others. It was something she was able to do *and be* precisely because she had done the work of opening to her own emotion over time. The art of listening deeply. Gena had it. In the following chapters I'll try to walk us slowly and clearly into what this looks like in practice, and what it requires.

But as a prelude—I will move us forward into the science of it—the neuroscience of what we're doing as psychodynamic psychotherapists, to be precise. This will be exciting to some; it is to me! For me, it adds legitimacy to things in psychodynamic practice that might otherwise seem, at some level, ethereal and inexplicable.

3

THE SCIENCE OF IT

We know from multiple sources, initially from psychodynamic theorists such as Freud and Winnicott, but more recently from interpersonal neuroscientists such as Siegel, Schore, Damasio, Panksepp and others, that the process of attuned listening involves much more than our ears and our left brain's language decoding mechanisms. Listening deeply goes well beyond the words spoken. It would have to. The words we speak to one another account for only about a third of the meaning in any communicative exchange (Hogan & Stubbs, 2003). Then there is the other, bigger part, which often freights the much more important load of it. How do we go about listening for that?

Particularly as psychotherapists, it's important to know how we might go about "tuning into" the part *not spoken*—or sometimes not even really *felt* by the other. How do we access the sometimes deeply buried affective emanations that lie within, behind, or well beneath the explicit verbal exchanges in psychotherapy? This may seem an elusive pursuit, and it *is*. But it is a crucial one, because if we don't get this, we can miss the emotional truth that is the real target of our work as psychotherapists.

In this recent era of burgeoning brain science, we are coming to understand some of the mechanisms underlying this rather ethereal "tuning in" process. This is important because the science of it can help to demystify the art of it. (Never entirely, of course.) The scientific picture is just emerging and is far from complete. But neurobiological research and advanced imaging techniques during the past decade or so have exponentiated our understandings of the mind's emotional underpinnings. And what we do know at this point can help ground us as we go forward in the clinical conversation about listening deeply. So, in this chapter, we will do a brief tour of our neurological equipment for the job of listening deeply. First a quick fly-over, and then we'll move in closer for a better look.

Fly-over

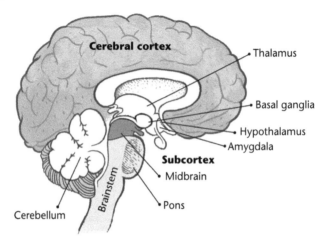

FIGURE 3.1 The Brain

From bottom to top, inside to outside, most primitive to most evolutionarily-advanced, we have three major brain regions. The bottom-most is the brainstem—pons, medulla, and midbrain—which control the basic functions that keep us alive: consciousness, respiration, heartbeat, blood pressure, etc. Also categorized with the brainstem is our cerebellum, in charge of balance, coordination, and learned movements. The second major region built atop and around the brainstem and middlemost in the brain is the vast sub-cortical area that includes the limbic system (hippocampus, amygdala, cingulate gyrus, and dentate gyrus), the diencephalon (thalamus and hypothalamus), the basal ganglia (caudate, putamen, globus pallidus, and substantia nigra), and the fluid-filled, shock-absorbing ventricles. This middle region is commonly associated with emotion, learning, memory, and voluntary movement. Third and top-most (and outermost), we have the "thinking brain": the cerebral cortex, with its myelinated white matter underneath and its convoluted gray matter on top. We divide the cortex into two hemispheres (left and right, with their respective verbal and non-verbal functions) and four lobes: frontal (pre-frontal, pre-motor and motor subdivisions), parietal (in charge of primary sensory functions), temporal (auditory processing and memory), and occipital (visual processing).

A Closer Look

Now, let's look more closely at the neural territory responsible for us as emotional beings. While it is correct to associate emotion with our (cortical-level) right brain and with sub-cortical structures such as the limbic system and hypothalamus, our emotional architecture actually reaches even farther down into the deepest centers of our brains, all the way down into our brainstems. Yes, the parts of our mind that

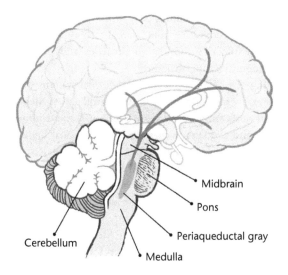

Midbrain

Pons

Periaqueductal gray

Cerebellum

Medulla

FIGURE 3.2 Brainstem Structures

are most fundamental in the genesis of our emotional experience lie at the very deepest level of our brains, well below our conscious, thinking, intentional selves.

These deeply-imbedded emotional centers—down in the periaqueductal gray and midbrain regions of our *brainstem*—respond to a myriad of internal and external stimuli on a moment by moment basis (Panksepp & Biven, 2012). Current neuroimaging studies have identified seven separate but intertwined emotional brainstem-based systems that play the affective "background music" of our experiencing selves all the time. They are making moment by moment emotional evaluations for us, giving us instantaneous promptings about all of the following: our safety; our desires to engage in the activities of life; our attractions; our angers; our drives to attach and nurture; our feelings of sadness and grief; even our urges to play. Panksepp puts it this way: "When we do an accurate archaeology of the mind, we find affective experience at the mind's foundation" (Panksepp & Biven, 2012: p. 423).

This is *big*. Neurologically, *affect precedes cognition.* Down at the bottom of things, at our brains' deepest and most life-critical centers, we have emotional brain structures that are quickly, quietly and constantly monitoring things for us *outside our conscious awareness*. We *feel* first; we *think* later. Sometimes milliseconds later; sometimes not at all (Panksepp & Biven, 2012).

Affect precedes cognition. This is true developmentally as well as neurologically (Gerhardt, 2004; Lewis et al., 2001; Panksepp & Biven, 2012; Schore, 2009, 2012; Siegel, 2012). As infants, we gradually build our advanced cognitive capacities— language, forethought, imagination, etc.,—*on top of* and (when all goes well) *integrated with* a solid foundation of emotional experience, mediated through our interactions with our primary attachment figures. Schore points out that the first eighteen months of our brain's life are spent predominantly on the task of wiring up our right brain's emotional circuitry, only *then* to be followed by the dendritic explosion of our more cognitive and verbal selves (Schore, 2009, 2012). Developmentally, our affective foundation precedes and provides the essential grounding for our cognitive superstructure.

And *this* is *also* big. All of our most basic emotional systems—even at the level of our brainstems—are *experience-dependent* (Gerhardt, 2004; Siegel, 2012). From bottom to top, our genetic emotional systems are trained and trimmed by emotional *experience*. As infants and toddlers, sectors of our emotional brains become more dendritically proliferated, or less; made more prominent or less; up-regulated or down-regulated; made more or less sensitive to neurotransmissions. Our early experience inclines us to be more trustful of others, or less. It makes our emotional warning systems more apt to trigger action, amplified emotion, heightened or distorted perception, or less. So sculpted, our basic emotional systems remain within us, all the time, doing their silent, vigilant, life-preserving and life-promoting work. In other words, our experience-trained emotional brains constantly provide to us—without our "thinking" about it—the foundational affective data for our encounters with the world beyond us (Panksepp & Biven, 2012).

Atop the brainstem sit the structures of our subcortex, responsible for emotion and movement, which we will revisit later. Above and around these structures is our cortex—our crowning glory as humans, our thinking brain—layered atop and coordinated with our emotional brain. It's a cortex that is meant to help us navigate through the intricacies of daily living, attending to the important messages of the below-the-cortex, or "sub-cortical" emotional brain, but also charged with the important job of evaluating and inhibiting its learned over-reactivities. By elegant design, then, our emotional-cognitive architecture is *meant* to be *nested* and *integrated*.

But our thinking/languaged/conscious selves are layered at some neural distance downstream from our more primary brainstem and sub-cortical affective strata, and can, at times, become quite disconnected from them. Of course, disconnection between feelings and verbal discourse is a routine part of daily life. "How are you today?" "Fine, and you?" goes the algorithm. Disconnection between what we talk about and think about and what we may be experiencing at the core of our affective selves is one of the slowly mastered marks of human maturity. We move gradually from the emotional immediacy of babyhood to the emotional circumspection of adulthood. This is a normal, adaptive progression. It allows us to function with efficiency and emotional control in a world filled with survival tasks, and, more importantly, a world filled with *others*. But—and this is *key*—our nested connection to the realm of our own emotion is never meant to be severed, or to be somehow outgrown.

Unfortunately, it often is. The compromises of early development and insecure attachment, the ravages of poverty and disease, the traumas of life and the accidents of ordinary living can disrupt this meant-to-be elegantly integrated affective-cognitive architecture.

This disruption can have many looks. We can be trained by experience to disattend to parts of our own emotional background music; to over-attend to learned fears and angers; to underestimate the trustworthiness of others; to down-regulate our willingness to engage with life. We can become disconnected from our own receptive and expressive emotional capacities. We can come to overvalue the powers of cognition. We can leave the warm glow of human emotionality sealed off and cemented away from ourselves and from others.

Freud made the observation that cognition and affect are often found to be shorn from one another—in either direction—sometimes with emotion overtaking reason; sometimes with cognition becoming emotionless (Breuer & Freud, 1999). When affect takes over, emotional dysregulation ensues, often wreaking devastating interpersonal damage. Sometimes, *intra*personally, such dysregulation requires extraordinary measures to quell its demands: sometimes spawning addictions or violence; sometimes dangerous risk-taking activities; sometimes self-injury, etc. (Cloitre et al., 2009).

[margin note: disentanglement of cognition and affect.]

On the other hand, when cognition takes over—when contact with our core affective experience has become inaccessible to us—we operate bereft of some of our most valuable and enlivening human qualities, and absent vital information for surviving and thriving in our intra- and interpersonal worlds. We wind up in this way emotionally handicapped just as we would be physically handicapped if our bodies lost their capacity to send us signals of sensation, pleasure, pain.

Listening Deeply, Revisited

So, what does all this tell us about the nature of listening deeply? Now we're getting to it. Because no matter what has happened to disrupt the nesting of cognition in affect, or to disimbed affect from cognition; however we have managed, through experience-dependent learning, to distort or distance ourselves from the emanations of our emotional selves, they are there nonetheless, all the way down to our brainstem, sending us signals all the time. They continue to operate, quietly and steadily, all the time, in the background—functioning to decipher the emotional truth of things for us, making reads for us at the deepest levels of our minds, drawing us forward, driving us backward. All the time. While we are alive, they are alive.

Attuned listening targets this affective bedrock of the communicating other. Attuned listening takes as its target the emotional emanations of the other, moment by moment, whether these emanations match or are discrepant from the narrative the other is speaking, and whether the person we are listening to is aware of their own affective experience or not. It attunes to what is being said and to what is *not* being said, but *felt* (or in some cases, *not even felt…*).

Just as a simple example, here's a snippet from the classroom exercise described earlier: "So you really wanted to get to the 10K event on time…" might have an entirely different emotional feel to it in the moment, and might, more honestly, be rendered: "So, right now you're talking to me about the 10K event. But I wonder whether what's really more prominent as you're talking to me now is a kind of anxiety about the exercise we're being asked to do. I wonder whether we could put words on that part of things right now between us…" Attuned listening listens for the emotions at the bottom of the verbal (or non-verbal) pile, so to speak. Why? Because emotion and cognition are meant to be complementary. It's a design feature of humanness. When they are disconnected, as they so often are in modern culture, we become, neurologically and psychologically speaking, a house divided against itself.

Attuned listening. Listening to the emotional emanations of the other—emanations that may be far from a person's own awareness, and quite afield from their verbal narrative. This may seem an elusive task, vastly vulnerable to listener-error, and perhaps far too nebulous to depend on as clinicians. But in daily life we, as humans, rely on this faculty routinely. We call it variously intuition, perception, sensitivity, "reading" the other, our sixth sense; it goes by many names. We read the happiness, sadness, agitation, equanimity of the other, rather automatically, and make automatic micro-adjustments based on that information without even necessarily "thinking" about it. And of course, every parent of a preverbal child uses this capacity constantly to attune to what their little one is wanting or feeling.

A Bit More Neuroscience

So, what is happening in these moments as we're attempting to "read" the emotional emanations of another? We now have parts of the answer to this question; other parts remain to be discovered. But let's assemble at least some of the pieces.

First and foremost, these brainstem-level systems we've discussed, designed to keep us safe and to move us toward the pursuits that will sustain our continued existence as humans, are all the time busy reading the "other" without our even thinking about it. And while their reading activity is silent, their outputs are not.

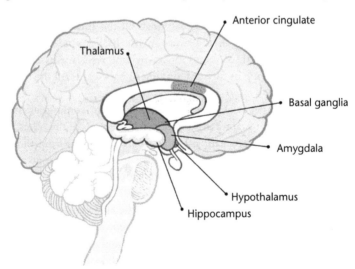

FIGURE 3.3 Subcortical Limbic Structures

They register in us as *feelings*—not necessarily worded, but there nonetheless—as we interact with the interpersonal world around us. They exhibit themselves primarily as unnamed feelings within us of safety or anxiety, as energy for engagement or not, as a sense of interpersonal attraction, or a pull toward or away from nurturing, as a sense of playfulness, as subtle feelings of irritation or anger, or sadness or grief. These "reads" are happening all the time, just as the monitoring of our own heartbeat and blood pressure is happening all the time, but outside of our awareness. They register in us as *feelings*—as bodily-based emanations we can attend to or ignore; information we can mine or discard. But this most primary emotional system, buried at the deepest level of our brains, is working all the time to give us vital information about what is happening in *us* as we connect with this particular *other*.

Then, moving up a step from our brainstems, but still in the less consciously-mediated middle level of our neural strata, we have massive neurological equipment for "reading" the other, and for "feeling" the other. We have, for instance, an amygdala and a hippocampus deep in the (non-consciously thinking) limbic area of the brain whose silent job it is to monitor all the time what's going on in our interpersonal environment, and how we're responding to it. It alerts us to interpersonal danger instantaneously. It learns from experience. For instance, research shows that those who have survived violent or emotionally tumultuous environments in their growing-up years are demonstrably quicker to identify the emergence of anger in an other than those not so trained by their experience (Pollak et al., 2000; Wilkowski & Robinson, 2012). We may think of it as intuition, or just a "feeling," but it's there as part of our limbic system's survival equipment.

In addition, we have our own autonomic nervous system on call 24/7 that takes its (non-conscious) cues from the hypothalamus buried deep in the middle structures of the brain. This system stands ready to super-charge the sympathetic branch of our nervous system in times of perceived danger (affecting heart rate, respiration, blood pressure, blood flow and tension states in large muscles, etc.), *or* to power us down (parasympathetically) in times of perceived safety. We don't *decide* to have our hearts jump out of our chests when the earth shakes beneath our feet (writing in California). Our hypothalamus makes that decision for us. Interpersonally, it's the same way. Sometimes, we just subtly *feel* unsafe in the presence of another, and we can observe our own body's reactions to our anxiety without even necessarily having identified the what or why of it.

Then, as we move up to the level of the cortex, we have the many ways in which our cortical brains harvest the information from their sub-cortical systems in order to tell our consciousness what we are feeling. Our right and left cerebral cortices dance in elegant partnership; our right brain, with its vast connections to our bodily experience and its inherent capacity for visual representations of emotion, passes signals through the corpus callosum to our left brain, which, like a U.N. interpreter, receives, orders, and translates this information into words for us so that we can "know" what we are feeling. But not only what *we* are feeling. Our brains also have resonators to tell us what the *other* is feeling as well.

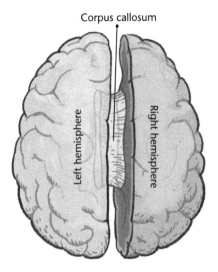

Corpus callosum

Left hemisphere

Right hemisphere

FIGURE 3.4 The Cerebral Cortex: Hemispheres

"Feeling" the Other

So at this cortical level, we have a spider-like web of neurons—*actual brain tissue*—that extends from the right brain's cortex all the way around the *heart* and the *stomach* as registers and amplifiers of emotional feelings (Siegel, 2008). This is part of our emotional architecture. Who has not had the experience of having one's heart ache or stomach twist in emotional pain? But who has not had similar sensations in response to the emotional pain of an other?

Now, why does *their* pain register in *our* heart or stomach? The answer is that we don't know yet. Damasio (1999) has suggested that one of the mechanisms enabling feelings of emotion to emerge in us is the activation of neural "*as if* body loops." These circuits, he argues, activate internal sensory body maps within us which we read as emotion. Damasio has further proposed that the activation of such "*as if* body loops" can also be triggered by our observation of *other* individuals, suggesting at least one neurological pathway for our experience of empathy.

Neuoroscientists have likewise identified what have come to be called *mirror neurons* in our premotor cortex, inferior parietal lobe and anterior cingulate, which function to anticipate and even mimic *in our own bodies* the actions and the action-related *intentions* of the other (Rizzolatti *et al.*, 1996; Iacoboni et al., 2005). Indeed, 10–20 percent of the sensory neurons in these areas appear to be devoted to these mirroring operations (Decety & Cacioppo, 2011: p. 526).

Neuroimaging research has just begun to extend this line of inquiry to the realm of our empathic capacities. We know, for instance, that if I am poked with a pin, my anterior cingulate neurons fire. If I watch someone stick *you* with a pin, my pain-simulating mirror neurons also fire, giving me a mirrored sense of your affective experience (Saarela et al., 2007). If I watch you smell a noxious stimulus,

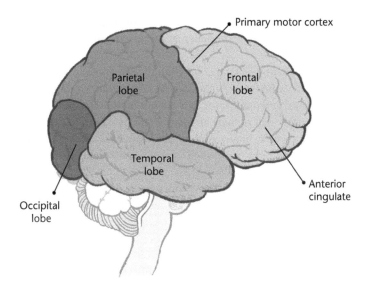

Primary motor cortex

Parietal lobe

Frontal lobe

Temporal lobe

Anterior cingulate

Occipital lobe

FIGURE 3.5 The Cerebral Cortex: Lobes

my "disgust" neurons fire (Wicker et al., 2003). These operations occur automatically, without our conscious attention.

So, while this research has not yet extended its understanding all the way out to cover the whole panoply of emotional states of the other, this is an active line of inquiry. Whether or not neuroscience has identified the specific neurological mechanisms involved in our capacity to "feel" what another feels, attuned clinicians routinely report that their physical bodies map on and mimic what the other is feeling bodily and emotionally in the moment.

Then, of course, in a way that is much more fully understood, we are equipped with a whole network of sensory-based receiving and decoding mechanisms distributed throughout our bodies. As is well known and easily-accessible through conscious experience, we have receptors sites across all five senses, distributed down to our toes and fingertips, whose (non-linguistic) information feeds through the thalamic middle of the brain to the associational areas in our cortex's parietal lobes, and syncs up to give us sensory impressions of the other: the sights and sounds and smells of it (smells actually skip the thalamic part, going more directly to the emotional parts of our temporal lobes). We are making sensory-based, cortex-level evaluations of the other constantly. These impressions are gathered up and register as emotional impressions in our consciousness. In other words, we "read" the other's body language and get a "sense" of what they are feeling.

In addition to all these tools, we have our (experience-dependent) orbitofrontal cortex (located in the pre-frontal region of our cortex right behind our eyes) whose complex job it is to make integrative emotional sense of all of the above, in ourselves and *in others*. Those whose (experience-dependent) orbitofrontal cortex is under-developed (due to neglect) or damaged (due to physical compromise) are unable to experience accurate empathy for the emotions of another (Gerhardt, 2004).

One last piece for now. For many, it will be the most compelling piece. All these systems I've described—the brainstem, the limbic system, the hypothalamically-mediated autonomic nervous system, our "neurological" stomachs and hearts, our bodies, our five senses—all of these are neurologically connected to, and feed their information to our *right* brain, our right hemisphere's cortex. That is their destination point. The right brain, then, makes sense of and integrates all of these inputs.

Its *outputs* within our minds are largely non-verbal, but register in our experience as internal mental pictures, feelings, bodily sensations, intuitions, reveries, songs, etc. Simultaneously, the right brain deposits *outputs* into the intersubjective space between two humans (through our facial expressions, eyes, tone and prosody of voice, body posture, etc.) without our consciously directing these expressions. Finally, the right brain hands a distillation of all this information to its left-brain counterpart, so that, finally, we are allowed to "know" (in words) what we're thinking and experiencing.

This is so crucial to the art of listening deeply! We live in a highly verbal culture. We depend on words, for sure. But the art of listening deeply to another human being in therapy involves learning to open ourselves to the huge flood of non-verbal data presenting itself to our *right brains* moment by moment. It involves harvesting what is not necessarily verbal, but nonetheless accessible and real. Modern neuroscientists are accruing a growing pile of evidence that the change mechanism in psychotherapy lies "not in verbal exchanges but rather in a background of the empathic clinician's psychobiologically attuned interactive affect regulation, a relational context that allows the patient to safely contact, describe, and eventually regulate their inner experience" (Schore, 2012: p. 138). In essence, the fulcrum of change in psychotherapy appears to be not so much our prescient moments of verbal insight and intervention, but the overall relational context of patient-therapist, therapist-patient, right-brain to right-brain exchange.

Change

In long-term psychodynamic psychotherapy, people actually change. Their habits change. Their emotions change. Their view of themselves changes. Their relationships change. Their *brains* change. Glass observes the following: "Recent research in brain imaging, molecular biology, and neurogenetics has shown that psychotherapy changes brain function and structure. Such studies have shown that psychotherapy affects regional cerebral blood flow, neurotransmitter metabolism, gene expression, and persistent modifications in synaptic plasticity" (Glass: p.1589, as cited in Schore, 2012: p. 143). This is our deeply exciting potential. But to do it well as therapists, we have to learn to listen to all that our non-verbal brains and bodies offer to us.

OK, so now, let me pause. The neuro picture is huge; a 100,000-piece puzzle. We're only beginning to have the tools to assemble it. I've given you a few pieces of it in this chapter. There are many more emerging. It's important, because what we do as therapists—the tools that we develop and access in our brainstem, our sub-cortical systems, our bodies, our right brains, and finally, our left brains—these are the tools of our trade. We need all of them in order to do our best work as psychodynamic psychotherapists.

Punchline

But here's the real punchline, and it will be important for the rest of the book. Listening deeply—listening the way our friend Gena listened—is a contact sport. Our own bodily and emotional experience in the presence of another is our brain's way of telegraphing to us something *hugely* important about the physical and emotional experience of the other in our presence, *often* beyond and beneath their verbal report. While it's true that our facility for making sense of the verbal messages of the other is absolutely crucial to our work as therapists, often—*very often*—the verbal narratives of our patients are incomplete, incoherent, or disconnected from their own emotional experience. Very often, this is exactly why they have come to us as therapists, whether they are able to put this into words or not (usually not).

So, let me say it again. Listening deeply is a contact sport. It is not an intellectual exercise. It takes the *whole* of us: physically, mentally, emotionally. If we don't show up with our hearts, our stomachs, our nervous systems, our muscles, our eyes and ears, mirror neurons and right brains open and ready for the receptive task of taking in the other, we can miss the deepest, most unworded parts of them. If we disattend to our own physical and emotional experience in the presence of the other, and don't count on our *nested* brain to give us all the information it's capable of giving us, we can miss the first and most important part of listening deeply. If we listen only to the verbal stream, we can miss massive amounts of emotional data available to us as therapists.

We may attend or disattend to this information, but our bodies and psyches are constantly receiving the affective signals of the other; functioning all the time as a giant satellite dish to pick up the physical and emotional emanations of the other. The signals are sometimes powerful, sometimes subtle. But they are always there. With practice, we can learn to attend to these signals with more and more precision.

Now we leave this very brief sojourn into neuro territory and turn once again to the art of it. The next part of the listening deeply process is the whole business of making sense of the signals we're receiving—translating the signals picked up by our satellite dish so that we can respond in a way that is accurate; that is attuned. That's what is next.

4

THE CHAIN OF EMOTION

I started our journey in this book with the art of listening deeply simply because that's the *sine qua non* of doing therapy; without this, nothing. If we can't attune on the most basic levels to where a person is in *this* session at *this* moment, the rest of the perspectives of psychodynamic psychotherapy won't make one an attuned therapist. So in this chapter, I will take us another small, but important, step down this pathway, and hope to keep you with me as we go.

As therapists, we are in the business of listening to people's stories, and listening *for* their feelings. We somehow know intuitively, or are taught along the way, that the medium of "the talking cure" involves having people move awareness along a gradient within them from unthought/unknown, to barely detectable, to feelable, to speakable, to elaborate-able, linkable, and ultimately transformable; from unconscious to conscious, if you will. We are taught and probably know from our own experience that there is something powerfully freeing about birthing a formerly unworded feeling into words. When we're truly scared, or aggrieved, or angered or even surprised, it helps to name the thing. It helps because an emotional experience seems to hold part of our being hostage in some kind of way until we've been able to move it into worded symbols for ourselves, usually by talking to another human being about the experience.

I will never forget seeing the real-life film footage of a Vietnam vet in therapy during my time at the V. A. His mind had been truly colonized by what he had experienced in battle. He had terribly intrusive nightmares that played the same scene over and over in his head. He woke up screaming each time. His waking life had become overtaken by efforts to numb himself as much as possible to the scenes that he carried in memory.

In the therapy, the therapist was having him recount what he remembered of the recurring scene, session by session, over time. In each session, the therapist would induce deep relaxation in the vet before each progressive attempt to go more fully into the details of the recurring scene, so as to keep this recounting within tolerable limits. Each session, the vet would be able to put into words a little bit more of the traumatic scene that had so arrested his psyche's attention.

Toward one of the final sessions of the therapy, the vet recalled with terrible anguish a scene where he and his friend had been foxholed several dozen yards apart, with a small group of enemy soldiers (Viet Cong) coming toward them over the crest of a hill. He related through fitful sobs how the soldiers, in a hail of bullets, seized his friend and held him upright while one of them first cut off his ears and then his nose with a knife; all of this while the vet watched from the shelter of his own foxhole yards away. This had been the secret he had not been able to put into words for himself. It had been unthinkable.

Minutes passed, then the therapist asked a simple question: "Did your friend scream?" "No" said the vet. After a long silence, the therapist gently filled in the blank that the vet had failed to complete in his own mind: "He was already dead" the therapist whispered. Several seconds later, the vet barely audibly repeated to himself and to the therapist, "He was already dead." The vet had omitted this realization from his wordless, torturous, internal narrative. We tell ourselves incomplete emotional stories.

There is something powerful about taking pieces of our experience, locked tightly within us, and bringing them into the words of day. Words make us make sense to ourselves. Words fill in the blanks that we leave, as children, as adults. Words give a feeling or an experience somewhere to live, so that it need no longer live everywhere within us. I once had a patient who wrote out in tiny print the text of an entire session as she could remember it. Laced tightly around the outside margin of the text of the session was the repeating phrase "You now live *here*, so you no longer get to live *everywhere*." When Freud penned the observation that words *bind* anxiety, I'm sure he had something like my patient's experience in mind.

Words can be powerful because they allow for the revision of memory, perception, experience, and the self we've constructed on their basis over time. But what is often unaddressed in the training of therapists is that words are the endpoint of a multi-linked chain of emotional experience. Understanding this chain is crucial to our work. In this chapter, we will attempt to de-couple the links of that chain so as to understand the trajectory of an emotion; to see what precedes the delivering of an emotion into speakable words. It's so important!

The "Mentalization" of Emotion

The process of harvesting our emotion from the deep, inaccessible reaches of our primitive brain is a crucial one indeed. Lecours and Bouchard (1997) refer to this as the process of mentalization—"mentalizing"—moving the messages of our emotional brain to our conscious, thinkable, speakable awareness. These authors explain that the awareness and expression of emotional experience follows a gradient from infancy onwards, and that this gradient describes the architecture of adult emotion as well. It includes four distinct "registers" or "links in the chain" of emotional experience: the somatic, the motoric, the imaginal, and the verbal.

Lecours and Bouchard put into words something that we all run into as therapists: that some people clearly have emotional experience but cannot yet use words to describe it. Indeed, some do not even know that what they are experiencing is emotional. If we as therapists can learn to receive their emotional signals in each of the different "registers"—perhaps "languages" would be a better word for it—our capacity to understand the emotional world of our patients is greatly expanded. If we can acquire an ear for the different tonalities of emotion, we are much better able to detect and resonate with emotions that are pitched well below the verbal threshold.

Often, the training of therapists begins with and *privileges* the medium of the verbal, and can leave out some of the essential links along the way. But early links in this chain of emotional experience cannot be readily translated into words. Each register has its own legitimate place that needs to be recognized, respected, explored, and sometimes lived with for a long time before it is ready to be transformed into something "higher" on the mentalization chain.

What comes to mind is the story of my friend Beth, who walked out into the garden in their first summer in California to find her husband, Eric, gently peeling back the leaves on their newly budding roses. "What are you doing?" she asked. "Helping them bloom" he replied. Sometimes our eagerness as therapists to get feelings into words can get in the way of a delicate process, perhaps disrupting what might have bloomed more fully and more beautifully in its own way, in its own time.

Links in the Chain

Let's start with Lecours and Bouchard's description of the process of "mentalization." "Mentalization," they write, "is the early activity of transforming the *somatic* drive-affect excitations into symbolized mental contents, and of maintaining these excitations in a symbolic form." Mentalization, in other words, is the process of transforming bodily-based states into meaningful, thinkable emotional elements. These authors describe and elaborate four distinct and progressive ways of registering emotional experience: the somatic, the motoric, the imaginal, and, finally, the verbal. We'll look at each.

The Somatic

The first link in the chain of emotional experience is *somatic* (physical) experience. Our earliest and most primitive experiences of emotion are entirely *physical*. The body is a baby's first vehicle of emotional registration, before they have any language with which to call a need a need, a feeling a feeling, an emotion an emotion. In an infant, these authors observe, emotion is first experienced as excitations (pain, tension, nausea, etc.) at the level of the internal organs (stomach, heart, etc.), the head, the musculature, and the skin. The body itself, albeit passively, becomes the organ of registration of our earliest emotions.

As we develop beyond babyhood and into adulthood, the body continues to be emotion's "first language." The body is the first receiver of emotional signals that arise—remember—from deep within our brainstem and our subcortex. The body is really a *transceiver* of emotion. It *receives* signals from the subcortical parts of our emotional brains, and *moves them forward* in the chain of our experience. It does this using sensory and motoric outputs that we can (potentially) feel.

The body is *first* in terms of the mechanisms that help us know our own emotional experience. As emotion arises from the deepest parts of our brains, it is passed along to the subcortex, registering in the body's autonomic nervous system first and in the right brain (visual/emotional part) second. Only then can it be transmitted to the left brain (thinking/languaged-part) as an afterthought.

And this is *key*: the body remains the ultimate emotional backstop throughout our lives. In the absence of any other form of emotional registration or expression, when all other vehicles of emotional perception are blown out—either due to the magnitude of the trauma or to developmental compromises—"the body keeps the score" (van der Kolk, 2006). We store in our bodies what we cannot afford to know in our minds. Joyce McDougall's (1989) thoughtful book, *Theatres of the Body*, explores this topic in depth.

Lecours and Bouchard's perspectives on the somatic register overlap with and draw on the earlier work of Winnicott in this realm. In his paper entitled "Mind and its Relation to the Psyche-Soma" Winnicott (1949) proposed that at the start, we as infants experience emotion first and fundamentally as a *bodily experience*. Needs arise within us (or are provoked from outside), tension states come to the fore, disturb us, agitate our bodies, impel our expressions of physical distress. In response, we are acted on by our interpersonal environment. We are soothed (or not). He proposed that this rhythm, responded to and managed by our (invisible) "environmental mothers," allows a developing infant the metaphorical space they need to stretch out gradually into their internal psychic world. Winnicott wrote that given a closely attuned environment, there is a natural elaboration of physical experience that begins to occur in the infant; that there begins a natural move within the infant toward increasing awareness of his own experience. He called this process the development of the *psyche-soma*. *Psyche*, soul; *soma*, body. Linked. Meant to be linked. Our psyche—our self-awareness, our awareness of our own experience as selves—is built, in Winnicott's words, upon "the psychic elaboration of *physical* experience," and has its *root* in physical experience (1949).

In session

Our first organ of self-awareness and awareness of what we are feeling emotionally is the body. True for infants, and easy enough to recognize in an infant. But how might this initial link in the emotional chain look in a patient in therapy? This is an important question, because for some, this somatic level might be the only language they have for the registration of emotion.

The somatic might exhibit itself in a session as the sudden emergence of nausea or dizziness amidst a patient's description of a past event. Or it might be represented by the partial reliving of a trauma through unexplained autonomic activation (racing heart, gut pain, shaking, sweating, etc.) during a session. Or we might see the eruption of a psychosomatic symptom, such as eruptions of skin rashes or headaches as emotional content is beginning to be brought forward in the work. Outside a session, emotion may occur as the intrusion of extreme bodily/psychic discomfort when certain triggers occur, as often happens to adult victims of childhood abuse or molest. Emotion not experienced as emotion, but encoded as *somatic experience*.

Tuning in

Now I'm going to say something that we will explore together in more depth as we go on. But as I've already explained, we have more potential "receiving equipment" in our satellite dish than we are ordinarily taught to attend to in ourselves as therapists, and certainly more than current neuroscience fully understands. We definitely have the capacity to communicate across the space of therapy—brain-to-body, body-to-brain—without the intermediary of spoken language. If we are able to tune into it, our amazing brains can at times pick up some of the somatic experience of the patient sitting across from us without words.

How would this look? At times in session we may feel suddenly nauseated, or headachey, or uneasy in our stomachs, or hurting around our hearts, we may feel our muscles tense with anxiety, we may find it hard to breathe, we might have to fight off tears, we might feel cold. We might, as in the example to follow, feel profoundly sleepy in a session (unrelated to our own need for sleep). These are not parts of our experience that we are generally taught to attend to as therapists. It is common for us to ignore these signals, or to assume they are "just us." But if we can learn to tune into them, *there they are*. There they are, giving us perhaps as much emotional information as we would have if someone were to say in words, "I'm feeling sad." Such somatic signals allow a level of attunement quite a bit more profound than what is ordinarily available outside of therapy—a level more akin to what attuned mothers give to their infants—reading the unworded physical/ emotional signals.

It is now not an uncommon part of my own practice to notice what I am feeling physically in the presence of my patients, and to wonder about it, first within myself, and sometimes also aloud with them. It might be, for example, that I feel my stomach tighten. I might wait for a while to see if the sensation persists, then I might ask the patient if they are aware of what's happening in their body as they're trying to talk to me. If they come up blank, I might query a little further, "Hmmm. I'm wondering if you feel anything here?" (I might gesture toward my stomach). If someone has had the habit of disattending to their own somatic sensations, that extra question often allows them to recognize the tightness, and to put their own words on it. It then allows us to wonder about what might be causing that tightening just now. They may not know. The emotions may only be at the somatic level. If so, efforts to word their emotion in that moment might well be premature, even intrusive. But it matters that we've *felt* it—that we've *gotten* something of their physical/emotional experience with them; that we've wondered about it with them. Over time, for most patients, the recognition of something going on in their bodies affords entrée into part of their emotional world that would otherwise be missed by patient and therapist.

We can't always be right about the signal, of course, and some people so thoroughly disattend to their experience that they're not able to feel even what their own body is feeling in the moment. But there is a whole stream of information available to us as therapists when we pay attention to the somatic in session. When we *get* people at this quite primitive level, they feel *very* understood. There's an intimacy to it, and a level of attunement that for many might have been missing in their own primary caregivers.

Yesterday in consultation group, a therapist presented the problem of being profoundly sleepy in the presence of a particular female patient. She had not been sleepy in the session that preceded this one, nor in the one that followed it. As we listened to her description of what this patient was saying, and how she was saying it, the group commented that the patient seemed completely disengaged from her own emotional experience (which was dreadful and hopeless) as she spoke. We surmised together that the only emanation coming from this woman was at the lowest possible position on the chain of emotional expression—at the level of the body—and that she was in essence bringing her therapist into her emotional world through a body-to-body communication, staying away from the pain of her own hopelessness by lulling herself (and the therapist) into sleep.

It is, of course, possible to bring our own somatic experience into the therapy room. The following is a true story. My dear friend whose infant son had rendered mom and dad sleep-deprived for a period of months, once heard himself asking a patient this question out loud in session: "Now, just exactly where were you standing when your grandmother emerged from the spaceship?" To his horror, he had fallen asleep, was dreaming, and had awakened to his own voice speaking these words. Fortunately, my good-humored friend was able to step up to it honestly in the moment, and to explore the impact of this *faux pas* on his patient. So yes, we all have our own bodily-based issues, of course. But if we can learn to keep track of them (as my friend did in the aftermath with this patient), and if we can use our own satellite dish to tune into the somatic level of emotional experience, our attunement to our patients' proto-emotional experiences is greatly enhanced, and our therapy, greatly deepened.

Gathering it up so far. Sometimes, as humans, we are missing links in our own chain. Sometimes we have no words for our feelings; sometimes we have no *feelings* for our feelings. In times of trauma or emotional overwhelm, we can even have no memory for the events that have left our feelings scarred and gnarled. But although all other links in the chain may be washed out or inaccessible, the body does indeed keep the score, holds the memory, registers the feeling. It does so in two ways: internally and passively, in the ways we've just discussed, and actively, motorically, as we're about to explore together.

The Motoric

We are—at the bottom of things, at our foundation—emotional beings by design. We have elaborate equipment with which to feel and decode our own emotional experience: what it is, what it means, how we should act in light of it, or not. We have this equipment because the nesting of cognition in emotion is important to our survival and to our quality of life as human beings. As therapists, we have to understand how this equipment is designed to work, and what to do when some or all of it seems to be missing.

The next transceiver of emotional experience—beyond having things register in our internal organs, skin, head, and muscles, as we passively observe—is the active enactment of emotion *motorically*. In the infant, this would be seen as squirming, wiggling, crying, arching, smiling; all active expressions of different somatic/proto-emotional states. These are all direct enactments of a felt somatic state; putting somatic feeling into *action*. But in an infant, these actions are reflexive. They are without any intervening mental processing of the emotion involved. In a slightly older child with more advanced equipment for mental processing, tantrums would certainly fall into this motoric category.

In an adult, the motoric level of expression might be easily observed. Have you ever walked into someone's house and encountered a hole punched in a wall? There was a human on the other side of that punch, who, in a moment probably not translated into words in themselves, was motorically expressing an emotion. People do this when they slam their fist through a wall, when they kick a door, when they trash their rooms, cut themselves, shake their baby, or find themselves face down in a binge-eating episode. They put into *action* something that is in their bodies and in their psyches as an emotion, but that has not been consciously elaborated within them and has no alternative means of expression.

A classic picture of emotion trapped in the body motorically comes from the experience of World War I veterans with what was then called "war neurosis" (now PTSD). Postwar film footage shows many of these men exhibiting profound neuro-muscular disturbances in their ability to walk and maintain their balance. They would walk a few steps with great shakiness, and then fall to the ground. Although quite young, they looked like people with advanced Parkinson's or Huntington's disease. In his account of his work with these veterans, Kardiner (1941) recounts that when they were able to capture their war memories consciously and gradually to make them verbal (last link in the chain of emotion), their quite severe motorically-based movement disorders resolved.

The motoric level of expression represents an unnamed and unrecognized emotional state which makes its way from an excitation in the body to a motoric act of release. The "motoric" part of emotion is captured in the derivation of the word "emotion," which comes from the Latin *emovere*, where *e-* means "out" and *movere* means "move."

The recognition that motor activity, in its vast array of forms, can proxy for emotional expression may be crucial to understanding the internal psychic world of a particular patient. Likewise, the understanding that motoric expression may be the "highest" form of expression available to a particular patient at a certain time can allow us to meet that person where they are rather than requiring that they come all the way into *our* verbal comfort zone before we can "hear" what they are saying to us; before they are ready or able to "speak *our* language."

For many people, explosion or implosion are their only options for emotional expression. They *move*—toward or away. Toward, with eruption, violence, attack; away, with silence, withdrawal, leaving, quitting. The activity involves using their muscles as the vehicle. Parenthetically, some people's verbal eruptions have more in common with a muscular release than they do with communication. A frontal attack that seems to be without anything rational or meaningful is often just that: a form of motoric release.

As therapists, we might see agitation in a session. Or we might hear a patient say, "I don't know what I was feeling, I just *had* to leave the room." Or "and that's when I needed to cut myself." Or "last night, I threw a tantrum. I don't know what I was feeling."

I remember one night in our group for chronic overeaters when one of the group members explained to the group that she had had a busy day—an exhausting day for her—and "just found herself" at a restaurant ordering and eating her way through a large plate of nine potato fries. As the group questioned her about her day, she came to the realization that the *action* was a response to the *feeling* she had had of being taken advantage of and dismissed by her husband. She had worked all day to clean up a computer glitch he had created. She had not *known* that she was feeling used and unthanked by him in that way that whole day, and had not connected eating the potato fries to her internal state of emotional agitation *at all*.

These are motoric expressions of emotion. *Activity* as a proxy for understanding and verbally expressing an emotion. When people use the motoric level of emotional expression, they often do not know that there's an emotion the action is covering for. They commonly say "I don't know why; I don't know what I was feeling, I just did it" (whatever the *it* was), and the "it" is often something that brings them shame, because it makes so little sense to them, and sometimes causes such interpersonal damage. Therapeutically, the *it* may not be ready to be delivered into words (and sometimes should not be), but should be recognized by us as therapists (sometimes silently) as the proto-expression of an emotion.

Here's how this looked in a session with a 45-year-old patient several years ago. She had been in weekly therapy for a few months and came into the office this particular day looking pale and depressed. She settled into her chair, looked all around the office, and finally spoke: "It's not going to be a very good day in here today." Then, after a brief interlude of silence, "I feel like I want to die." "I feel split open right down the middle of me" (somatic register). She took me to an argument with her boyfriend that weekend, and described what she called having a "meltdown" in the aftermath. Her meltdown consisted of crying incessantly, staying in her pajamas all weekend, and feeling liked she wanted to die. There was a notable absence of specificity as she reflected backward on the argument. She felt on the verge of several *action* plans: maybe dumping her boyfriend, maybe quitting her job, maybe just taking her life. These were all motoric—all in the motoric register—taking action in response to an unidentified, unelaborated emotion.

What was happening here? She was experiencing emotion trapped in the body, and seeking expression through action. The level of emotion she was experiencing ("meltdown") was familiar to her, and was discernibly not a response commensurate with her current experience with her boyfriend. She knew that much.

She had been raised in a home with a needy and misattuned mom. She had no doubt had many scenes as a baby and child of having had overwhelming physical and emotional excitations that were uncontained, ignored, and allowed to continue, unabated; terrifyingly so for a child. She was a 45-year-old experiencing the intolerable states of emotion she used to fall into as a child, "flashing back," as it were, emotionally. Because she was completely unversed in understanding her own emotion, her only recourse was to evacuate the feelings into possible action patterns: breaking up, quitting, taking her life. This is a sample of what the motoric register might look like in *action*. We will return to this incident in the next chapter to explore how we, as therapists, might respond therapeutically to such a moment.

Before I leave this depiction of the motoric register, let me offer one more piece. Sometimes in session I find myself in fantasy wanting to punch something or kick something or to move in some way as I listen to what a patient is talking about. I might in such a moment ask a patient about their own state of activation. In response to one such moment, I once asked a male patient what he was experiencing in his body. Tightness in his arms and legs, (unsurprisingly) matching what I had been feeling. My next question was this: "and if you were to move [motoric level] in response to what you're feeling right now (in fantasy)?" His surprising answer was "I would dance." Tears. Followed by a touching flood of memories from boyhood, connected to the events preceding a childhood performance in a play, the events leading up to it, and words/emotions he was never able to voice with his own parents. It was truly a lovely yielding of the motoric into links much higher on the emotional chain.

The Imaginal

The next "channel" or "register" to develop as the pre-verbal infant "stretches out" into his psyche beyond the somatic and the motoric is *pivotal*. It is the capacity to use *mental imagery*—mental pictures and ultimately mental scenes—as a way to represent bodily experiences and associated excitational states. This is a *large* developmental step forward, because it involves the *representation of experience*. It moves experience from the thing in itself, which cannot be reflected on, to a stable mental image of the thing, which can ultimately be elaborated: replayed, re-imagined, and even reformulated (Freud, 1915a; Sandler & Rosenblatt, 1962).

This step into mental imagery is a step that takes place during the early pre-verbal months of infancy, when right brain development is burgeoning and before the language circuits of the brain become active. It introduces a degree of mental/psychical flexibility into the developing mind of the infant. The capacity to conjure up the memory of a mother's face or the soothing scene of being fed and rocked to sleep, or even the capacity to fantasize an assault on the caregiver—this developmental capacity begins to give the infant an internal life beyond reflexive reactions to what comes upon him from his internal or external environment. It buys a child *time* between the arising of an urgent state and its excited expression.

If we think about it, introducing the element of *time* between the eruption of a disturbance inside us and the motoric enactment of that disturbance is pivotal to the psychological maturation of a human being. With the introduction of the element of time, the world of thoughtful reflection begins to become possible, and with that comes the possibility of developing and trying out alternative explanations, attributions, even the choice to act or not to act.

Mothers intuitively sense in their babies the incipient development of this channel in a child's emerging capacity to wait just a little longer for her ministrations; just a little at first, then a little longer, and then a little longer still. Winnicott (1949) felt that the increasing latency between the arising of a child's need and the point of intolerability allowed for the growth and elaboration of the child's imagination (read "image"ination). But, like Beth and Eric's budding roses, this process cannot be rushed.

How might we encounter the emergence of this visual register in therapy? For a child in therapy, they might visually represent their emotional world in the colors and shapes of two-dimensional drawings. Most of us have encountered the darkly disturbing drawings of children in abusive or neglectful homes. They look and feel very different from the drawings of children in stable and attuned homes—dark in color, emphasized in line, exaggerated in proportion—giving us the internal sense that something's just not right.

When we work with children in non-directive play therapy, we often see children orchestrate scenes, three-dimensional *visual* representations of their emotional worlds. A child might arrange sand tray figures, script scenes with toys, or even cast us as therapists into roles in the scenes they direct. These are drawn from a child's capacities to begin to transform raw somatic/motoric emotions ("beta elements," in Bion's parlance (1962b)) into visual representations of their emotional worlds.

In an adult, the visual/imaginal level of mentalization might present itself in therapy in a variety of ways. Images might be drawn from a patient's current or past experience, or perhaps from a book, a movie, a poem or a piece of art they've seen. The patient might describe a scene from their childhood. The imaginal might exhibit itself through the patient's use of metaphor. It might even be exhibited through a patient's presentation of their own art as an expressive medium in the therapy. Or it might be present through the recalling of a dream scene, which is our regular, nightly venue for translating emotional experience into visual moving pictures for ourselves.

A patient might be just a tiny step away from the motoric "I felt like throwing him through a window," but importantly, this *visual* rendering of a feeling begins to *represent* the emotion, rather than performing the action. This pivot from the motoric to the imaginal register provides time and room for elaboration and reflection. When such a moment occurs in therapy, it is important to stay *with* the patient, to stay in the *image* with the patient, by getting them to describe the scene as fully as they can, to imagine more of it. If we are too eager to "translate" their emotion into words for them—"wow, you were really angry"—we steal from them the opportunity to use the medium they are *able* to use, as fully as they are able to use it.

The imaginal might exhibit itself as a static image: "I feel like the subject in Edvard's Munch's *The Scream*" or "I don't know, I'm just a raw nerve," or "I just feel like I'm in quicksand." I once had a patient describe to me the image of an orb slowly turning in his mind's eye. He could describe its exact look and velocity to me, and while we eventually did use the medium of words to deliver its full meaning as an image, it captured for him non-verbally something about what was happening in the therapy between us in those moments (we'll return to the orb in Chapter 5).

Sometimes the imaginal emerges as a scene that comes to a patient's mind, prompted by a query from us as therapists, as was true of my patient who remembered his dance performance in a school play, triggering a whole set of memories and feelings. Sometimes a patient's spontaneous attempts to explain something in the present lead them to visual recollections of childhood that bring them into a whole treasure trove of emotion. "My boss was so cruel to my co-worker yesterday. It was so upsetting. It felt like one time when my father was yelling at my little sister; hitting her and shouting at her repeatedly to stop crying."

Very often, the imaginal is exhibited in the use of metaphor, "I felt pinned under a bus by her comments," "I feel like I'm in a vortex pulling me down, down, down." Images and visual scenes can be rich expressions of an emotional truth, often not quite ready and not even needing to be reborn into our standard list of emotional words. Staying with a patient in the visual registry—getting someone to fully elaborate the image or scene as they imagine it—is really important. The visual is a fertile and emotionally evocative medium, and pliable, really, to elaboration. But this should be the patient's elaboration because what someone's image evokes in them may not be at all what it evokes in us. It's *their* emotional experience that is the target.

Neurologically, there is good reason for why the visual channel might be a pivotal vehicle for the representation and expression of emotion. Images arise in the right hemisphere of the brain, which is also the locus of our connection to our own bodily (somatic and motoric) experience (Schore, 2012). The right hemisphere is the highest emotion-processing center of the brain. It mediates the first three links in the chain of expression of emotion we've been discussing. This hemisphere maintains constant back-and-forth communication with the body, and it is only after the right hemisphere has consulted with the deeper emotional centers of the brain, and with the body's organs and musculature, that it can move an emotion along to the visual channel. Only then is it "ripe" enough to be transported across the corpus callosum into the left hemisphere for ultimate delivery into spoken language.

It is little wonder that in the emotional world, one picture is worth a thousand words.

The Verbal

The final modality in the chain of emotional expression is the verbal one. Verbalizing emotion—elaborating emotion in words and stories, explanations and insights about our feelings—is the pinnacle of our emotional architecture. Verbal language bestows unique capacities in the expression of emotion that cannot be accessed in its absence. Although in "last" position in the mentalization chain, language gives us the powerful capacities to translate our emotional experience into word symbols, and to use those words to make our emotions make sense to us. Words allow us to hold an emotion in time; to turn it in space and view it from different angles. The verbal allows us to link past emotional experience to present emotional experience in ways that can be truly transformative. Language allows us to deconstruct and reconstruct how we see ourselves, past and present, and to transform how we act based on such alterations in our own self-definition. Finally, words link us intimately to others, allowing us to convey our world of meaning to another.

This last-in-line position of *language* in the trajectory of an emotion makes sense. In early development, we develop the language with which to express emotion only after we have developed the capacity to feel, to motorically enact, and to picture an emotion. We spend the first eighteen months of our life essentially pre-verbal, in an intensely need-filled, dependent, emotional relationship with a primary attachment figure(s). All the while, our experience-dependent brains are wiring up our emotional experience: what it feels like to have a need, to express a need, to have that need responded to, or not. We wire up what it feels like to be in a relationship—to be understood, valued, loved, cherished, held, smiled at, played with, enjoyed, cared for well enough—or not. We develop trust in the world around and infer a sense of our own worthiness to receive care—or not. Our brains learn. They make us equipped to live in the emotional terrain we find ourselves in. They do all of this work while our left hemisphere (language/logic part) awaits its developmental turn (Schore, 2012). Indeed, the foundational parts of our emotional and attachment architecture are proliferated for the most part in the *absence* of expressive language, which comes on board in a prominent way during the second eighteen months of life. Attachment and emotion *first* (right brain), language and logic *second* (left brain).

But with language comes freedom. Words allow us to link basic (bodily-based) experiences with images and word symbols that stand in the place of that experience. Such representation of emotion gives emotional experience its transit pass, so to speak, so that it is no longer stuck to its bodily moorings and immediate motoric expressions. Once an emotion, or series of emotional experiences, can be represented by pictures and words, it has the freedom of time travel. Emotions can be identified, and linked, one to another, over time. They can even be put on "pause" and revisited later. Emotional experiences—even recalled emotional experiences—can be replaced by their word and picture equivalents, and freed from the necessity or compulsion to be acted on or enacted in the moment. Through image and word representations, we are no longer "lived by" and compelled by our emotions; we gain the power to author and edit our emotional responses.

Wrap-up

We move, then, in the process of mentalization, from being the passive stage on which physical/emotional experiences are played out, unbidden, to creating our own script—finding images and words to describe the physical/emotional excitations. This translation process allows for linking basic bodily-based experiences which cannot be thought about (because they just "are") to images and words that stand in their place. It enables us to step back from them in time, where they can be compared with one another, labeled, given symbols to stand for and represent experience. From there, they can be owned, expressed as a felt emotion, and ultimately be flexibly elaborated as thoughtful constructions about the self—as opposed to concrete, intractable responses to internal and external experience.

Bion (1962b) has described this process as "alpha function": the metabolizing and transforming of intolerable internal events, experienced as concrete things in themselves (beta elements), into tolerable, "thinkable" experiences. This is also congruent with Freud's (1911) notion of "secondary process" thinking: using our left brains to think in words about emotional experience. He felt that such thinking was key to releasing the kind of built-up energy that characterized neurotic and even psychotic functioning, and blocked optimal adaptation to external reality. Pondering our emotional experiences can lead to the revisioning of memory, the ways we perceive and act in reality, and ultimately the degree to which we experience the freedom to become our full selves.

So, levels of mentalization: the somatic, the motoric, the imaginal, the verbal. All crucial to the art of listening deeply. An art acquired with practice, over time. In the next chapter, I will help you see what these levels of mentalization look like in session, and how we, as therapists, can listen for and make use of their expression in order to deepen the therapeutic work of transformation.

5

THE ART OF LISTENING DEEPLY

In the Room

So how do we use what we've been talking about so far in session? How does it look, in motion? It's one of the strange quirks of training to be a therapist that we can't observe the thing we're trying to learn first-hand, as an apprentice surgeon might observe and observe, and then finally do—but only under the moment—with close supervision of an expert surgeon. As therapists, we can't identify a master-clinician and follow that person around in their sessions, watching the detail of how they handle this and respond to that. We rarely have the benefit of video recordings of therapy in motion. When we do, it's typically only a snippet, and then often with actors playing the part of patients in therapy. It makes perfect sense that we can't stand around and watch, given the crucial element of privacy in the psychotherapeutic setting, but it presents a learning challenge of the first order. We have to rely on after-the-fact accounts of our own work and that of our mentors, but it's never the same as being there.

I know that as a therapist in training I longed to watch one of my supervisors doing therapy. I thought that if I could copy her words, her cadence, the way she did the work, I would be much closer to the mark. But (thankfully) psychodynamic therapy isn't something you can copy. It's not a set of techniques; it's not something you *do*. It's something you *be*. Words, insights, resonances, understanding of feelings come from deep within us; they are uniquely *us*, as much as writing a poem would be uniquely us. The learning of how to listen deeply is about cultivating the ability to tune into the emotional experience in the room, to get alive to what's happening in us so that we can tune into this person, in this session, in this hour. After that, there *is* the further step of understanding the signals we're receiving and how they fit together in this person's emotional world, but we will talk about this in later chapters. For now, we're working on the first part: the emotional receiving and experiencing part.

In this chapter I will again attempt to slow things down. I'll give you what I can of some real life sessions, knowing that painting word pictures isn't the same as sitting in the room, observing the nuances. But perhaps an honest rendering is the next-best thing.

Let me first recap a bit. The world of feelings has an anatomy, an architecture: somatic, motoric, imaginal, verbal. For anyone, the ability to explore a feeling—to move it into consciousness, to let it expand and ultimately to become more understandable—is a developmental achievement. An expanded consciousness of our experience as humans—what we feel, and what about us in terms of temperament and history causes us to react and respond emotionally in the ways we do—allows us to see the emotional truth about ourselves, and to "un-tape" the keys of our own emotional keyboard. In essence, it allows us to become more fully human.

But this is not an achievement that comes easily. In the words of Tom Ogden (2001: p. 113), therapy is a process

> in which two people [patient and therapist] may become more fully capable of living with, of remaining alive to the full range and complexity of human experience. These efforts are made in the face of conscious and unconscious wishes to evacuate, pervert, subvert, or in other ways kill the pain of being humanly alive.
>
> Perhaps the almost irresistible impulse to kill the pain, and in so doing kill a part of ourselves, is what is most human about us. We turn to [psychodynamic psychotherapy] in part with the hope of reclaiming—or perhaps experiencing for the first time—forms of human aliveness that we have foreclosed to ourselves.

The full range of psychological dysfunctions—from substance use, to dissociation, to splitting, to narcissistic disorders, etc.—can be thought about as attempts to bottle-stop pieces of our human experience from coming fully into our awareness. Why? Because we fear (and know) that such experiencing might overwhelm us (sometimes even bodily) and ultimately force a revision of how we see ourselves, our history, and our interpersonal functioning. And because the emergence of emotional truth is birthed almost invariably through the medium of psychological pain, we reflexively stay away from it. But the "mentalization" of our experience as humans—moving our emotional life from its roots (and ruts) in the body, past our motoric impulses to get rid of bad feelings, and into the light of image-based and verbal awareness—can be a source of continual and life-long transformation, leading us to fuller degrees of living in an alive way.

So let's watch this process together in one session in a patient I will call Lyndsey. She is the patient I described in the last chapter who came this particular day on the heels of an incapacitating weekend of emotional "meltdown," feeling "split down the middle," and wanting to alleviate her (somatic) pain by taking (motoric) action: breaking up with her boyfriend, quitting her job, or killing herself.

As Lyndsey came into session and began to share her experience with me that day, she cried heavily, telling me that "meltdowns" had been a part of her life for as long as she could remember. I remember being moved by her tears and her helplessness in the face of what seemed to her to be a force that would overcome and inhabit her for days at a time. My natural response was that I wanted to provide comfort to her, and assure her that things would be OK. But such reassurance, while a "natural" human impulse, has unintended consequences that are anti- *supportive / uncovering -* therapeutic (Feldman, 1993).

It stops the process—the exploration and elaboration of the pain—in its tracks. It blocks the potential for this experience to move from bodily-based feelings ("split down the middle") and motoric actions ("break up with her boyfriend," "quit her job," "suicide") to higher, more integrative forms of mentalization (imaginal and verbal). So my job as therapist in the moment was not about reassuring either herself or me, because reassuring would have short-circuited her expression of feelings and truncated the process of mentalization we've been talking about. No, my job in the moment was to contain my own anxieties and impulses in the face of her pain and her anticipated actions.

Now, *this* is hard work—that's the emotional truth of it. It's as though someone comes to us with a deep cut, bleeding profusely, and we say, in essence, "let's just let that bleed for a while and see what happens." This is hard to do. The art of listening deeply involves opening oneself to the pain of another and bearing—not stopping—that pain. It means using the "satellite dish" of our own bodily-felt emotions to receive and stay with the emanations of our patient in the moment.

I have heard new therapists recite to me the instructions of their supervisors that they must be able to witness people's pain without taking it on, or taking it into themselves; that they can't let it affect them emotionally. This could not be further from the truth. In the work of listening deeply, the pain evoked within us—in all its nuanced and sometimes searing forms—allows us to join in the work of mentalization accurately, compassionately, legitimately.

So back to the session. Shortly into this session with Lyndsey, I remember quieting myself down, and consciously resisting the urge to do a suicide safety check—which would be substituting *my* action for resonating with her feelings— feelings that were heavily somatic in those moments. There would be time for considering the seriousness of her suicidal impulses later on in the session, if needed. I also remember experiencing the urge to examine and perhaps talk her out of her other anticipated actions (breakup, quitting), a pathway equally unhelpful, again, because it would drag us away from her internal, somatically-based emotional experience. For now, the job was to listen deeply to what she was feeling.

I remember the tension I felt in my sternum—the physical constriction that moved up the middle of me, all the way into my throat. I remember being moved almost to tears myself, and inhibiting my own impulse to cry (because that would pull the attention away from her). I felt a whirling sense of chaos, panic, sadness, of not knowing what to do. I felt the youngness of the feelings, the sense of bewildered overwhelm and burning emotion that one feels as a child of three or four years old with no one to help contain the hurt.

How did I avail myself of these feelings? How did I know they had anything to do with what she was feeling, and weren't just *my* feelings? Go back and take a look at our discussion of our neurological satellite dish equipment in Chapter 3. When we can quiet ourselves and tune into the feelings that are emanating from one person to another, we *resonate*: we have the capacity to feel in our bodies something like the mirror image of what the other person feels in their body. Knowing how to locate and trust this is part of the acquired art.

I've had the unique opportunity to do numerous sessions of live therapy in front of classroom groups in my graduate seminars. My instruction to the student audience is always the same: attend carefully to what you feel in your body, and any images that come to mind. As we de-brief, and students report on their bodily experience, they have the opportunity to check it out with the volunteer patient. Almost without exception, the physical experiences had by audience members map directly on the physically-registered emotional experience of the patient at the different points in the session.

So again, back to the session. Sitting quietly (and painfully) with the somatic feelings in the room, and continuing to be with her in these moments, I began to allow my mind to wander, and to wonder. This may seem a strange thing to do if my job is to stay with her feelings. But having gotten a full sense in my body of the kind and intensity of pain she was experiencing, and having lived with it for a long while in the session, I allowed my mind to present whatever pictures it was forming. So in this moment I was allowing my own mind to move to the *imaginal* register.

Sometimes, nothing comes to mind, just the pain of it. But sometimes, a picture or scene presents itself to my imagination. Bion (1962a) would call this "dreaming" the experience. This time, a picture of a distraught 3- or 4-year-old child dressed in a little gray coat with white shoes came to my mind.

As I let that image remain in my mind's eye, what came to mind next (moving to my left brain's "thinking" verbal register) was that my patient had been raised by an emotionally needy and ill-attuned mom. I became aware that she had, no doubt, had many scenes as a baby and child where she would have had overwhelming physical and emotional excitations that were uncontained, ignored, and allowed to continue unabated. It became evident as I sat with the pain and associated pictures in my mind that she was a 45-year-old *experiencing* the intolerable states she used to fall into as a child; flashing back, as it were, emotionally. She was having the same bodily-based, emotional experience that she had had many times in her life, so much that she had a name for it: "meltdown." To her, meltdowns just *are*. She had never been able to "mentalize" this emotional experience beyond the somatic and motoric levels. Her meltdowns had never been able to be thought about or linked to other experiences or perspectives.

You may be wondering how all this was going on inside me while I simultaneously audienced my patient's verbalizations. The answer is that at some level, *allowing* one's mind to wander and wonder means de-riveting from the detail of a patient's discourse *just enough* to allow one's own right brain to move into imagery. We often have images (sometimes music) at the sides or in the backs of our minds, sometimes just fleetingly, at its narrowest margins. We typically disattend to this dream-like stream as we move through our daily activities and conversations. But as therapists, in order to access the images our right brains are naturally offering us along the way, we have to let go of getting every detail of the verbal report of our patient *in the service of* getting the "whole picture." For Freud (and for many psychodynamic psychotherapists), this de-riveting was facilitated by his use of the couch. For me, this means that I tell patients early on in our work that I often don't look directly at them as I listen, that closing my eyes or looking deeply into a picture on the shared wall between us helps me sink more fully into their experience, and to listen to them in a fuller way. It also means that I disengage from the obligation to speak back and forth as one would in regular conversational cadence. Both of those things allow the space our right brains need to make meaning—again, in Bion's words, to "dream" our patient's experience.

So with Lyndsey, my internal picture-maker moved the "meltdown" experience she was having up the mentalization chain to the imaginal, representing it in an image (4-year-old girl, gray coat), and then to the verbal, allowing me to think about, link, and make meaningful associations to this repeating, but never-understood emotional state that she would fall into.

Now, here's a really important thing about this almost dream-state that I'm describing to you. At times—*often*—it begins to provide an environment in which the *patient* will also get images. "Dreaming" the patient's experience generates a kind of shared dream state between the therapist and the patient. It gets silently picked up by the other (perhaps through *their* mirror neurons), such that our internal representations as therapists create the environment in which they also begin to have images and representations of their own experience.

It went this way with Lyndsey in this session. In the midst of my silent picture/thought stream, without my verbalizing *any* of it to her, she presented an association, a scene—a memory, she thought—of when she was little, perhaps 9 months old (but the precise age didn't matter so much). She had climbed up onto the bathroom counter, trying to brush her teeth by herself, but fell to the ground. She made her way to her mom in the other room with the injury. It was three days before her mom took her to the doctor. Her arm had been broken the whole time.

What was happening here in the session is that my capacity as therapist to "contain" her emotional experience—to feel it, image it, and think about it—was providing her the psychic room to begin to do something new with her "meltdown" experience: to expand it up the mentalization chain, not through intellectualization, but through an image-based representation of the experience.

As the two of us sat with this scene, we considered together the physical and psychological pain of a little girl being missed by her mom on such a basic level. In the midst of this, the client said to me, unexpectedly, "I have no memory of childhood. I wish I could remember."

Now, never mind that she had just that moment presented a memory of childhood. This would have been emotionally off track. After a long silence, I shared what had formed in the imaginal and verbal registers of my mind. "You know," I said, "I think you *do* remember, but maybe in a form that doesn't *feel* like memory. I think that meltdowns are direct samplings of what it may have been like for you to be utterly uncontained in frighteningly painful moments as a child … I wonder if that's what it feels like to you?" Almost instantly, she began to settle in her body. The tension and strain in the middle of her torso was lifting, and we could both feel it. I noticed the shift out loud, saying, "It seems like you're settling." "Yes," she said, "I feel like I can breathe."

Ogden (1994) describes what happened in the session this way:

> One of the most integrative, and therefore "supportive," things that we have to offer a patient is the power of verbal symbols to contain and organize thoughts, feelings, and sensations and thus render them manageable by the patient. Words help bring that which has been experienced as physical objects or forces into a system of thoughts and feelings that are experienced as personal creations that stand in a particular relationship to one another. Symbols help create us as subjects.
>
> "words bind anxiety"   (p. 186)

What happened for her in this session was the experience of what Bion (1962a, 1970) calls "containment." Not unlike a mom with a pre-verbal infant, I was encountering her somatically-based experience, and allowing it to fully impact me in my *body*. Then, I was allowing myself to move it around inside me, to "dream" it into pictures and finally into words (in that order). This "living with her experience inside me" gave her the (probably not conscious) feeling that the "meltdown" wasn't intolerable to me, so *she* could tolerate it differently. She could make room inside herself to entertain pictures and thoughts inside her that would represent and expand the experience (her scene of brushing her teeth and falling), rather than just doing something (motoric) to get rid of the feelings as she had always done before.

This was the first of a series of times when she came to our sessions in states of emotional disarray. Each time, we would live with (dream) the experience together. Each time, she would be able to "stretch out" into more and more meaning-making herself. Now, two years into the therapy, she no longer has "meltdowns" as she used to experience them. She has moments of piqued emotional experience, but she is able to do something different with them, noticing the bodily-based feelings they generate, holding herself from action-based discharge of the feelings, and tuning into herself to make sense of what they might mean.

It may be important at this juncture to point something out. In no way do I share this material to demonstrate my *unique* talents as a therapist. I share it because it describes a level of attunement that's part of the acquired art, but not an inaccessible part. What happened in this session is a sample of the ordinary potentials of therapy; something I see develop even in the work of grad-students-in-training in our program. But it requires a different kind of "being" in the room. It doesn't have the normal feel or pacing of ordinary conversation, and one must learn to set this rhythm and to tolerate the process it affords.

Carl Rogers commented toward the end of his life that he felt he did his best therapy when he found himself in a kind of meditative state in the presence of his clients (1989). This quieting down of the self—the allowing of a slower, less-pressured kind of cadence, this letting go of the ordinary rules of conversation in favor of creating the space for the therapist-patient dyad to linger with the crescendos of evoked feelings—these are all parts of the art of listening deeply. They take time to develop as a therapist, and in particular they take a quelling of one's own anxious need to be "helpful." But the level of attunement available is well worth the effort.

Orb

Let me now take you to another patient—one I also mentioned in the previous chapter—to give you a different example of the process of mentalization in action in session. This patient, whom we will call R. J., was in his fourth year of twice-a-week psychodynamic therapy. He had come to therapy at the bidding of his wife because of his out of control conflicts with his emerging teenage sons. I had initially experienced him as a consummately unrelated patient, who early in the therapy had insisted that our work together was strictly a "business arrangement," with no interpersonal or relational aspects to be talked about. His sessions indeed felt impersonal to me, ranging from his accounts of his own boredom and interpersonal miscues at work to his reflections on how the therapy was not helpful to him.

As time went on, particularly when we shifted from once to twice a week, there seemed a gradual warming up of what went on in session. He enjoyed coming more, found it more useful to him, and had even come to enjoy finding out what he was thinking and feeling.

During this particular session, after his always rather formal greeting to me, "Hello," we had sat comfortably silent for what seemed a long while. (A long while is perhaps five or ten minutes.) He then spoke, describing to me a moving picture that had formed distinctly in his mind's eye (imaginal register). It was an orb slowly turning in space, brightly lit, like one of NASA's pictures of a far distant planet. He described its exact look and velocity to me, and that he could make it turn faster or slower in his mind's eye as he wished. He found it beautiful and arresting, and truly loved that he could determine its speed. "Yes," I said simply, "it gets to turn at your pace." That was all I said.

Now, what was fascinating about this particular scene was that in the minutes of settled silence before he described the turning orb, *I* had been seeing a beautiful slowly-turning orb in my own mind's eye as well. I had let it quietly turn in my mind, not knowing why it was there or what it might be representing. As he described to me what he was looking at in his imagination, I quelled my impulse to share with him my inexplicable viewing of the exact same scene (although *that* was *more* than fascinating to me!). We were clearly in sync about something sacred to him, so I held it in my mind in a spirit of reverence within me. He finally spoke quietly, moving inside himself to the verbal register. "It's a picture of what happens in here between us. I come. We sit together. I go at my own pace. There's no rushing me, no need to go faster or slower than where I am in the moment. You match my pace. That's what we do. It's like nowhere else I've ever been in my life. I'm allowed to go at my own speed, without feeling rushed or pushed at to be or do anything differently." "Yes," I said quietly, with a slow, nodding motion of my head.

We had visited together a sacred representation of the freedom he felt in our sessions to be himself, to stretch out into his experience of himself without demand or intrusion from the outside. His image was the beginning of a representation to himself of many things: that he had never felt honored for just being himself; that he had always felt that he needed to sense and live up to the expectations, first of his parents, then of so many others in their wake.

It was the beginning of his realization that our relationship had indeed become special—had become sacred to him—that he felt my profound respect for him, and the room we had created for him between us.

All these things followed. And while we eventually (over the ensuing weeks and months) were able to use the medium of words to deliver the full meaning of that image that day, it was not for that day. That day, we were witnessing his right brain's way of capturing (largely non-verbally) something about what had been happening in the therapy for him for some time. Images and visual scenes can be powerful expressions of emotional truth, but sometimes, they take a while to be fully born into words. They may need time to come to full term.

He later verbalized to me that the way we sat and talked was something he had longed for all of his life, but didn't think possible. Now he wanted it in his other relationships. He wanted to sit with his wife or his best friend as though there were a fireplace like the one he imagined we had between us, that we both stared into while together, allowing all the time in the world for thoughts and feelings to come up from within.

In both of these cases, with Lyndsey and with R. J., we—first I as therapist, then we as a therapist-patient dyad—co-created a kind of environment in which feelings could be felt and lived with. Holding the space for feelings—allowing for them to stretch out and register their full force within—is hard and often anxious work. It's a practiced art to resist the urge to bandage a wound immediately, or to call 911, or to make the wound seem less serious than it really is. To be clear, this is not something I do successfully all the time. But the commitment to quietude and attunement in the face of psychological pain is the essential first step in the art of listening deeply. It allows the environment our minds and spirits require in order to truly engage in the process of living all the way through—mentalizing—our emotional experience.

Another side note that may be important: my feelings, impulses, images and thoughts—however present they feel in a session—may be *on*, or they may be *off*.

In a profound way, the patient is the author of his or her own experience, so the things that come to me, in whatever registers they present themselves, need always to be held with a certain tentativeness and humility within. But if and when we choose to offer something of what comes to us in somatic or image-based ways to our patients, it may or may not fit for them in the moment (although surprisingly, it often does).

Misses are OK, especially if they are offered tentatively. Even something that's off in the moment may add to or clarify the analytic discourse. It's also important to know that some things that come into our quietude and consciousness in session may just need to be lived with for a while—not spoken. Winnicott would say that if something has come to us, it is often on the verge of coming to our patient as well, and the better part of valor is to allow it to emerge from them (1962, 1968). If you noticed in the examples I used, we created the space in which the patient, much more than I as therapist, came up with the pivotal images and verbal meanings. My job was primarily to create the space in which we as a dyad could "dream" together.

The art of listening deeply. An acquired art and yes, a delicate art. We'll elaborate one more piece of this art in the upcoming chapter.

6

CREATING SPACE

Yesterday, on the eve of Christmas Eve, I received a card from a patient I've seen several times a week for eight years. The card was beautiful on the outside, embossed and embroidered colorfully with five horses (she owns two). Inside, the card was blank, except for the simple words she had penned:

> you have given me myself.
> thank you for the rest of my life.
> I will live it well.

We do sacred work. It is no less than that. It's because of the potentials of this work that I write, straining to orient, demystify, and make accessible what might seem beyond our reach. The acquired art of psychodynamic psychotherapy involves a whole symphony of skills, and slowly mastered capacities to read and feel and play music of various intensities, with just the right touch at the right moment. The nuance can be daunting. But there will be time for nuance and touch and timing. There will be a lifetime for those things. We are, together, sketching out some of the basics of it that nuance will enhance as time goes on.

Imagine a two-clef arrangement of the music of psychodynamic psychotherapy. Until now, we've been talking about what you need to be able to play with your right hand: the treble clef, so to speak. It carries the melody (most of the time). In our work, this involves the art of listening deeply, listening in an attuned way, listening in a way that is surprisingly different from ordinary listening. The other clef—the bass clef—provides the background music that gives context and meaning and depth to the melody. This plays on your left hand (for most of us, the less dominant hand), and is perhaps mastered more slowly. This clef involves the art of understanding what you're hearing in the therapy *over time*, and what is going on within the music that you and your patient play together.

But for now, I will take us one further step in the art of listening before we turn to the art of understanding. We will touch on what goes into creating the space of resonance, attunement, and potential that I've spoken of so far. How do we find the place from which listening deeply occurs? What does that space look like and feel like within and outside, and how do we optimize the chance that moments of meeting will occur?

In Old Testament symbology, when God directed the building of the temple, he described its construction in detail, including the ark of the covenant, which was to be housed in the holy of holies in the temple; the innermost sanctuary. The ark was to have a platform of solid gold with two gold seraphim (angels) at each end. Between these angels, there was to be a blank space, a place of nothing— nothing but air. That sacred, uncluttered space was to be the place where these most holy meetings between God and man were to occur.

The art of listening deeply requires space, within and outside. Space uncluttered by ordinary social rituals, by the warmth of niceties that are unconsciously but continuously extinguishing anxiety for us before it can find its voice. Space big enough and still enough to hold the aloneness of the one, in the presence of the other. These holiest of meetings, between the unthought, unuttered parts of the one and the listening stillness of the other, these require the disciplined space of potential, or "potential space," as Winnicott would call it. Gaston Bachelard, in *The Poetics of Space*, puts it this way:

> Immensity is within ourselves. It is attached to a sort of expansion of being that life curbs and caution arrests, but which starts again when we are alone. As soon as we become motionless, we are elsewhere; we are dreaming in a world that is immense. Indeed, immensity is the movement of motionless man. It is one of the dynamic characteristics of quiet daydreaming.
>
> *(1969: p. 184)*

Psychodynamic psychotherapy takes place in this space of immensity—in the space where the aloneness of the one can meet with itself and come to know itself in the presence of the other. And this space of meeting is delicate, indeed! Years ago, I worked with a senior therapist at an early point in my training who would stride into the waiting room of our clinic, find his (usually male adolescent) client, and, with a sweeping gesture, would slap the client on the back, and say in an upbeat voice, "How ya doin' today, buddy? Come on back!" I couldn't help thinking at the time that in his well-intentioned enthusiasm to set a welcoming and upbeat tone, he had ended the session before it had had a chance to get started.

The internal space of listening deeply requires first and foremost that we collect ourselves inside for the encountering of another person in a kind of raw, unadorned form. Raw and unadorned. Several days ago I visited my friends' newborn baby, Emma, on her second day of life. She was completely without shield or cover— having not yet learned the ways of being human—having to take in the gaze and the energy of any who would come into her space. It was precious and disarming, but it also struck me as dangerously unprotected. We learn beyond our very first days the art of wrapping ourselves—in social ritual, in bravado, in cleverness, or warmth, or humor, or distance, or authority. It becomes our invisible protection, constantly and unconsciously keeping watch for us against the dangers of the other.

The space of listening deeply, should we want to enter this space, requires an unwrapping of ourselves as therapists—a shedding of the normal cocoon of protection that is our ordinary second skin—a making room for the full force of the other. This means many things—some of them seemingly very small—that mark out this space as big enough and still enough, and steady enough to contain what may want to come forth.

We do many things reflexively (unconsciously) to cover this space ordinarily. The things I write about in this chapter may threaten these coverings. You may be inclined to dismiss them out of hand because they "don't fit" your style, or seem too small to matter. I offer a note of caution in this regard. In 1867, Joseph Lister first proposed the practice of keeping a sterile field in surgery. At that time, the post-surgical death rate was 50%. The aphorism, "the surgery was successful, but the patient died" was the true and common parlance of the day. Lister's methods, although simple and unobtrusive, were met with skepticism and indifference, even hostility. His interventions were perhaps seemingly too small to be of consequence. But some small things really matter. In psychodynamic psychotherapy, they can make the difference between a treatment that lives and one that does not.

Starting Moments

The therapy starts from the moment of our first encounter with our patient-to-be. Our moment of greeting (even our first moments on the phone) must say, "This is a *different* space. In this space, there will be more room for you than you've become accustomed to. In this space, I will wait—we will wait—to encounter you on your terms."

As we prepare ourselves for our first encounter with a particular patient, the clamor of thoughts and concerns that beset us as new therapists (often as old therapists) about our competence, about how this first session will go and what this person will say back to their referral source, about whatever else assails our attention before the moments of meeting, need to be recognized by us and turned aside from, so that we have the space of our own receptivities available. It means that our hearts must be uncluttered with our own need for this person to see us in a particular way or to have a particular response to us. In its place, there should be a simple openness and curiosity of spirit. We don't know what will happen here; what will emerge from this person and in this relational field. We don't know what will be brought forth from them or in us. It is ours only to provide a space where the unknown thing might come forth.

Concomitantly, there should be the recognition that for this person, our new patient, this moment of meeting will be daunting and difficult. They will have thought about this all week, they will perhaps not have slept well the night before.

They will have had to negotiate the (conscious or unconscious) anxiety of choosing the clothes they would wear this day to present themselves to us, finding our office, and getting there at the appointed time. Then there will be the moment of meeting us in person when they have to do the quick internal work of adjusting the image they had formed of us in advance, based on the sound of our voice in the first phone conversation and whatever other information they've gleaned about us in advance. They don't know how it will go in this first session, or what will be asked of them.

Setting the Tone

First moments are pivotal; they set the metric for all that follows. The first few minutes of a therapy are that blank space of meeting that set the tone for the whole of it. As much as our social training has taught us the trade of dispelling anxiety, our job at the outset of a therapy is the opposite: to make a place where anxiety can live in plain sight; to make a place where, over time, a whole range of hidden feelings can live in plain sight.

So, instead of the reflexive launching ritual that includes such para-greetings as "Welcome. Did you have trouble finding this place?" or "I hope this meeting time wasn't too inconvenient for you," there is a blank space, appointed only with the inquiry, "Brett? I'm Dr. Quatman. Please come on back." Instead of a little filler chat about the weather as we make our way down the hall to the therapy room, there is quietude. Instead of the social back and forth as we are seated that might include, "Oh, I really like your office." "Thanks, so do I. I've been here in this building since 1992," there is a blank space. There is an unspoken honoring of the anxiety involved—for the therapist and the patient—in starting a therapy.

This is a practiced and disciplined blank space that is entirely the therapist's responsibility to create. We as therapists can choose to fill up the space of initial anxiety, but in so doing, to paraphrase Ogden (1989), we have committed an act of robbery, having robbed the patient of his or her unique way to find themselves in our presence and their own, and to start the voyage of their own therapy. This is not a *rule* of doing the work, it is a *tool* of doing the work. Setting the tone is a way of communicating from the first moment that we will be with one another in a way the patient hasn't been with another before.

One of my consultees worked in her internship at the local YWCA. The distance between the waiting room and the therapy rooms was an L-shaped hallway that extended half a city block. The discipline of walking all that way each time, well enough ahead of the patient so as to quell that person's attempts at idle chatter was nothing short of valiant in my mind. But necessary to the work, and my fleet-footed consultee could feel that this was true.

The Room

Once we are through the not insignificant first moments of meeting, greeting and seating, there is the all-important first volley. But let me back up. Seating is important. It's important to be clear about where a patient should sit. It is not OK to indicate that they may sit anywhere. Your seat is a pre-designated space that is set up in a particular way. Your clock is visible to you; what the patient may see in terms of artwork and windows, etc., is something you've set up in advance. Should the patient, by mistake, head for your chair, it's of no small importance to interrupt their movement and reset where they will sit. This is a claiming of your space, which will occur in a temporal sense with the ending of each session. Also, the physical space between the chairs is important. It should be enough to allow their aloneness in your presence; a little more than how you might space normal living room chairs. And here's an extremely practical but utterly critical part of things: I use a digital clock for my sessions, seated on a table to the right of my chair. I routinely have a mug of water that sits on that table. If my mind loses track of the time with my own internal clock, a motion to lift or replace my water mug gets me a good look at the clock.

Office décor is also important. Bion conducted his therapy in an entirely bare room. Pictures of your family or your vacation trip to Hawaii pull the fulcrum of the therapy away from the inner life of your patient, and toward your own personal life. As intimate as a therapy will become, this is not to be the ground on which the therapy is conducted. These are some of the silent background pieces of a practiced therapy.

First Volley

Back to the all-important first volley. As difficult and "antiseptic" as this may sound, it's important to allow the patient to start the session, however they can, with whatever awkwardness or lostness this evokes. This is a signature moment, and it should be signed in the patient's own hand.

In my own practice, I wait. Some starting patients aren't sure what the silence means. They guess their way into the space. "Am I supposed to start?" I nod in response, slowly, with warmth and resoluteness. "I don't know what to say. Why don't you ask me some questions?" "You seem anxious," I might say in response. "Can you tell me what feels anxious about trying to tell us why you've come?"

In such a moment, we've begun together to tell the emotional truth of it. This is exactly what we will try to do the entire way along. There is also the inevitable patient who wants to start with how therapy works, or what your particular therapeutic orientation is. A simple response that says that it will be clearer if we show them rather than tell them is a helpful way to get the onus of starting back where it belongs.

From the beginning, here's what's happening: the patient is beginning a relationship with you that is destined to be the same as *and* different from all other relationships they've ever had. The same as, in the sense that we as humans have a certain pattern that defines and bounds how we are used to "doing" ourselves and being with another person. We try as much as possible to color within these familiar lines with every other we encounter. A relationship that is different, in that we together will look at and consider these lines and patterns, with all of their various meta-communicative and emotional pushes and pulls, in order to understand their familiarity and function (and constriction). This is what's in play from the first moments. To insert ourselves too patently into this space at first is to usurp from the patient their attempt to enact the familiar with us, so that someday, we can together create the unfamiliar.

Initial Considerations

A note to therapists in agency and training settings. First sessions are desperately important. They set the metronome for the whole of it, as we've said. As new therapists in random training sites with assorted supervisors, there are the inevitable requirements for a structured history-taking, and an elaborated explanation of the exceptions to confidentiality, etc. As much as possible, it's important to start the therapy in a different space from those up-front concerns. Some make their way through this territory by having the legalities and exceptions to confidentiality occur in the initial screening and session set-up process; others, by presenting these things in a written statement before the beginning of the session itself. Some alert their supervisors that they want the history to emerge organically, to be part of the way the patient introduces themself to you. These are realities of training sites that have to be negotiated.

The Space of Quiet

Quietude is the coin of the realm in the beginning. It is the chrysalis from which something of new form will slowly emerge. Sitting quietly with a patient allows us to feel their (somatic) energy, to experience the psychic pulls that they exert on us. It allows us to begin the process of losing ourselves in their presence (and they in ours); of yielding to the thoughts and reveries their presence evokes in our internal (imaginal) theatre.

I'm reminded of an entertaining story told at a local psychoanalytic society gathering by one of the guest speakers. He had decided to begin his own therapy with a well-respected psychoanalytic psychotherapist in the area, finally getting the courage to phone with his inquiry about perhaps starting a therapy at some point. Not thinking that he would be successful in his foray, he was surprised and shocked that the analyst could accommodate him that week at 7:00 a.m. two days from then.

Getting over the jolt of it, the speaker agreed to the meeting, considering privately that it was quite a distance and *quite* an early appointment time. On the appointed day, he rose early in the morning to make his way to the therapist's office. He drove the long distance, arrived at the therapist's office, was greeted and found his way into the therapy room.

He knew in advance that he would probably need to start the session himself, so he did. He made his way anxiously through one topic, then the next, and then the next, finding himself more and more fitful and uncomfortable as the session continued. At minute 48, he had heard nothing from the therapist—not a word. He considered all the emotional energy that had gone into the decision to see this man, all the hours of nervous anticipation, his fitful night of sleep followed by the inclemently early point of rising. It was all too much for him.

He launched into an end-of-session diatribe. "Fuck you," he said, "and fuck this! I've come all this way to see you, borne all of this anxiety and anticipation and inconvenience. I have talked this entire time, and you have said nothing! This is a fucking waste of time!" To which the therapist at last responded, "Well," he said, "if you could do *that* more often, I suspect you wouldn't need to come here anymore." The speaker knew that he had hit on the truth of it, and felt uncommonly seen by the comment, understanding that in the silence, the whole time, the therapist had been getting to know something quite close to the essence of him. This precipitously tumultuous start was the beginning of a long and successful analysis.

There are huge upsides for the therapy when there is space from the beginning. Often, we are presented with a microcosm of the patient's way of being as they first try to introduce themselves to us. We are, from the beginning, immersed in a field of psychic particles that each person emits. We feel their particular anxiety and their particular way of being with, or positioning the other, around that anxiety. We register their presence in our own bodies—often quite subtly—and feel different energies from the different people we meet in this way. But the art of it lies in creating and allowing the space for this; a space quiet enough for us to detect the barely detectable signals of the patient's inner world.

Creating Space in the First Session

Let me see if I can give us a sense of this creating space from the beginning of things, which facilitates a taking in of the patient's energy, and in turn gives us an experience "in microcosm" of this patient, and why they've come. I'll use moments from the starting session of two patients.

Tedi

The first, I will call Tedi. She was a health ed counselor in the mental health field. She had encountered me in a continuing education workshop I had co-taught, and felt from that venue that she might be able to work with me.

We started the session as I normally do, allowing her to stake out the territory as she wished. She spoke fast, but with a certain emotionality that seemed at first alive to me. As the session went on, I (in my quietude) began to feel a slight sense of agitation. I couldn't describe it to myself. It was no doubt registering itself at the (somatic) level of my body. I remember at first looking into the picture on the wall just adjacent to her, trying to disengage myself enough to locate my experience of what was going on as she talked to me. I eventually took the freedom to close my eyes and attempt to feel what it felt like to be in her presence.

After 30 or so minutes of continuing to listen to her, I saw in my mind's eye (the imaginal register) a stacked set of two large television sets. The upper one—the one at eye-level—had nothing but static on it; the lower one was playing a TV program, but I couldn't quite see what was playing. It struck me that the energy in the room was well described by this split-screen arrangement. I sat with the image for a while, allowing its meaning to suggest itself further to me. I wanted to be able to say something to the patient that was emotionally true to what was happening in that first session.

I stopped her monologue at some point, and with the aid of the picture that had formed in my mind said to her, "You know, there's something I'm noticing as we've been sitting here together. It seems there are two things going on between us today. One is the conversation we're having; the other is in the background but may be more important, because it seems to be carrying more of the story—the anxiety that perhaps you're feeling as you're with me today, but wanting to distract yourself from, and me as well. I wonder whether you feel that in here as we're talking?"

She said that she did, and that she often was aware of a background of anxiety in herself that she didn't know what to do with. She said that at one level or another, it was always with her. She said she was embarrassed that it showed, but relieved at the same time that we could name it and that she wouldn't be required to cover it up as she usually does. Our efforts to slow her down and allow her to feel and understand this anxiety were to become central to the therapy, there in small measure from the first session. Had there been no psychic space for me to consider my internal experience in her presence, this first session might have steered the therapy in a quite different direction.

Barb

The second patient, whom I will call Barb, came to me from a colleague of mine who had led a short-term outpatient group that Barb had attended. She began talking, letting me know that she had had therapy in the past, and that she knew how this went, so to speak. She said this several more times, and I remember being put off by this. To my mind she was suggesting from the outset that nothing new was to be happening in this therapy.

It felt to me as though her description of this initial encounter was roughly akin to the process of having a mammogram—a procedure one has repeatedly over time, where the humans involved are incidental. I also felt strangely uncomfortable, crowded by her presence and the volume of her voice, as I would be on a hot July day, standing in a grocery line with someone's bare arms next to me, occasionally touching into me. I felt a sense of discouragement, not knowing if I would be able to work with this person.

In addition, toward the end of the session, at about the two-more-minutes point, I was suddenly presented in my mind's eye with a picture of Niagara Falls, roaring with power, unstoppable. I braced myself for the moment, sensing that the patient (undoubtedly unconsciously) was about to launch into an end-of-session fight for an unstoppable extension of the normal time frame. Armed, I was able to say to her that I sensed that what she was attempting to talk to me about was emotionally important, and that I did not want to dishonor it by squeezing it into the thin sliver of time we had left together.

At the fifty-minute point, I stood up from my chair and moved over to my desk area where I typically make out a receipt for the session. As I turned to pivot back toward the patient's chair, I found her standing just a few inches from me. "Can I have a hug?" she asked importunately. "I actually don't do that," I managed to return (relieved to have found words for this moment), "but we can talk about it the next time you're here."

This was a moment when the patient was unconsciously maneuvering to ground the relationship in the familiar for herself. It was a desperately important moment for the therapy, because in addition to being her attempt to drive down the anxiety stirred in her by the session, it communicated in microcosm the impingements inherent in *being* the patient, and my own willingness as therapist to freeze the dance mid-motion in order to *understand* it rather than to (motorically) *enact* it.

The preceding moments of the session had also been part of the microcosm. I was to come to find out, as the therapy moved forward, that she had suffered insufferable impingements of her bodily person and her sense of ownership of her own time and space, from babyhood, at the hands of an off and on psychotic mother. These were the impingements she was putting into motion with me in the therapy from the beginning moments of it. Even my sense of the therapy's feeling *generic* was a foreshadowing of something she had felt on the receiving end of her mother's care. Had I made it my goal to make us both comfortable in that initial interchange, much of what she was communicating to me would have been covered over, perhaps never to be unearthed. In large part, although she did not know it at the time, my experience of her in the first session was at the heart of why she had come to the therapy.

First Session Comments

There are two more pieces I'll mention about creating the space of psychodynamic psychotherapy during the first session. The first is something I've just mentioned. That is, that as much as is possible, I try in the first session to say something of the emotional truth of this encounter between us. This will be my effort the whole way along in the therapy, but if I have the words for it in the first session, I try to say something of it. This communicates to the patient and to myself that this will be the territory of the therapy—that we will be letting the emotional truth between us emerge and be worded as it can (so that it can be transformed). If it has not otherwise surfaced, I often ask a patient at the end of the session if they can tell me what it has been like for them as we've met together today; how they've experienced it, themselves, me. This begins to put their experience of our relationship into play.

The second is something extremely hard to achieve as a new therapist: simply ending the session. This is an unbelievably potent expression of the "space" of the therapy. If the session is allowed to go beyond its appointed time—to spill over "out of bounds," so to speak—we've communicated many things besides our gracious generosity toward and interest in this patient. We've said simultaneously, "I'm afraid of you," "I'm afraid of my own aggression," "I'm afraid you won't like me," "I don't value my time," and "This space won't be steady enough and sturdy enough to hold you and what you bring to it." We've said, in Winnicott's parlance, that there won't be the space for "hate" in this room, so there can't be the space for authentic love either (1947). These are all unconscious communications that take place from the beginning of the therapy, and this piece, though seemingly small, is another pivotal part of creating the space of it.

Necessary Disciplines

We started this chapter with the question, "What does creating the space of psychodynamic psychotherapy look like and feel like within and outside, and how do we optimize the chance that moments of meeting will occur?" The parts and pieces I've shared with you in this chapter have been meant to make sense of the kinds of disciplines necessary to this acquired art. A closing story might put this in better light.

My friend's daughter pursued ballet at a professional level. One afternoon, when I was a guest in their home, she tried to teach me the positioning of one's body that is part of the art of ballet. Amidst my irrepressible laughter and futile attempts to follow her instructions, I could not believe that all that *contortion* was the backweave of such beautiful choreography. But she had acquired it over time, muscle by muscle, bone by bone. And in the end, it equipped her to dance with incredible grace and beauty. It was, for her, truly an acquired art.

7

UNDERSTANDING, THE BASS CLEF, AND INTERSUBJECTIVITY

We've been talking in the previous chapters about listening deeply; listening with our whole bodies; listening through the full architecture of emotion from somatic, to motoric, to imaginal, to verbal registers. We've talked about creating the space in which listening deeply occurs: the quietude, the openness, the disciplines. In the following chapters, we turn to the *art of understanding*—of developing an ear to hear the bass notes that play in background of the therapy.

Over time, and with much practice, we can begin to appreciate fully, and even to participate in, the music of what happens in the therapy. The art of understanding is truly an acquired art. It involves perspectives developed over the past one hundred years from Freud onward. It involves clinical sensibilities exceeding the span of one's lifetime to develop. But there are always beginning steps, and it is my job to take us on some of these.

In the next chapters, we will look together at the intersubjective field in which the therapy takes place (we've already begun to do that, without calling attention to it). In this chapter, we'll discuss intersubjectivity itself, and the co-created place of the analytic third within that field. Next, we'll talk about the patient's "object relations"—their internalized set of relational structures that determine and bound how they relate to themselves and others in their world. Then, in the chapters that follow, we'll look at transference as a special manifestation (externalization) of this world of internal "objects." We'll look at the role (and usefulness) of our own countertransferences, and how to distinguish our "stuff" from the "stuff" of what is happening between the patient and us. We'll talk about the underlying anxieties that orient and determine a patient's way of being with us and themselves (and resisting being with us and themselves). We will do all this, with an eye to what the experience of psychodynamic psychotherapy is truly purposed to accomplish: a fuller and richer living of a person's humanity.

The Goal

To begin with, let's consider more fully the goal of our work as psychodynamic psychotherapists. At its most fundamental level, to use Ogden's words, psychoanalytic psychotherapy takes as its goal helping the (patient) "become human in a fuller sense than he has been able to achieve to this point." He then continues, "The effort to become human is among the very few things in a person's life that may over time come to feel more important to him than his personal survival" (1997: p. 15).

In the beautiful following passage, Ogden uses Goethe's *Faust* to capture the quest for full humanity inherent in the psychotherapeutic task:

> And I'm resolved my most inmost being shall share in what's the lot of all mankind that I shall understand their heights and depths, shall fill my heart with all their joys and griefs, and so expand myself to their and, like them, suffer shipwreck too (p. 46).

(Ogden, 1997: p. 16)

The goal is no less than this: becoming human in a fuller sense. This goal, as easy as it is to state, is uncommonly difficult to achieve, and none of us ever achieves it completely. Becoming human can be lost in the ordinariness of life. It can be sacrificed on the altar of achievement. It can be suffocated by grief and disappointment. It can be impersonated by falling in love. It can be siphoned off by the quest for financial gain. It can be strangled by the legacy of family dysfunction. It can be sucked away by addictions. It can be substituted for by perversions. It can be lost in the pursuit of happiness.

The Work of Understanding: Getting Oriented

The art of *listening deeply* takes us a long way toward the goal of helping another become truly human. The gift of this kind of listening is rare and precious, indeed. But there is more to the psychodynamic task. The true genius of psychoanalysis, since its inception, has lain in the work of *understanding*—understanding what we're hearing (in the bass notes) session-by-session, and over time. Increasingly, over the last fifty years, the attention of psychoanalysis has shifted toward seeking to understand what is being put into play not just *within* the patient, but relationally, *between* patient and therapist. Thankfully, for this part of the work—the work of understanding—there are some orienting axes, handed to us by Freud himself.

Many think of the accidents and accents of formal psychoanalysis—sessions 4–5 times a week, the use of the couch, institute training, use of the words "analyst" and "analysand"—as the markers of real or *bona fide* psychoanalytic psychotherapy. Freud was not of this mind. He said that "anything that takes as its concern transference and resistance, and the existence and role of the unconscious deserves to be called psychoanalysis" (Freud, 1914). So these—the unconscious, the transference, the resistance to growth—are our orienting *axes of understanding*. Whether we call it psychoanalysis, or psychoanalytic psychotherapy, or psycho-dynamic psychotherapy, or object relations therapy—whatever we call it—if we are truly orienting our work of understanding toward the axes of the unconscious and the transference, we are doing psychoanalytic work.

This is an important point to underscore before we go forward in talking more fully about the art of understanding. Many of us as psychodynamic (or psychoanalytic) therapists are not in a venue that allows for a 3-to-4-to-5-times-a-week psychotherapy. Nor will many of us work with a population able financially to sustain such a therapy. Many will consciously choose to serve a range of people that includes those barely able to afford weekly therapy. I think of my colleague's psychotic patient who folded laundry all night at Target in order to pay for her $15 per week therapy sessions.

The rich tools and perspectives on psychoanalysis should not be considered out of reach to such patients (and therapists). If we're about the goal of helping our patients "become human in a fuller sense," and if we can learn to orient toward the axes of the unconscious and the transference, then we are indeed legitimately doing psychoanalytic psychotherapy. To be sure, learning to orient toward these axes of understanding in psychoanalytic work is no small endeavor, but it is fully available to those who would commit themselves to the work of learning. We will orient toward these axes in the pages to come.

Intersubjectivity: One...

So, intersubjectivity: a pivotal concept. Psychoanalysis has been a living art form since its inception, and has changed and evolved with the additions of its contributors. The focus of understanding in Freud's work, as truly brilliant as it was, was in the context of a "one-person" psychology. That person came to an analyst to be *analyzed* (usually by a *him*). The analyst listened to the patient's free associations and made integrative sense of the unconscious roots of the patient's symptoms. The analyst worked with the patient's resistances to seeing and understanding his own unconscious motivational system, and observed the ways in which the patient related to him (the analyst) as part of that system. In the course of the analysis, if the analyst experienced emotional disturbance or disequilibration as he worked with a patient, this was a sign that something was going awry within the analyst, and it was his job to resolve his countertransference issues so he could get back to analyzing the patient.

...Plus One...

Increasingly, during the past sixty years, the locus of the psychotherapeutic encounter has shifted in theoretical terms to include the contributions of the patient *and* the therapist. From Winnicott's observation that there is no such thing as a baby (in the absence of the mother who attends to and provides for that baby) (Winnicott, 1960), we now recognize that there are not one, but two linked people—two "subjects"—in the therapy room whose respective "subjectivities" are in play in the therapeutic encounter the whole time. These two people comprise what we have come to call the "analytic dyad." To be sure, the roles of the two people involved are asymmetrical. The therapist, in Winnicott's language, is involved in providing a "holding environment" for the other, facilitative of the patient's psychological growth; the patient's role is, over time, to come to be able to use such provision in whatever ways truly promote that growth.

...Equals Three

Increasingly, through the influence of Bion's writing (and many others), we have come to recognize that these two together—the patient and therapist—co-create a "third" space that emerges between them, an "intersubjective" space, contributed to in different ways by both, but owned or authored by neither individually. Within this space, the conscious and unconscious products of both people form, inform, and contribute to the moments and to the understandings that will occur in the therapy.

Ireland (2003) uses the metaphor of subatomic (psychic) particles to describe this intersubjective intermixing. It is as though the protons, neutrons, and electrons of the two people mix together, and attract and repel one another, forming something new in their mix. This "third" space, which represents the co-mingling of the subjectivities of the two people, Ogden has called the "intersubjective analytic third." The "analytic third" contributes profoundly to the work of understanding in the therapy, and has been well described and elaborated within modern psychoanalytic literature (see Atwood & Stolorow, 1984; Bion, 1952, 1959, 1962a; Ogden, 1982, 1994, 1997, 2001, 2005, 2009; Sandler, 1976; Stern, 2004 for elaboration).

The Third Space

Now that we have some terminology, let's think slowly and carefully together about this. We're really saying that somehow, by virtue of how we as therapists open to and position ourselves within the therapy, we create the possibility of a third area of experience, that itself yields what neither the therapist nor the patient could produce single-handedly (in terms of insight, understanding or experience). This third space—this "possibility"—is not created automatically when any two people gather, or when a therapist and a patient decide to work together. It is not the natural byproduct of just any random therapeutic encounter. The conditions for its creation are quite specific, and include the elements we've talked about so far in terms of space, quietude, listening deeply, therapeutic frame, and some of what we'll discuss here. Given these conditions, this intersubjective analytic third is more likely to emerge.

Intersubjective Co-Creating

So what is it that emerges, potentially? Let me first use the simple metaphor of a pregnancy. Under normal circumstances, a pregnancy requires two people involved on the meeting ground of a sexual encounter, which itself requires close, open intimacy. Under ordinary circumstances, this sexual meeting expects nothing but the encounter of the other. However, in sacred moments, it is surprisingly generative of something new—a third—carrying parts of each, reflective of each, but replicative of neither. This new being—the third—will carry something beyond what either party could contribute on their own. This "third" will arrest their attention, and will provide a unique and intimate meeting ground between the two partners. It will need to be apprehended by each, learned from by each, recognized by each. It will bring forth new things from each. It will grow and change over time. So, from the contributions of both partners in a couple, a third is created, carrying parts of both, but being more than and different from the one or the other, or even the two together.

In the intersubjective space of psychodynamic psychotherapy, what can emerge in the analytic third is exactly what the previous metaphor suggests. Something *new* is born—a different feeling, a shared emotion, an otherwise inaccessible image or metaphor, an insight that could not have been born through sheer deduction or even by listening attentively to the other over time. This space provides a level of access to the inner experience of the other, and ultimately an understanding of the other that could only be yielded by a co-creational process, and that is, at the same time, a mystery and a gift.

Reverie

One form in which this something *new* presents itself is through the therapist's (and often the patient's) engagement in *reverie*, a process akin to sleep-time dreaming, while awake. Reveries waft into the consciousness of the therapist (or patient) in the form of "mundane, quotidian, unobtrusive thoughts, feelings, fantasies, ruminations, daydreams, bodily sensations, and so on" (Ogden, 2001: p. 21). Reveries present themselves in somatic, motoric, or visual (even auditory) registers (see Chapters 4 and 5). They happen only as we give ourselves over to the quiet inner space inside us to listen deeply and to open the aperture of our being to its fullest extent. They occur subliminally in the therapist during the session, seeming to be mental rubble to be brushed aside in the listening/understanding process. But drawn *as they are* from the co-created analytic third, they may, in moments, contain raw elements connecting the therapist directly to the inner experience of the patient, leading to moments of uncommon connection and to otherwise inaccessible insights. It is as though, for moments, we share one mind (that belongs to neither of us). Such moments help us to piece together what it is like to be this patient, and to be in a relationship with this patient. I'll illustrate this part of the process as we move forward in this chapter and the next. So hang onto this thought for a few minutes, and we'll come back to it.

Now, preparing oneself and the therapeutic space for co-creating the analytic third is part of the acquired art. It is certainly built on listening deeply. But it perhaps goes just one step further. In this intersubjective co-creational process, we as therapists must make a tacit agreement to open ourselves to feel and to be affected by the psychic energy of the other. It is as though for this work, we voluntarily adjust our normally semi-permeable psychic membranes to become more permeable, more easily penetrated, affected, breached by the psychic "particles" of the other.

Intersubjectivity: A Messy Process

Let me be as explicit as I can. While we take control of the therapy's frame (start, stop times, pacing, who speaks first, etc.), we try, from the first, to put ourselves on the receiving end of (and thus to get a core sample of) how this person is. In the service of this effort, we adjust our own permeabilities and allow the patient's particles to "hit" us however they hit us, trying to notice what it feels like to be on the receiving end of their energy. We allow it; we feel their particles crash into, affect, and sometimes re-arrange our own psychic particles. We sometimes lose our psychic footing in the particle blast (or undertow, or seduction, or poisoning). We observe ourselves having lost our footing (however this happens), and at some point we (hope to) make sense of it for and with our patient.

At first, this can take many forms. We might feel suffocated in someone's presence, or be *really* happy to see them. We might be gratified that they are so good looking and personable. We might feel feelings of not being smart or clever enough to keep up with them. We might hate the volume or cadence of their voice. We might feel pleasurably idealized, or desperately insecure. We might feel pulled to do our practice a slightly different way. We might find ourselves unusually anxious or chatty or helpful. These are all ways I have certainly felt with various patients.

There's a feel with everyone. Everyone emits psychic particles. Our job is to open to the particle blast (or bath or ooze), and participate in it (sometimes unwittingly), but all the time to hold onto something inside us that is the therapist, and is observing all of this happening, often only over time. That's our job, although making such observations conscious is almost always inaccessible to us at first, often for what can seem a long time.

A "Particul-ar" Example

Perhaps a quick example of this process would be helpful before we go forward. Last Thursday I was anticipating seeing a patient I've seen only for three weeks now. He is a prominently Type-A businessman, and his stated goal for therapy is to find ways to more effectively override the stress messages he is receiving from his stomach—hmmmmm. At home before the day's sessions, I found myself taking particular care in picking out what I would wear for the day. I rejected several also-rans, and finally put on an outfit I'd never worn before, with a shawl given to me by a friend in Thailand. I wanted to feel like I looked put together and sophisticated that day, but wasn't conscious of why.

This is tiny, but it's one in the stream of things being created within me with this particular patient in our particular intersubjective space. I might be feeling the subtle impact of his own internal pressure for perfection, spilling over into my psyche, and re-arranging my particles (including my unconscious clothing choices).

Here's another piece of the same new therapy. When we finished the session last week, I noticed as I walked to the water cooler that my entire upper musculature had tightened up, and that I was breathing more shallowly. I realized that I had felt under pressure the entire session. It seemed as though I was under pressure to offer him practical solutions, which I resisted doing, but only with great effort. What little I know at this early point in the therapy, however uncomfortable I am for a while, I do know that my particles are picking up and living with something of what it is to be on the *receiving* end of this patient. So far, my "particles" feel tense and under pressure to appear "put together" and to "deliver the goods." Over time, as the intersubjective mixing of particles proceeds, I may indeed come to know more, particularly to know something of what it is to *be* the *him* who creates such tension and pressure in me, and doubtlessly in himself. I will give more in-depth examples as we go forward, but wanted to ground the discussion just momentarily in a current, just beginning-to-emerge, real-life experience.

So under the essential conditions of *listening deeply*—and these are absolutely essential to this process—we can learn over time to open ourselves to the awareness of the psychic impact of our patients on us as therapists, to be more and more attuned to this in ourselves. Everyone has an impact, an energy, an effect on us. Becoming aware of this effect, and how we are moved around by it inside—how we become subtly *different* in our physical experience, our feeling, our thinking, and our behavior with this particular patient—this is an important building block in the process of coming to *understand* the inner psychic terrain of this other. Then, with the unique intersubjective intermixing of their particles with ours, there can emerge the co-creation of the unexpected—in a birth-space we call the analytic third.

I will present a case example of this intersubjective analytic third in slow-motion in the next chapter. But first I'd like to see if I can walk us more specifically into this intersubjective space together, and parse this process into a quasi-temporal sequence.

I will call the elements of this sequence "moments of meeting," "moments of swirl," and "moments of precipitation"—shorthand terms I've created to talk to myself about the intersubjective process.

A Reminder

A quick reminder: the territory I'm now walking us into is the explicit province of psychodynamic psychotherapy. Supervisors and colleagues from other perspectives operate with different theoretical frameworks (usually focused on relieving the symptom), and will generally not focus specifically and preferentially on your experience of the therapeutic relationship. We hold some things in common with other therapeutic schools; some things not. We certainly hold parts of the art of listening in common.

But the *art of understanding*—making sense of what we're hearing and experiencing in the analytic third—is a definite point of departure from other schools of therapy, represented by a different *goal* (helping someone become more fully human) and by a different *process* (working in the analytic third with the unconscious, the transference and the resistance). Your progressive training and experience as a psychodynamic clinician are what optimize the likelihood that you will operate in and benefit from the space of the analytic third.

Three "Moments"

So let's look together at these three elements—three moments. I'll talk about the first of these three components first, "moments of meeting," but you may recognize that I've been making reference to these moments the whole way along.

Moments of meeting

In the permeable intersubjective particle mix of therapy, unexpected "moments of meeting" can occur. These are moments where we come to know what we otherwise could not know, or we come to share what we otherwise could not share.

In my classes, we have developed a metaphor to describe these moments. We imagine together a great big soup pot sitting between the patient and the therapist. Into that pot go the (often unspoken) psychic contributions of both people (carrots, celery, bay leaves, etc., from one; onions, chicken, garlic, etc., from the other). The soup simmers, and the mixed flavors of it waft into the shared space (the analytic third), sometimes stimulating memory, insight, desire, experience, or suggesting this flavor or that, as the soup cooks.

These co-created waftings come to the consciousness of the therapist in the form of *reveries*, which present themselves in somatic, motoric, or imaginal (visual or even auditory) registers. As I have explained, reveries occur subliminally in the therapist during the session, seeming to be insignificant mental rubble, perhaps even distractions to the listening/understanding process. But drawn *as they are* from the co-created analytic third (the soup), they may, in moments, contain raw elements (flavors) connecting the therapist directly to the inner experience of the patient in entirely unexpected (and frankly unexplainable) ways. In the co-created soup, it is as though, for moments, we share one mind (that belongs to neither of us). This is better illustrated than explained, so I will first illustrate, then explain.

On this particular day I was sitting with a patient who was a retired professional orchestra conductor. As usual I was quiet in my listening, allowing the space for him to stretch out into his experience of that session, and for me to stretch out into mine. He was emotionally guarded as a patient, having endured much loss in his life, and allowing little of his emotional world to show to himself or to others.

As an aside, it will help you to know that often in the course of daily life, I have a song playing in the back of my mind. It's just part of my particular DNA. It's most often just quietly there, and I might even have to look around inside to find out what happens to be playing, and what it might be telling me about how I'm feeling. It doesn't typically happen when I'm with someone else—usually only when I'm alone.

In this session, which was about my patient's struggle with the pending outcome of some medical tests his male partner was undergoing, I began to hear the symphonic sounds of Smetena's *Moldau* in the back of my mind. At first, there were the quiet sounds of the first movement—the sounds of a tiny rivulet beginning its tentative journey down the contours of a mountainside. I continued listening to my patient, and as he went on, the music continued. The piece itself gains strength and volume over its various movements as the rivulet becomes a stream, then a rushing current, but in this session, the audible volume of the music in my own mental background began to rise. It became so prominent that I was having to work to focus my attention on my patient's narrative. As usual, I allowed myself to wonder about this experience—a musical reverie—and why this music might be playing in this session at this time. I was clueless.

In a way that was technically sort of gauche (and I don't recommend), I finally spoke to my patient, saying simply, "You know, today as you've been talking, I've had the Moldau playing in my mind as part of our session the whole time. I'm not sure what it means." "That was the first piece I ever conducted in a professional orchestra," he responded with a hint of surprise.

This was a surprising "moment of meeting" (for both of us)—one that as a therapist I could not have invented. But it was drawn as reverie from the commingled psychic soup pot between us. It was a moment created inexplicably and non-consciously between us, a moment whose effect was to bond us in a different way in that moment and in moments to come. Unbeknown to either of us, the emotional tenor of that particularly minor musical piece was to presage the dark real-life scenes of tragedy that were to emerge over the next two years in this patient's life.

I'll give you another brief example of a "moment of meeting" from my practice on Friday, only stunning in its simplicity. As I listened to my patient, back from Christmas break, I noticed myself lightly rubbing the tops of my hands. I often notice my hands as I look down in thought during a session, but this particular time, I was noticing their unusual dryness. I found myself running the fingers of my right hand over the outer surface of my left hand, and being surprised at the dryness I found, almost to the flakey point—extremely uncommon for me. I returned my attention to my patient, who was talking about how, in the wake of the three-week Christmas break, she had begun to be self-critical across a range of fronts. Influenced, perhaps, by my in-the-moment physical experience, I used the word "autoimmune" as a shorthand way to describe the purely psychic way in which she was beginning to attack herself. Not responding to the observation in the way I had intended it, she responded "Yes!" with enthusiasm, "My *hands* are terrible!" (holding up her hands for us both to see). "They've *erupted*, this whole time over break! I think it's been my body's *autoimmune* response."

Here's what happened. In the soup between us, her bodily experience had been mirrored by my bodily experience (my dry hands); my word choice "autoimmune" had come not randomly from my own mind, but more meaningfully from the soup between us. As simple and concrete an example as this is, it is illustrative of a kind of connectivity—in this example, my body (hands) and my speech ("autoimmune")—mirroring her experience without my awareness. This kind of event is something that seems often to occur in this space of reverie coming from the soup pot of the analytic third.

Gathered up with the other examples of such moments as the ones I've shared so far along the way (the "orb," Niagara Falls, split-screen TV, little girl–gray dress, etc.) these "moments of meeting," through in-the-moment reverie, truly suggest an element of mystery, which our current neuroscience strains to catch up with. But such mystery is the routine experience of attuned (parents and) therapists, and is beginning to yield itself to the inquiries of science.

Daniel Stern, M.D. summarizes current neurobiological research on the realm of intersubjectivity as we've been discussing it, as follows:

> Our nervous systems are constructed to be captured by the nervous systems of others, so that we can experience others *as if* from within their skin, as well as from within our own. A sort of direct feeling route into the other person is potentially open and we resonate with and participate in their experience, and they in ours… We are capable of "reading other people's intentions" and feeling within our bodies what they are feeling… We are quite good at this "mind reading," even though our intuitions need verifying and fine-tuning.
>
> *(Stern, 2004: p. 77)*

Why might, at some levels, we be equipped to "read the mind" or the experience of another, or, in the terms we've been discussing, to catch the waftings of the co-created soup? We need think no further than the survival of the species to imagine the basis for this capacity. Were we not able as humans to decode the signals of pre-verbal infants, few would survive babyhood.

And, moments of meeting in the therapy have a *function*. They allow us to access preconscious, inaccessible thoughts and feelings in the patient (more open to us in the analytic third)—an access that makes that person feel seen and understood at a quite profound, often unworded level. Further, such attunement prompts (often) a further opening to themselves and to us. So, "moments of meeting" are potentially accessible as we open our own permeabilities to the other in the analytic third. This is a part of listening deeply, but also the beginning of the *art of understanding*.

Moments of swirl

Let's now turn our attention to the second element in the *intersubjective experience*: "moments of swirl." This part is of even more importance to the *art of understanding*, because it comes closer to Freud's axes of the transference and resistance, and takes place on the stage of the unconscious.

So let's go back to our tacit agreement to open ourselves to feel and to be affected by the psychic energy of the other. As we've said, this involves voluntarily adjusting our normally semi-permeable psychic membranes to become more permeable to the other person's "particles." From the first moments of the therapy, we enter into a relationship with the patient. Better put, we (only somewhat voluntarily) enter into a dynamic interplay with the patient—an interplay that generates not only the kinds of "moments of meeting" discussed earlier, but that also positions us somewhere within this patient's relational world.

The relational interplay that will start in the first session and evolve over time will be the cross-product of them as patient and us as therapists, unquestionably. But if we as therapists position ourselves properly, the interplay—the relationship— will be predicated on the internal and largely unconscious "object" world (internal relational world) of the patient. If we make proper room for it—if we don't anxiously clutter up the space with our own personal ways of being, relationally— we will find ourselves on the receiving end of the relational templates that the patient has used as his familiar, orienting forms for being in relationship with the others in his present and historical life.

This is close to the heart of the matter in psychodynamic psychotherapy, and is *definitely* part of the acquired art. The interplay set in motion between the patient and us gives a first-hand experience of the "object relational" world of the patient, and allows our understanding of it, *from the inside out*, so to speak. When people talk in therapy about the world of relationships they inhabit, we get an *outsider's* view of their relational world. When we allow ourselves to become (psychic) participants in that world, we get an *insider's* view. We become participants so that we can be observers, and ultimately, perhaps, co-transformers of it.

This means at the very least that for a while we give up playing on our own (relational) home turf. We enter into an interpersonal field with them, where, for the most part, the rules are unconscious, so we can't know them in advance. We must harvest slowly for ourselves what it feels like to be playing on their turf. Despite our holding of the symbolic frame of the therapy (the "rules" and "disciplines" of the therapy), we allow ourselves to be cast as a character in another's (interpersonal) play. To do this, for a while we must abandon or suspend our claim to our own well-worn interpersonal script, a script in which we ourselves play familiar, self-assigned roles. We voluntarily give up the privilege and the comfort of that script and enter a world governed by someone else's rules and privileging someone else's perceptions.

For example, when a patient shares with me that she feels I look at her with a combination of irritation and disappointment, it is not mine to protest her casting, and share with her how I "really" see her. It is mine to live with the discomfort of being misperceived, and to use the feelings generated in our dialectic to further understand the patient's internal world. When a patient is sure about the meaning of my five-minute delay in starting the session, it is mine to probe and understand her feeling world, rather than to preempt it with *my* ("the real") reality. More subtly, and more unconsciously, when I find myself treating one person with deference and another with eruptions of contempt, it is mine to hold and wonder about the position I have been angled into in their interpersonal drama (I will give you a slow-motion look at this process in the next chapter).

The ways we are seen and the roles we are assigned are confusing, confounding, and de-centering. But this voluntary conscription puts us into more intimate contact with the patient, such that we can feel with fuller force what it is to be within and outside of the patient's inner world. Undoubtedly, part of what has led this person to seek therapy—and a large part of what has arrested them in their quest to become more fully human—is the set of relationship predispositions the person carries within. These are the subtle expectations of relational life that have been formed before they (our patient) had any voice in the matter: that people are dangerous, or not to be trusted, or ultimately disappointing, or needing constant support; or that they are vampirizing, or fragile, or disinterested, or punitive, or not able to understand them. These expectations go before them, carving out in advance what they will expect, and what they will experience of their relationships—including their relationship with us.

Our role as therapists will eventually be to instantiate a new kind of relationship that doesn't fit their pre-fabricated molds. But—and this is big—remember Beth and Eric's roses? If we try to substitute a new kind of relationship before the old kind is allowed to germinate, we will abort the process. For most new therapists and many old therapists, this is counterintuitive. Shouldn't we just be able to plant someone in our own "field of love" and have them bloom gloriously?

The answer is no. Because perhaps beyond all else, we are emotional truth-seeking beings. A person comes to therapy to show themselves and us what they have survived, what they have become as a result, and the profound sacrifices they have extracted from themselves and their potentials. We have a driving human need to make sense of ourselves: what is, and always has been. This is primary. We as therapists must meet our patient on this ground, understand it intimately, and *bear* being seen this way or that, before there will be a psychic openness within them for something else.

This makes total sense, if we think about it. We construct our entire lives with certain postulates in place: given this, then this. Everything about us is silently predicated on our "givens." Without our consent, the "givens" were given to us, in most cases, early on, while our brains and psyches were in their most formative stages, during our earliest experiences of attachment relationships. From that point, the "givens" were normally reinforced within a consistently recursive family system over time. Once in place, the "givens" operate to filter the reality we encounter within and beyond the family system, such that the "givens" operate as an interpersonal selection device and a self-fulfilling prophecy.

It's a given, for instance, for some people that others will need to be taken care of. Congruent with this, they unconsciously choose people in their lives who need to be taken care of. As they come to therapy, they will unconsciously try to exert this force on us as therapists. "You look tired today, are you? Maybe we should end early today." It's a given for others that the other is always on the verge of explosion or implosion (and they will inject this energy into the swirl of the analytic third), such that we feel in ourselves an odd explosiveness in their presence. It's a given for others that no one will ever see them or show up for them (which they will unconsciously experience in the therapy, and may even cause to happen in the therapy). This will inevitably be the patient whose appointment time we forget.

So we enter the "swirl" in the analytic third. This living in the swirl of someone else's interpersonal world is critical to the *art of understanding*. Here we encounter the bass notes that play in the background—that give the music the patient plays in the foreground day-to-day shape and form and context. This space, built on the art of listening deeply, and helped along be "moments of meeting" in the analytic third, defines ground zero of the psychodyamic task. Our goal is to help our patient become human in a fuller sense. The biases, predispositions, and givens that a person brings to the interpersonal theatre unconsciously constrain and choke off their humanness before it has a chance to be. This is where we operate; this is why we came.

But it's at first, and often for a long time, a "swirl"—meaning that we, at first, have no way of knowing where we are on the field, or what role we're gradually to occupy. It's completely non-obvious. We are gradually, unconsciously positioned by the other to feel certain ways and act certain ways as we're with them. This often goes on for a *long* time—sometimes months, sometimes years— before it's the least bit recognizable. And then a longer time still before there are the words to speak about it with ourselves or with the patient.

I need only walk back through my last clinical week to give a sense of this. With my Type-A businessman, I am tense and performance-oriented, and much more conversational than is my normal, studied style. He pulls me off my game. I'm playing on his turf for now. My job is to try to get back on my game, and to notice how and why I can't. With another patient, my mid-week female, I'm scared: scared of my incompetence, scared she'll fire me, after first eviscerating me. I go forward nervously, but with my gut in a twist each time. With her, in her world, I can't find my emotional footing. With my end of week male patient from a destructively Asperger's-like home, I have found talking about the relationship with him almost non-existent. This is not how I act with any other patient. But he pulls me onto his home turf, which we have just begun to explore. It's a home turf where any interpersonal interchange in his family of origin was used as an opportunity to tear the other apart. So he has unconsciously positioned me away from such conversational streams. This has made our relationship safer for him, but also more familiar, because it replicates the aridity of his impersonal family of origin. I've only recently begun to talk to him about us: what it feels like to brace for, but never receive, brutality from me (he says he finds it relieving and confusing). Finally, with my largely silent patient, I find an unusual yearning in myself, a wondering each time in session how I can make the therapy valuable to her. I feel an intense pressure inside to provide a life-line to her in her sessions, and at this point in a new therapy, all I can do is wonder about that pressure, and what it may mean in our being-newly-created interpersonal theatre.

As therapists, we live in the swirl of the other, whether we effort to get conscious of it or not. As psychodynamic psychotherapists, we live in the swirl voluntarily; we invite it. But—and this is important—we try with whatever part of us lies outside the swirl to understand what is being enacted in the swirl—how we feel with *this* patient, how we see ourselves with *this* patient, how we're different with *this* patient, which of our normal ways of being we violate with *this* patient, how we feel and act differently—and what all of this tells us about the inter- and intra-personal world this patient has occupied in their life, and invited us into as their personal guest. Often, these understandings come to us in moments, which I will explain next. But what we're talking about here—living in and making sense of the swirl—this is indeed an acquired art, and comes quite slowly to us in our development as therapists.

So, so far, moments of meeting—so nice. But moments, sessions, months, years of swirl. Living inside the relational world of our patient. Straining to see it, to describe it to ourselves, to make it make sense, first to us and then ever so gradually to them. A lot of work. And then, thankfully but rarely, moments of precipitation…

Moments of precipitation

The last of the three elements, available through the space of the intersubjective analytic third, is that this space provides experiences, thoughts, feelings, and reveries that can be accrued *across time*, and used as puzzle pieces to form and inform our understanding of the patient's intra- and interpersonal world. These accrued experiences in the swirl of the analytic third finally yield their meaning to us in imperceptibly quiet "aha" moments—moments I will call "moments of precipitation."

Let me first explain the underlying metaphor behind the phrase "moments of precipitation." Back in high school chemistry, we did experiments wherein we would mix two elements together, like salt and water. We would be instructed to stir the solution, then gradually to add more and more salt. At an unanticipated moment, the salt would suddenly precipitate—would separate itself out from the swirl of the solution and fall to the bottom of the beaker, identifiable as itself—salt.

Gradually, over time, we create a relationship with the patient that is unique to them and us. We add to it the elements of time and experience, and we stir. While we stir, we may have many "moments of meeting," as detailed before—drawn from the analytic third—that serve to help the patient feel more seen and understood in the moment. We bear the stirring process—the swirl—whatever it inflicts on or extracts from us.

But in moments often unanticipated, the analytic third can serve up even more profound understandings—meta-understandings of the swirl, if you will. These understandings often come in the form of a suddenly accrued wondering: a "what does it mean that…?" moment. "What does it mean that only with this patient, for five years, I've gone consistently five minutes over time, and am just now letting myself notice it?" "What does it mean that I look forward to this patient's entertaining and irreverent way of presenting herself to me in session, and even visualize her somewhat devilish smile as I hold her in my mind's eye?" "What does it mean that I just had a nearly irrepressible urge to call my patient over the weekend to suggest a name for her new dog?"

Sometimes, without our bidding, moments of precipitation call us to see what we have not seen; what has been suspended in the solution of the relationship the whole time. These moments of precipitation are often mediated by our capacity for reverie—our capacity to let our bodily or motoric or imaginal (or auditory) registers arrest our attention momentarily, as would a fleeting dream fragment. These moments of precipitation are not so much flashes of lightning as they are detections of something sitting in plain sight in a dimly-lit room. Something in our thoughts or daydreams or ruminations calls our attention to some aspect of the relationship that's been there the whole time, but just out of sight to our consciousness.

The reason this is important is that it is the vehicle whereby we as therapists wake up to parts of the relational parameters we've been operating within with this particular patient. These moments, accrued and precipitated as they are from the repository of the analytic third, allow us to see these parameters (and our participation in them), whereupon we can begin to think about them, and can ultimately gain contextual understanding of them in the patient's life. From this honestly-*earned* vantage point (inside out), we gain the right to speak to our patient with a certain accuracy and compassion. Precisely because we have lived and strained inside the patient's intrapsychic world, our words carry an appreciable combination of grace and truth. And this is the powerful medium in which deep psychological change—change that invites and allows our patients to become more fully human—can and does take place. Ireland (2003: p. 17) sums up the process this way:

> In any analysis there is a constant dynamic movement of the patterns of … psychic particles between the analysand and analyst, whereby their two patterns mix with, connect, and repel each other, moving back and forth between them, the patient seeking unconsciously to maneuver the analyst to match a familiar unconscious imaginary pattern concerning her/his ego and the other. The protosymbolic particles within the analysand metaphorically flow into the interior of the analyst, through a process of verbal and nonverbal exchanges, only to be subsequently returned to him or her. This cycle will be repeated again and again in the treatment, such that with each influx to the side of the analyst, cumulative effect begins to accrue. In this accumlation,

the analyst allows her/himself to become saturated with the transferential experience until, as Bion noted, a "selected fact" seems to emerge, enabling symbolic elaboration to begin to take shape within the analyst. It is like Braille slowly emerging to the touch.

This is the analytic process in the sacred space of the intersubjective analytic third. We open ourselves affectively and relationally to the patient. We enjoy access to "moments of meeting"—in and around many, many "moments of swirl." We are graced with "moments of precipitation." We speak from these moments with authenticity and compassion. Our speaking of the emotional truth, so accrued, allows our patient to see what to them was always there, but very dimly lit. This seeing allows the possibility—the potential—of something new, something more fully human—initially with us, but ultimately extending into the sphere of their life outside of us—which is why they came.

8

THE SILENT PATIENT

In this chapter, I want to bring you in camera-close to a sequence of sessions—my words, my thoughts, my therapeutic flaws—that I think best illustrate the parts of the art of listening deeply and the art of understanding that I've laid out so far along the way. One can only go so far in describing concept before the inevitable urgency of showing the thing pushes itself forward. So I've chosen a series of sessions to present word-for-word, thought-for-thought. It's as close to being there in the room and in my mind as you can get.

There's a real risk I take in sharing this particular footage with you. I have not altered or edited this transcript to make my work appear better or different, except for the necessary disguising of my patient's identity. It's raw and without makeup. The patient I present and the person I am as therapist are, at the same time, wonderfully illustrative of the presence I try to achieve in the intersubjective space, *and* completely *not* that. You'll find that the therapist you observe in these pages conforms magnificently to the fundamental task of listening deeply, and listening analytically, but that she breaks some of the most basic rules of the psychoanalytic rubric along the way.

I know in advance that some may not like the work; may argue with my unorthodoxies; may criticize my not waiting her out, not challenging her defenses. Some may be made uncomfortable by how self-revelatory I am to my patient and to you, my reader, especially in a work aimed at therapists relatively new to the psychoanalytic trade. And I agree. But if we dive underneath our orthodoxies down to the stiller waters below, it in fact presents the point of it all—using all of the tools I've spoken about so far, and some I've had to invent on the spot—to find and to meet *this* person.

So I'll let it be. Maybe my use of this particular patient is good. The truth of it is, at some level, all of us do this combination in our work all the time. We all approach our task with the bible of orthodoxy tucked under our arm but then find ourselves in interaction with this *particular* patient, in this *particular* particle storm, and we must find a way to be.

So before we launch, a moment of preamble. I have theoretical axes that frame and inform my work as psychodynamic psychotherapist. I will take you further and deeper into these in the ensuing chapters. But I have *personal* orienting axes as well—personal values and ways of being that define me as an individual within and across the fabric of my life. We all have these. My *personal* orienting axes, clinically and privately, are, I think, the qualities of grace and truth—a phrase borrowed from my Catholic school days out of a passage in the New Testament. I've found no better way to express my personal dialectic as I walk the path of therapist. Grace perhaps comes more easily to me. I think I received my mother's grace, and walk in it comfortably, as I would in an old pair of shoes, without thinking about it. Truth, on the other hand, has been harder won. I'm careful with it, respectful of its power to cleanse or to destroy. So, as much as I can, I try to keep these in balance with each patient, and to keep my eye on it when I can't.

When all else is darkness about me, these are the stars that guide me. They guide me as a person. They guide me as a clinician in moments when nothing else makes sense to me. As much as there are technicalities and techniques to acquire in the art of psychodynamic psychotherapy—and there *are*—there is the heart of the matter that precedes and underlies them all: that we are the bearers of, in Freud's words, "a cure through love," and our souls need to line up behind this (Bettelheim, 1984).

So in this spirit, I now wish to present, with humility and respect, several real-time sessions with Sara, a young woman in my practice. I will attempt to use some of my experiences with her to show you in slow motion what "moments of meeting," "moments of swirl," and "moments of precipitation" might look like in the context of listening deeply.

Several things to keep your eye on as we wander into these sessions. First, this is different from other cases you might read. It isn't all done; it's barely started. We're in the first painstaking months of a therapy that will go on for a long time, and could and should be multiple times a week. For now, it's once a week.

Second, it has me well off my normal rhythms and game plan as therapist, because the patient, Sara, is profoundly (distrustfully) silent in sessions, and seems to require some access to my experiential world in order to share hers with any safety, or at all. So in that way, the case represents a non-modal patient and in return, a non-modal example of my work as therapist. It certainly suggests a vastly more self-revelatory stance than I would ordinarily occupy or endorse. But for now, and as long as it serves the progress of the therapy, I will go with this, although I suspect that it will change over time.

Third, one thing to notice in particular is that my direct sharing of my own experience with this patient seems a prerequisite for her building of any kind of trust at all in the relationship. But also try to notice that my implicit goal is to talk to her *not* about *my* experience of the relationship with her, but of what the relationship might seem and feel like *to her*. It's also important to note that this patient has indeed come to this therapy (after ten years with a previous therapist) in the quest of becoming more fully human, which always needs to be acknowledged as an inordinate act of courage for anyone who chooses that path.

Finally, as I begin to present moments of "meeting," "swirl," and "precipitation" with this patient, I'm reminded of what it was like to play tennis as a younger person, and now to watch the major tournaments on TV. The difference between being on the court and watching from afar is misleading. From afar, it's all clear, makes sense, and frankly, looks easy. On the court, the pace is intense, and you can only hope that your trained instincts get you through decently enough. So let me take you onto the court with me with this silent patient, Sara. Try, as you read, to be alert to my use of reverie as a guiding light, and the sense of quietude necessary to spawn such internal thoughts.

She is, as I said, silent, only making occasional contact. She is 32 years old, but seems much older, as though life has rubbed the gloss from her. It feels like a bit of a contest with her: me, anxiously trying not to disturb her silence; her, wanting to let me in but at the same time, not wanting to. She occasionally breaks our silence with the question, "What are you thinking?" In this way, there is an adolescent quality to our interactions. She requires a certain quotient of authenticity from me as an ante before she can or will venture out, as though these are the minimum terms of safety for her. Finally, a reminder: the experiences of meeting, swirl, and precipitation I will share with you, drawn from the analytic third, are not unique to my work. An array of other psychodynamic authors have relayed their parallel experiences of working in this way, as have my colleagues, and consultees in my practice.

In the following, I will include excerpts from seven sessions, drawn roughly from months four and five of the therapy. The sessions are consecutive, and (as a warning to you, the reader) build slowly. Strap in for ultra slow-motion. But slow motion is an intimate and fertile point of observation, so with your permission, I will take you on this extended, camera-close walk. For clarity, I'll use italics to indicate my own thoughts, wonderings, and reveries, and also any commentary I make to explain something to the reader.

Session 14 (3½ months into the therapy)

In this session, after ten minutes of silence in which I had allowed my mind to be in the feelings in the room and to wander in reverie, Sara noticed something on my face.

"What are you thinking?" she asked. I responded honestly, "I was thinking about my friend who is dying." I was thinking about her simple advice to me on that Sunday afternoon. I had spoken to her about my 17-year-old cat, whom I thought was in the process of dying that afternoon. She had advised me, "Take him into the vet. He may be suffering." Hearing the story, my until-then completely silent patient responded, "I have a 17-year-old cat. His name is Notch." She went on to tell me stories about Notch: how she came to have him, how he got his name, what he is like. "I didn't name him," she said. "I got him by default. My roommates left him. I've been with him ever since, all these years. He walks with me—like a dog—on my walks. He likes to sit in the sun. I hold a shade for him; he has a skin cancer on his nose. He's such a cool cat. I trust him. He's the only living being I trust."

It felt in these moments as though Sara had brought me into the inner sanctum of her life. I was touched by the experience. This was a "moment of meeting," in that my silent, random thoughts had drifted in her presence toward my 17-year-old cat, to be followed by the strangely coincident event of her having a 17-year-old cat as well. It linked us, psychically, for those moments.

Session 15

I'll skip to the next session. Lots of silence. Lots of time to let my mind wander where it would. Reverie requires space, and the willingness to let the currents of your mind take you this way and that. Most patients don't engage in such prolonged silences as this patient does. But as therapists, our practiced ability to disengage from the back-and-forth of normal social conversation (so we can "lose ourselves" in the drift of what comes) allows and invites the space of silences into our sessions. This is a crucial part of the acquired art, and, as you'll see, a crucial part of my work with Sara.

Somehow, in the quietude, she noticed an expression register on my face as I sat across from her. "What are you thinking?" she asked again. Again, it seemed an honest question, somehow in the service of establishing safety for her. I attempted to relay the scene in my mind that had come as I was trying to sit with her in such a way as to avoid putting pressure on her to talk. The scene that had come to mind was a dream-like image of a young girl, perhaps in fourth grade, with a dirt-streaked face. She was in a corner of a room, facing outward. In my mental scene, she looked terribly scared; immobilized. It seemed that any movement would scare her more. I related that scene to my silent patient. She responded that she had once written a poem about being in a corner, and that her "internal critic" was compelling her to stay in that corner.

I knew once again that we had had a "moment of meeting"; that the image that had formed in my mind was drawn from the soup between us and again, linked to her experience in a way I could not have made happen were I trying to make something happen. It was more a yielding to my internal emotional scene-maker (right brain-mediated) than it was something I could directly have figured out. Again, the reverie linked profoundly to her personal experience. I was reminded of Freud's observation that "it is a very remarkable thing that the unconscious of one human being can react upon that of another, without passing through the conscious" (Freud, 1915b: p. 194). My internal response to her sharing about being in the corner in her poem was that I felt somewhat surprised and humbled, as though she had brought me into a world I imagined no one else had shared.

Session 16

This next session, two weeks later, I'll present in its entirety to give you a sense of the back-and-forth, and the background thoughts and feelings of a session, real-time.

On New Year's Eve—the Friday after Christmas—she came in furtively, as always, dressed all in black, except for the simple gold design on her black T-shirt. There had been a week's gap since our last meeting. It was the end of the Christmas holiday. She sat across from me, settled into the chair, looked around the office for several moments. She finally looked up and said "Hi," in a tone and with an expression that carried a hint of warmth, perhaps of relief. I matched her tone. "Hi," I said.

She became silent, as she always does at the beginning of the session, but this day her face and dyed black hair were unusually dark. She looked down and to her right, leaning forward a bit in her chair, pulling her hair down to partially cover her face.

I felt uncertain, knowing (and fearing) that the entire session could pass without a word from her. At the same time, I've come to know that she battles while she's with me to word what she's feeling, and also battles with how much she would want me to know of her inner world. I'm left to wonder whether she wants me to come toward her or to yield her all the space of her silence. This is my "swirl," virtually ever-present.

After some minutes had passed, and she had shifted around in the oversized chair a number of times, occasionally looking up at me, and I at her, I tried my first hopefully unobtrusive volley. "How long have you been back from your folks' house?" I asked. "Since Monday," she replied, not looking quite at me, but making some contact. Moments passed. I interrupted the silence, "You've been in this space since then," I offered tentatively, not so much posing a question as offering my best guess of things. She paused a bit, then said, "Yes."

I was momentarily satisfied that I had located perhaps the source of her unusual darkness, and had made contact, so began the job of settling myself down with what was her evident pain and the unbreachable silence in which she held it. There was some sense of panic inside me (in the swirl). I wondered how she experienced the silence of our sessions; whether it was of any value to her to have come to me during these months, with so few words exchanged between us. I thought about my consultee several years ago, who met with a middle-schooler for eighteen weeks without a word from the child, and sparse few from the therapist. I thought that if Wendy could bear that anxiety, I could as well (the therapy made huge shifts in the middle-school girl's adjustment outside the sessions). I reminded myself that my part was to feel my way into what she was experiencing, as much as I could. I allowed myself to wonder whether her darkness was signaling a suicidal space within her. She had told me several weeks before this that she was discontinuing her antidepressants. My anxiety went higher. I didn't know if this would be our last session. I needed to calm myself down inside. I pictured myself in the usually empty church I used to visit with regularity as a child, using the space and quietude of that place to come upon and be with my own insides for long times. This allowed me to settle.

As I settled, I was able to drop down into the palpable feelings in the room. I could feel a sensation in my upper stomach, like what it might feel like to fall through endless, dark, inchoate space. I allowed the feeling to grow inside of me, drawing my breath silently toward it. It seemed boundless and inescapable. I sat a long time with this barely tolerable feeling— fifteen minutes or so—long enough to have a strong sense of her in it (this is the somatic register, in action. I've learned to trust that it is drawn from the affective soup in the analytic third).

I spoke first to the sense I had of her this day (my sense of what the relationship might feel like to her right now). She had shared with me that as a child, she would retreat to her fort some distance from her house, and guard her solitude with all the might at her disposal. I said to her, "I sense that you're not in the fort today. Am I right?" She looked up from her darkness, making eye contact. "Do you have words for what you're feeling?" I asked as softly as I dared. She immediately shook her head, no. After a silence of a minute or two I followed up, "Are there thoughts?" "Yes," she said. "Can you share any of them?" After pausing to consider my question, she again shook her head, no.

We were back to the silence, but I felt inside that she knew I was trying to be with her in it; that I wasn't allowing her to fall in endless space entirely alone. I wondered what this state that she had silently installed into me (in the soup) might be communicating about her internal experience; whether my own uncertainty and anxiety were reflective of feelings she had had to bear in her own history. I thought of what she had shared in a session a couple of months previous about her depressed and sometimes violent mom; that she had been hit, but her older sister, more. We had spoken of the scariness and the confusion. I left my thoughts and came again into the space of falling in darkness.

After what seemed a long time, there emerged into my consciousness a scene from my junior high school years. I had had a teacher for fourth and sixth grades—a nun—whom I felt very close to and somehow seen by. I would often stay after school to visit and to help out with classroom stuff. In the scene I was remembering, we had made our way this particular day to the book storage area near the front office, perhaps affording safety for a different kind of conversation. She sensed I had something weighing heavily on my 13-year-old mind, and said to me in an inviting tone, "Out with it. What are you thinking?" In the scene that was coming to mind, I remember wanting for all the world to share my angst with this trusted teacher; to let her in on the inner terrain that was so hard for me, and hard for me to articulate at that point in my life. She waited a long time, I remember, and I was only able to communicate the barest sliver of what was swirling inside. I truly had not the words to express it, but felt met in it nonetheless.

I lived with the very deep feelings of this personal scene, and (assuming this impactful reverie had something to do with the soup between us) formulated my next inquiry (drawn from the feel of the scene in my reverie).

"Does a part of you want me to know what you're feeling in there?" I asked with a softness. She looked with a sidelong look and said, "A part of me does, and another part doesn't." She looked a bit tortured by her own response. I nodded slowly, knowing again I'd made contact with her.

(Her silence and reticence in no way represent a game to me or to her. It doesn't have that feel at all. It seems much more the stance of an injured but wary animal; needing to let someone intervene, but profoundly distrustful.)

Alone again with my own thoughts and feelings, after a series of random thoughts, a new dream-like scene presented itself, again presumably drawn from the soup. In the scene, I was standing at the circular edge of a 2½-foot-high cinder block abutment that encircled a deep, *empty well shaft. My patient was at the bottom of the shaft, barely visible except for her dark eyes, looking up without recognition or hope of rescue. She seemed like a helplessly trapped animal at the bottom of the shaft. In the scene, I considered options as to how to get her out, but they all depended on her strength and willingness to grab hold of whatever hoist I could devise. I was stuck (in the scene), but felt that I had to come up with a way to get her out; even to get her trust and cooperation. Feeling at a loss, I told myself in the dream-scene to step back and think a bit. I allowed myself to shift internally, and realized that while I might not at that point be able to extract her, I could send something down to her. I decided to lower a bucket with a young kitty cat (something I knew she would welcome and respond to, given her devotion to her cat, Notch) and a sandwich; it might increase her strength, and let her know someone was up there. Some time passed and the scene elaborated one step further. It occurred to me also that I should hoist down something to write on. Writing has been her medium.*

The session was in the last ten minutes now. I asked her if she wanted to know the picture that had been in my mind *(this is something I rarely do because my training has taught me to speak* from *but not directly about the scenes that present themselves in my mind)*. She said she wanted to know, so I described the scene: that she was at the bottom of a deep well shaft, that I could see nothing of her but her eyes, looking up unaware of anyone's presence. I told her that in the scene I was unable to think of how to help get her out of there, but that I finally decided that I could get some things down to her. I told her I decided to lower a kitty cat and a sandwich into the well to her. She half-smiled.

I waited a minute, then asked her if she wanted to know what next came into the scene. She nodded her head, yes. I told her that it occurred to me that I should also hoist down something to write on.

I watched her response. She looked toward me, and it seemed as though she was deciding to say something to me, but that she stopped herself. "You were about to say something, but you stopped yourself," I said. She seemed stuck between speaking and not speaking. "What?" I asked. "I'd tell you, but we're out of time," she replied. "I'm not moving," I observed, somewhat playfully. "It won't come out," she finally said. "A part of me won't let it come out." I nodded again, slowly. "Can you write it?" I asked. "Yes." She said. "Is that OK with you?" I asked. "Yes," she said, again with a half smile.

We both got up to leave. It had been an extremely intense time for both of us, but it felt utterly connected the whole way, as though we had been witnesses to the same disaster. I stopped as both of us were en route to the door. Slowly and with marked emphasis I said to her, "The part of you that wanted me to know, *got her way.*" "I *know,*" she said, looking directly at me for the first time that day.

This was an extremely high-impact moment; her acknowledging that something had "gotten down" to her. It felt important in a way I wasn't able to understand, but could feel. As you may have noticed, this session was mediated almost entirely by my reveries. I felt in the dark (in the swirl) the entire way, and had to trust that the things that registered with most impact within me were steady enough to walk out on. These barely accessible thoughts and feelings in the soup between patient and therapist are facilitated by space and quietude, and, obversely, are made completely inaccessible by the practice of engaging in unbroken back-and-forth talk in any session.

Session 17

This next session was to be predicated on the previous one in a way that I could in no way have anticipated.

A week later, she settled in, not quite so dark. She was wearing a solid orange long-sleeved blouse beneath her normal black sweater and pants. She began the session silent, but we had leftovers in the relational field from the last session, so, as is important to do, I spoke to her about it. "Any thoughts about last time?" I asked. She squirmed and reshuffled in her chair. "Not that I can put words on." I tried again, "So, last week, at the end, I said to you that the part of you that wanted me to know, *got her way.* You said back to me, '*I know.*' I wonder what it was like to be seen in that way, what it felt like to either part of you?" This query was followed by minutes of silence. Finally, she spoke: "I felt relieved to be not alone in it." (Silence.) "And the part that doesn't want to be seen?" I asked. "It felt like I might be being judged or minimized," she responded.

After a few minutes, I pressed on, "What was it like for you when you got home, knowing you had in some way let me see you? Does the other part try to drag you back toward the middle?" "Oh, yah," she said, suggestively. "There's hell to pay?" I asked. She nodded her head.

I let several minutes pass. I thought about her words: "judged," "minimized." They seemed painful and tragic to me. I thought that at this point, she could have no idea that I had developed a deep respect for her. I wished for her to know that, but knew that that was a long way off. I struggled inside with these thoughts, and finally I had words.

"Minimized," I said, "in particular, packs a wallop, like a word in a poem that jumps out at you."

She writes poetry, so I trusted that the reference to words in a poem would work for her. I felt disturbed inside; I hated that this has been her experience, but checked my urge to say that to her. I knew that I should just hold that big feeling. (An important aside: there is no way to change someone's internal landscape by simply asserting something of our (the therapist's) intention or experience in such a moment as this. So I skipped the admittedly alluring option of telling her that I wasn't judging or minimizing her.)

In the silence that ensued, more and more, I thought about the sheerness of the 50–50 arrangement she had within herself; wanting and not wanting to be seen, split right down the middle in a "dead heat," in a "dead lock," were the words I used to talk to myself. Again, these ruminative thoughts would reveal themselves by the session's end to be non-randomly harvested from the analytic third.

Detecting something on my face, she asked, "What?" As usual, I answered her honestly. I told her I was thinking about the parts within her; that they were in such a *"dead* heat," motioning with my hands. "*Dead*-locked," I said, with emphasis, and that it must take a lot of emotional energy to keep them balanced on a razor thin divide.

Another silence. I pondered my grief for her; the fact that last week she said she would write what she couldn't say in the session. I wondered why she hadn't proffered the writing. I wondered about under what circumstances being seen, which she clearly longs for, became so dangerous and off-limits to her. I jettisoned thoughts about my particularity—my safeness— and tried to imagine. What came to mind in that moment (I had been completely in the swirl of it) felt like a "moment of precipitation," like a part of the Braille emerging to my touch. I had, all session, been longing inside to know her experience of the last session (the well shaft/ kitty cat session). I felt the longing intensely, but doubted that she would really comment on it. I had been sitting on that feeling, really the whole time since we started the session, and even before it started. It occurred to me that the place of longing intensely but feeling little hope of having someone respond might indeed be her feeling (historically and currently), placed into me for now. I then had a new thought (another "moment of precipitation"): in terms of attachment theory and research, she seemed to have been put in the torturous place of the "disorganized child"; a child whose caregiver/source of comfort is the very person who inflicts pain, leaving the child in a completely untenable place, frozen. I reflected that she hadn't given me much of the story, but that she'd had a depressed, sometimes violent mom.

In the wake of these reflections, I ventured forward with her once again. Picking up the strand of her ambivalence about being seen, I queried (honestly), "Should I *not* guess?" (meaning, should I not verbalize my efforts to find my way into her experience). "Why?" she responded directly. "Because," I said, "there's hell to pay afterwards." She shook her head "no," as if to say "no, don't stop guessing."

I was aware we had ten minutes left, and that she hadn't produced what she had said she would write about the last session; a session that had seemed so darkly pregnant with something unspoken.

I asked her when she had decided *not* to write about last week. She said "I did write." I then asked playfully, "When did you decide *not* to share it with me?" We both laughed hard. I said when we settled, "Laughter feels like a neutral zone. Does it to you?" (meaning that we could link up through laughter, and there didn't seem to be any hell to pay for that). "Yes," she shook her head.

At 4:20, it was time to end. I said, "You're on the verge of telling me something. Start the sentence and the words will come." "We're out of time," she responded, looking at her watch. "Stop it!" I replied firmly, *bending my normally firm commitment to the end of the session.* She let a minute more pass, and finally said, "Notch is gone."

I knew instantly that it meant that her 17-year-old cat had died. Knowing that Notch was her prized (and only) companion, it felt to me like I was hit in the stomach with a shovel. I was immobilized. Despite its being at the session's end, I sat for what seemed a long time. I said, after a few minutes, "Now I'm the one without words." I allowed myself to tear and to have a single strand of tears move down from both eyes. "My soul is deeply sad," I said. I let a couple more minutes pass. "When?" I asked. She answered, "A week ago Tuesday I had him put down. A vet came to the house."

I instantly and almost eerily realized that my image of hoisting a kitty cat down to her in the well shaft during the session a week ago was the session immediately (two days) after his death. I also realized that earlier in this session, my random use of the words "dead heat" and in a *"dead lock"* had been decidedly un-random references to death). These were *"moments of meeting."*

"I don't have good words," I said (somehow, I didn't want to say anything trite). I ended by saying, "I am very, very sorry."

In the space of my reverie in the previous session, I had been drawn toward the scene of the well shaft, and of hoisting a cat down to her at the bottom of the shaft. This occurred freshly (two days) after she had had to terminate her cat's life. In this session, my use of the words infrequent in my own vocabulary, "dead heat," "dead-locked," seemed uncannily drawn from the "third" space between us. I wondered why she had held this news through the entire session immediately after the death of Notch, but knew that it was perhaps too vulnerable, and that this was the best she could do at this point.

Session 18

I met her in the lobby as she came in the door. 3:30 exactly. I motioned her back to my office. We sat; I, aware of the session as it approached.

It was hard to settle down. I heard the creaking of her chair as she rocked in it. I wished I had had it fixed. The service guy had said he couldn't fix the squeak. I wanted the noise not to be in her way. I wanted her to be able to rock, unconstrained. My thoughts drifted to the groaning of the wicker rocking chair in Mom and Dad's bedroom in my growing-up house where we were rocked as babies. I remembered it as white, painted wicker.

I was aware that I was anxious, with the feeling of longing to be as attuned and connected as I had been in the previous two sessions. I was afraid that I wouldn't be as "on" this session. I thought again of my sixth grade teacher. I hoped that she (my patient) wouldn't ask me what I was thinking right then.

There entered my mind more thoughts of babies: Winnicottian babies, Ukranian refugee babies, baby Emma, in the hospital, that second day. Her eyes. I thought about my eyes, and how she experiences my gaze. I tried to settle myself. I thought about her mother, and wondered whether she had had an anxious mother, given the anxiety I feel with her. I wondered about how her mother beheld her, and about the vulnerability and permeability of babies.

I wanted to ask her how she was doing, how her day went, something.

Finally, I asked her, "How *are* you?" She shrugged her answer.

I watched her. She moved around, looking like she was aborting things she might say.

I said, "It looked like you were about to say something." She shrugged, no.

After a while of again trying to get myself OK with the silence, she asked, "What are you thinking?" I told her that I was wondering how I could be of any help in here to her today. She said, "Sometimes I wonder about the same thing." It felt strangely enigmatic, as though she might be saying that it might be useless for her to come here *(this wondering about the uselessness of our meetings will re-emerge in the soup in a bit).*

I let the silence be there. Eventually she spoke. "Did you know it was about Notch?" (meaning, did I realize during the very dark session that included the kitty cat reverie, or perhaps last week's session so punctuated by the words "*dead*-locked" and "*dead* heat," that he had died). "No," I said. I found more words. "I was entirely surprised, although it seems to have shown up in my images." Silence. Then I spoke, "What did you do with my reaction last week?" (I was referring to my reaction of feeling like I'd been hit in the stomach by a shovel, which expressed itself in my immobilization and tearing in the moment.) "At first, I didn't trust it," she replied. "Then I was surprised at my own detachment." I was unclear, so I asked, "Detachment in the time since Notch went down, or in the ending moments of last week?" "In the ending moments," she said.

I was disturbed inside, because I had reacted with such genuineness and unguardedness. I wanted to tell her that it had been one of the most unguarded moments I'd ever had as a therapist.

"I was entirely surprised in the moment. If I had known in advance, I would have reacted in a way that was more circum-something, circumspect, or circuitous, or something *(I know she writes, and enjoys the nuance of words greatly, so this was in my response)*. She half-smiled.

At some point a few minutes later, she spoke, "You talked the week before about my being in a hole, and you handing me a sandwich and a kitty cat. The sandwich I could use, but a kitty cat. Oh shit!" I laughed, knowing she was made uneasy by my seeming "clairvoyance" in that moment. I said with playfulness, "You give me so much space in here, I'm dangerous!" We laughed hard together.

Settling again, I had the numbers 50–50 come into mind. I thought about how tortured she must be to have me in her internal space. It seemed both safe and unsafe for her; trusted and distrusted.

I said, "It *must* be a real 50–50 experience in here with me." "Yes," she said, with affect. I said, "It must be like whiplash, one way, then the other." She smiled, seeming to connect with that picture.

I had little 2-day-old Emma come back to mind; her eyes looking out at the world.

"What?" she said, again noticing something cross my face. I responded, "Recently, I visited my friends' baby in the hospital on her second day of life. Baby Emma. Her eyes were remarkable. They were taking in the world, without knowing what they were taking in. She'll make sense of it much later on."

A minute later, I said that I had a question for her that I had tried to get away from, but that wouldn't leave, so I'd ask it. She waited. "How do you experience my eyes as I look at you in here?" I asked, not expecting much of an answer.

She didn't slough it off (surprisingly). She said, "I have to answer that with a disclaimer: that I have my filters, which may not be right, but they're there." She continued slowly, "Sometimes, I think I see irritation; sometimes disappointment. Other times, I don't know."

I was sad hearing the response, but reminded myself that in the transference, I was that distrusted figure to her. I thought of how smart I find her, and deep, and how I have developed a strong compassion and respect for her. I recalled her words in our first session about the disturbed kids she works with; that she had a "profound respect for them," she had said. All those things I thought about; what she can't at this point see in my eyes, which I feel are unmasked with compassion toward her, and tenderness.

I said, "I wonder whether there might be a way, in some altered universe" (she laughed) "where there would be room for something other than irritation and disappointment."

This is different from asserting as reality my experience of her. It presents an uninsistent possibility, which I don't in any way pressure her to agree with. It is directed for the most part to the unconscious parts of her.

I went on, "I'm thinking again of little Emma. She was taking things in before she knew what they were. They'll take time to develop. I think it might be the same in here."

She seemed to take it in, and then asked, "What do you think comes first, intuition or filters?" I thought about it, trying fruitlessly to construct something from my knowledge of right brain development, but nothing of that would come to me in the moment. "Intuition," I answered slowly. "What do you think?" I asked. "I don't know," she said.

Finally, as the end of the session approached, I asked her how she had experienced our interaction today. "OK," she said, almost quizzically. "How did *you* experience it?" I sorted through adjectives, internally, rejecting the word "alive" as too generic. "Contactful," I said. Then continued, "I thought about saying 'alive,' but that wasn't it." I exhaled to myself several times. She said, "You're taking deep breaths." I said, "That's because it was contactful." I rose. She dug the folded check out of her wallet and handed it to me. I said, "See you next week on Thursday." "Yes," she said.

Session 19

In anticipation, I noticed that I had had an unusual preoccupation with the upcoming session. I kept it in mind; wanted to be early and settled, looking forward to what we'd say to one another. I let myself wonder about my evident investment in what was coming. Now, the investment and anticipation are part of the swirl.

The session started. As usual, there was the beginning silence. No "Hi" even. I found it hard to settle. Heard the creaking of the chair across from me again. Again, the wish that I had had it fixed. Five to ten minutes passed. I finally observed to her, "It seems hard to settle in here today." "Yes," she said with feeling.

Several minutes more passed. "What are you thinking?" she asked. I've come to think of these queries as a way for her to make contact safely. I answered, "It's kind of a meta-thought. I was thinking about thinking about" (she smiled) "that I was feeling pressured to make something happen in here for you today. So I was noticing that, and letting myself wonder why." She received this, and after a minute I said, "What is it like having me tell you what I'm honestly thinking?" "It's refreshing, actually," she said with evident sincerity.

Several minutes later, I said, "I think I have an answer to my own question." (The question about my feeling pressured to make something happen.) She indicated she wanted to hear the answer. I said, "I think I'm experiencing a pressure you experience, like something wanting to be birthed, but not quite ready. It's a pressure." I paused, then offered something I was less sure about. "The second thought I had is that you might have experienced a pressure as a youngster, a sort of pressure to be vigilant."

She eventually said, after a long pause, "I resonate with the first part of what you said." I felt relief, and a sense of wishing I hadn't said the second part.

Silence. She then said, "I used to have a condition where I couldn't go to the bathroom for long periods of time. I was actually hospitalized several times. I would finally go, but in the aftermath vomit and vomit, every five minutes. Dehydration. I'm not sure why that came to mind."

I thought that it exactly mapped on the pressure I was and had been feeling: the waiting and waiting for something to be birthed from her.

At about twenty minutes to go, I said, "Seems like you have something to say today, am I right?" "Yes," she replied. I continued, "It's your normal rhythm to hold it to the end of the session. There's a lot of space, then at the end you say something. I want to see if you can say it earlier, and so have the space on the other side of saying it."

More silence, in which I visited in my mind the many things I'd read about the value of being able to put words on things.

I finally offered, "Perhaps you could say it in pictures." This didn't seem to spring anything from her, so we went on, in silence, again. She again noticed something register across my face. "What?" she probed. As usual, I tried to let her into my thoughts. I relayed to her that I'd had the image come to my mind of divers on a high diving board, but that there were two divers on the board.

This picture did not seem to yield anything much from her in the moment, but I thought further about the 1980s Olympic medalist, Greg Louganis, who seemed to take an eternity on the edge of the board before he would move, then with uncommon grace and beauty, would perform his dive.

The last five minutes of the session arrived. She asked, "Are we out of time?" "Yes," I said, "and no," unwilling to have sustained all this waiting with so little spoken from her. I waited. "Words," I said. I made and maintained eye contact for what seemed a minute, during which she also maintained eye contact most of the time. I wondered if it was too much pressure, too much eye contact. Finally, she said, shaking her head, "It changed." I guessed, "It changed? The session changed? We changed?" *(I'm frustrated here).* She shook her head. "Both," she said.

Finally, she asked, "Are you going to drop me from therapy because I can't find the words?" "Absolutely not," I answered with firmness, then returned fire: "Are you going to drop *me* from therapy because you can't find the words?" "Absolutely not," she said with matching firmness.

I observed to her that the therapy might reflect her physical (hospitalization) experience. We might have to wait a long time for things to come forth. It might be painful in the waiting.

I ended the session, reflecting to myself that we had, in some kind of way, ratified the therapy that day; talking (in her story about hospitalizations) about the pressured holding back of what would want to come out so much sooner, and the sickening pain involved in that holding. Then her highly unguarded question, "Are you going to drop me from therapy because I can't find the words?" I once again felt that something significantly impactful had taken place between us, and that no matter how slowly, there was a building sense of trust accruing.

Session 20

"Red," I said, as she settled, referring to her red shoes, red socks, and red sweater.

I reflected to myself that her choice of clothes might reflect unconsciously a good feeling about our last session, or a change in her mood. The color itself seemed like her opening volley.

I waited a few minutes, then perhaps a little emboldened by her clothes, or perhaps just unwilling to wait for her to put something in play, and also conscious that she doesn't start easily, I said, "How you doing?" She considered it for perhaps a minute, then responded, "I don't know. It depends on when."

This felt a little like we were starting a chess match, which I wasn't up for.

I said, "In the last seven days." She said, "It's variable." I said, "Give me the range." She said, "I've been missing Notch this week. And, I..." (something inaudible), I asked her what. She said she had wanted to kick different things at home several times that week as she had before: the dishwasher (which she dented by kicking), but didn't. "Over what?" I asked. She said, "I can't remember. Little stuff."

I had the thought that we were like two adolescents, trying to make contact. I thought that she might find it scary but enticing. I wondered what all this meant, waiting internally to understand the intensity. I'm in the swirl here.

I waited a couple of minutes more and said, "What was it like for you at the end of last week's session? You asked me if I was going to kick you out of therapy if you couldn't find the words." She responded quickly to correct my words. "*Drop* me from therapy," she said with emphasis.

Noting internally that she had recorded the exchange word-for-word in her mind, I said, "Sorry, *drop* you from therapy. I responded 'absolutely not,' then asked you the matching question, to which you responded, 'absolutely not.'"

She responded, "a part of me felt relief."

Whereupon I felt relief that she felt relief.

She then asked, "What was it like for *you*?" I paused and thought, and consciously decided I could make use of her excellent knowledge of words. I said, "You know the word 'report,' as in, the 'report' of a gun?" "Yes," she said. I said, "I liked the report of my answer to you. It was strong, and clear. I liked that, and I liked the coupling of the question I asked you back." After a short pause, I queried back, "What was it like for you to hear me tell you that?" "A part of me doesn't believe it."

I shook my head yes, but felt a sense of hurt and discouragement within me. I calmed myself a bit by thinking about how honestly (and with what pain) she had come to be distrustful.

I reflected for a while on how I seem repeatedly to work with schizoid patients. I wondered if that was perhaps a reflection of my own schizoid-ness and tried to let that in as a possibility. I let that settle inside me, all the while hoping she didn't choose now to query my thoughts.

She said after a while, "You seemed disappointed in me last week." Somewhat taken aback, I wrestled within about that. I didn't want to give her a quick, protesting response, so waited to get more honest with myself and her. I finally said that I was searching around inside to find a word that was a neighbor to "disappointment," but not quite "disappointment." I struggled to word my response; I didn't want her to bat it away, and didn't want to say something that wasn't entirely true. I finally harvested the picture that had formed in my mind. I said that being with her last week was like watching competing impulses (as in an electrical wire) get stuck before one of the two could prevail: the one that wanted to say something, and the one that wanted to muzzle it. I gestured to indicate a narrow opening. She asked, "Which one did you want?" I said, "The one that wanted to speak." After a long pause, I finally had the right feeling in mind. I said, "With your students, do you ever earnestly hope for something for them?" "Yes," she said. "It was more like that," I said.

We again moved into silence. Several minutes later, disturbing the silence, I laughed out loud at something that had come to mind; it was a little irrepressible.

"What?" she said. I shook my head a little, as if to say "No." "You can't laugh without saying what it is," she urged with a half smile. "OK. Let me see if I can trace it backwards." I said, with some effort, "I was thinking about your intensity … and then about my intensity. And I thought about how you must think some of what I say is total bullshit." (She smiled.) "I know you don't exactly think that, but that's how I talked to myself about it. Then, what came to mind: there was a professor in my department—Mary Ann Wakefield—in the mid-1990s. In her office was a large standing set of file drawers, and on the top of it was an aerosol can, with the label on it, 'Bullshit Repellant.'" She smiled again, and responded, "Yah, I actually think I've seen one of those a couple of times."

Then she spoke, "I'm surprised that you pick up so many strands of me that I thought I was hiding more successfully." After a goodly pause I responded playfully, "You'll have to hide better." Then, after a long pause I said with emphasis, "You didn't come *here* to hide."

I sat a long time. I had several pieces of poetry come to mind. First, Frost's Mending Wall.

> "Something there is that doesn't love a wall,
> That sends the frozen-ground-swell under it,
> And spills the upper boulders in the sun,
> And makes gaps even two can pass abreast."

This repeated several times, my trying to recite more of it to myself, and wishing I had committed the whole poem to memory. Why hadn't I? This was followed by phrases from Langston Hughes' "Harlem."

> "What happens to a dream deferred?
> Does it dry up like a raisin in the sun?
> Or fester like a sore … or sag.
> Or does it explode?"

I wondered why the rush of poetry; wondered if (in the soup) she was having poems come to mind.

Finally, she said, "What?" I responded, "I have several pieces of poetry colliding in my mind. I was wondering why. Do you know?" I asked. "What poems?" she asked. I said the most prominent one was "Mending Wall" by Frost. Did she know it? "How does it go?" she asked. I said with some discomfort, "it's almost too patent." I then recited slowly,

> "Something there is that doesn't love a wall,
> That sends the frozen-ground-swell under it,
> And spills the upper boulders in the sun,
> And makes gaps even two can pass abreast."

She asked if I'd read Raymond Carver's poetry. "No," I said. "He's my favorite poet," she said.

Again, it felt like a moment of accruing trust. Her private writing is close to the bone for her, and sharing with me the name of her favorite poet seemed like giving me access to something close to her emotional self.

It was at the end, and I asked her, "What was it like in here for you today?" She responded, "I never know what to say to that question." "One word," I suggested. She shook her head, no, then asked, "What was it like in here for you?" "Intense," I said. "Fair enough," she said, agreeing. Then she added, "I couldn't come up with anything at the end." "Yes, you actually did," I said. She looked surprised. "You shared your favorite poet," I said.

I walked to the door and held it open. She passed by without eye contact. "See you next week," I said.

This series of sessions occurred three months into what promises to be a long and challenging therapy. The challenge is and will be to go at her pace, and to bear the transferential distrust and misperceptions that characterize her perceptions of me. Most of what is presented here is in the swirl; my thoughts, my interventions, my reveries are confused and blind in most moments. Once in a while, there are moments of meeting, especially the kitty cat scene, my use of the words dead bolt and dead heat, which tell me that I'm close enough to her internal experience to have her feel somehow seen. Her words in the last of these sessions, "I'm surprised that you pick up so many strands of me that I thought I was hiding more successfully," tell me that. There are occasional moments of precipitation, when something of the patient comes out of the swirl and into sharper focus, notably the understanding of her perhaps "disorganized" attachment experience, and the understanding that my intense longings for her to feel seen might be reflective of the child's longing for her mom to be present for her. This is a therapy in its infancy, but perhaps illustrates as well as any the role of space, quietude, and reverie in connecting (through the analytic third) with the unspoken emotional world of the patient.

Afterword. Often in training books in psychotherapy, cases are presented where the end is known. I chose this one specifically so students could know how I sit with my anxiety and confusion, not knowing how it's going to turn out. But as I sit this morning with the task of editing and polishing this manuscript, three years after these sessions occurred, I'm happy with the bets I've made and the risks I've taken along the way in my work with this patient. She continues in the therapy to this day, now twice a week, is no longer silent, no longer experiences me with unrelenting fear and distrust, and is gradually growing in the therapy.

9

OBJECT RELATIONS

It's a shame if any child grows up not having been able to look down the barrel of a kaleidoscope. It's a magical world of colors, patterns and light that can be made to remain, momentarily, and then to be transformed into a whole new array with the slightest wish of the child's hands. The way it works is that inside the kaleidoscope there is a circle of mirrors containing loose, colored objects (beads, pebbles, bits of glass). As the viewer looks into one end, light entering the other end creates an endless array of colorful patterns, due to the reflection of the light off the mirrors.

We're about to enter a decidedly kaleidoscopic place together in this book journey. We can say that we're going to count out the bits of glass in advance: some green ones, some red ones, some yellow ones, some blue ones. We can arrange them in neat little piles and know their exact size and shape. But when they're loaded into the kaleidoscope of the psychotherapeutic relationship, they'll mix together, and the neat world of exactitude will give way to the swirling world of patterns and colors and shapes we've never seen before.

Let's at least select the bits of colored glass together: "object relations" in one big pile, then "transference" in the pile next to it, "countertranference" in another pile, with projective identification right next to that, and over here, anxieties—well, maybe defenses in that pile, too. We'll try to examine the piles one by one, but ultimately the wonder of it (and the swirl) awaits our mixing them together.

A Word on Theory

The piles of glass we're about to explore are ways of looking at the therapeutic relationship that are pivotal to our understanding of the individuals who come to us for therapy. *Understanding* follows listening deeply, and entering into the intersubjective field with our patients in moments of meeting, of swirl, and of precipitation. But *understanding* what we encounter as we listen—the *whys* of a patient's internal patterns, and the root systems that keep those patterns fixed in place—is rarely self-evident. Our capacity to understand the psychological truth at the bottom of things is an extremely important part of our job. The truth is a powerfully mutative agent. It can bring freedom where empathy alone may only bring comfort.

This is why, as psychodynamic psychotherapists, theory is our friend, and definitely helps in the art of understanding. Theory binds our confusion. It gives us words. It tells us where to look. It contains us. Theory puts at our disposal the perceptions of the geniuses of the field who have preceded us to this moment, to this patient. It focuses our lenses so that we can see what we might otherwise miss.

My youngest sister, Suzi, got glasses in seventh grade. She had never seen the leaves on trees at a distance, and had never known they *could* be seen. Her new lenses allowed her to bring into focus what, left to her own resources and under her own power, would have remained fuzzy to her. This is how theory works. It sharpens our focus; it allows us to see what perhaps would have remained indistinct to us forever, or worse, out of sight until we fell over it.

As you may be painfully aware from listening to media psychologists, we all operate with theory. Some make it up entirely from their own experience.

To quote Greenberg and Mitchell (1983: p. 3),

> Every analyst, even the most rigidly atheoretical, is at least implicitly a theorist. What one hears from a patient is informed by what one knows about living; it is shaped by a theory which the analyst may or may not articulate (even to himself) and which is derived from what he has read (within and without the technical literature), seen, and lived.

So let's look together at several theories that can deeply inform the work of *understanding* in psychodynamic psychotherapy. We will look first at the theory called "Object Relations." It provides a basic "meta-map" for understanding the unique ways that people orient themselves in their relationships: to themselves, to others, and to us as therapists.

Object Relations?

First, the name, "Object Relations." Some intergenerational names should never be handed forward. "Object Relations Theory" is one of these. It was named formally by Ronald Fairbairn in 1952 (Fairbairn, 1952), and was really named to credit Freud as primogenitor of drive theory (even though it would serve as the pivot point away from drive theory). Freud had defined three essential characteristics of a drive in his paper, "Instincts and Their Vicissitudes" (Freud, 1915b: pp. 121–122). A drive had its *source* (physiological), its *aim* (satisfaction: the discharge or expression of nervous system excitation), and its *object* (the eminently changeable entity toward which the drive was directed). The *object* of a drive could be food, or sex, or a particular human, or a whole range of interchangeable possibilities. Object Relations Theory picks up on this third aspect of the drive, and suggests theoretically that the *human* "*object*" is our most primary and compelling object. Object Relations Theory's focus on and elaboration of our relationship to the kinds of objects that are indeed *human* has changed the trajectory of the psychoanalytic discourse in the last sixty years. However, as rich as Object Relations Theory has come to be, we still have to live with the name. My high school was named Mother Butler Memorial High. Unwieldy, still.

But Object Relations Theory truly lives beyond its name. It gives to psychodynamic psychotherapy its intensely two-person focus. I will present the barest schematics of it here, because a large number of authors have beautifully done the conversation ahead of me (notably, Greenberg & Mitchell, Sandler, Ogden, St. Claire, McWilliams, and many others). But let me put out a few essentials. Let me also note, in advance, that the "theory" is really the "theories": the cumulative (and sometimes disparate) discourse of those who have written, over time, in this theory space.

Self and Other, Perspectives and Preferences

So, Object Relations. According to Object Relations Theory, our predispositions and patterns in relationships are based on three things, essentially. First, our conception of the *inter*personal terrain: who we think *the other* to be—their safety, their reliability, their trustworthiness, their capacity to understand us and to accept us, what they require of us, etc. Next, our relational patterns are based on our own *intra*personal terrain: who we think *ourselves* to be—worthwhile, not worthwhile; deserving respect, or mistreatment, or disappointment, etc. Finally, the interface between the two: our preferred ways of being perceived and treated—or what we seem to require of and pull for in the mix of *interpersonal* and *intrapersonal* terrains. These are the foci of Object Relations Theory. In addition, the theory seeks to explain how we acquire this set of relational perspectives and preferences.

Self

Each of us has a view of the *self*. We see ourselves in certain ways: talented, well liked, wise, embattled, misunderstood, alone, gentle, care-taking, thoughtful, alienated, invisible, ineffectual, competent, surviving, buoyant, dependent, awkward, depressed, powerful, admired, steady, anxious, paranoid, fractured. We see ourselves at the most fundamental level as deserving or not deserving to be loved. These self-descriptions may shift in the moment, or with life events, or with our moods. But we tend to have a certain consistent set of characteristics that define the range of who we experience ourselves to be.

Other

We all have certain *filters* through which we see others; filters that govern our selective perception of others. These can be general (you can't trust anyone, really)

or more specific (good-looking outgoing men are, at core, narcissistic). No one is
filter-free. We all see others as though through a pre-existing set of prisms. Each of
us has no doubt had the experience of comparing our perceptions of a particular
person with those of someone else, only to find that we have opposing "hits" as to
the observed person's character, motivation, likeability, sincerity, and so on. We
have all probably also had the experience of seeing someone initially a certain way,
and with time, gradually refining or revising our view. We see, especially initially,
as if through filters.

understanding biases

Interface

All of us have a certain preferred style of interface in our relationships: a way we
want to be perceived, a way we want to be related to, a certain way of being seen
and connected to that makes us feel comfortable. We have a certain *feel* that we try
unconsciously to achieve, and a certain way that we "pull" on others to see us as we
want to be seen, and to treat us as we want to be treated—usually across contexts
and relationships. We operate so as to be perceived and treated in ways that are
familiar to us. We use familiar methods and moves to achieve these ends. I've called
these our "spin" in relationships. It might be, for instance, that we want to feel
respected, or to be experienced as warm, or to be taken care of, or to be listened to,
or to be seen as self-sufficient, or smart, or creative, or to be the one who "takes
charge," or makes peace, or tells the truth, or any of these in combination. We
might consistently jockey to be "one-up" or "one-down," or we might feel more
comfortable being hidden, or even being overlooked and mistreated. We
unconsciously sculpt, predicate, and constrain our behavior in relationships—our
spin—in order to get what we are used to; what is normal for us.

Here's an important corollary: our conceptions of *self* and *other* and the ways we
desire to be seen and treated greatly influence whom we relate to as our closest and
most intimate others. It's as though we master a set of dance steps along the way.
We try these out with different people. Some people can't dance with us at all.
Some slide into our rhythm exquisitely well and even seem to know the backwards
parts of some of our steps. These are the people we feel we've known all our lives.
We tend to be most comfortable when we're getting, relationally, what we have
accustomed ourselves to and practiced along the way, because for better *and* for
worse, we know exactly how our part of the dance goes. For instance, if we grew up
in a chaotic environment where our role was to be observer and peacemaker, we
might long for the joys of a low-conflict relationship, but become unconsciously
bored by relationships in which there is no chaos for us to mediate. If we grew up
with little connection to parents and family members, we might dream of someday
having such connection, but feel smothered by those who would attempt to draw
us into more frequent or more intimate interaction. We tend toward what is familiar
to us; we tend to use the dance steps we have learned and practiced over time.

Our ineluctable attraction to the *familiar* is a huge axiom in Object Relations
Theory, and it would be hugely easy to pass by the observation that we strive to be

"perceived and treated in familiar ways," without giving it its proper due. So perhaps it would be well to stop a minute and consider the questions, "What is your particular spin?" "How do you want, need, work to be perceived by others?" "When you feel uncommonly *not* understood, what is it that someone is *not* getting?" These questions lead to the same endpoint: that we work (often unconsciously) to have others encounter us in certain familiar ways.

Object Relations Theory attempts to account for our relational "spin": how we position to be encountered and perceived; and our relational "filters": the underlying templates through which we view other persons and ourselves. The theory elaborates how we come to have such selectivities and relational valences.

Brief Commercial Message

Before I go further, I'd like to plug Object Relations Theory. So much of our job as psychotherapists involves people who come to us with counterproductive ways of seeing themselves and others (and us), and equally counterproductive ways of behaving in those relationships. But it doesn't take very long in practice before we discover that such ways of seeing and being do not yield easily to disputation or logic. What may appear to us as a pebble on someone's psychic terrain—easily kicked aside—often winds up being affixed to a much larger set of schemas, and attached to the center of this person's earth! So, having theoretical tools to equip us as clinicians to understand those hidden infrastructures (in ourselves and in our patients) helps us to operate with appropriate respect, appropriate perspective, and appropriate patience.

Origins of Self and Other: Experience-Informed "Models"

How do we acquire our views of self, and other, and our desired interface between them? In a simplified schematic form, what Object Relations Theory posits is that our "spins" and our "filters" begin to be acquired very early on in the process of human development.

Here's how it goes. We, as infants, are received into an interpersonal environment that preexists us. We enter that pre-existing environment with a certain mix of genes that constitutes the "nature" part of the "nature/nurture" equation. Then, we have a set of experiences (the "nurture" part) that causes us to build a psychic impression of the interpersonal world; to construct an interpersonal *model*, so to speak. (If we add in Lacan (1953) here, we might also mention that we are received into a certain cultural and linguistic environment that preexists us, pre-privileging and pre-limiting aspects of us).

This *model*, begun to be constructed in infancy, as the theory goes, includes a picture of how the *other* (the "*object*") behaves toward and apprehends us, and a picture of the *self* in that relationship. The picture of the other and the self is forming from the earliest days of life. To paraphrase Winnicott, we, as infants, put together a picture of ourselves through what we experience in our mother's treatment of us: how she looks at and beholds us. To quote him directly, he says, "The precursor of the mirror is the mother's face." Winnicott elaborates in the same chapter, "Ordinarily, what the baby sees [in the exchange of gazes with the mother] is himself or herself ... [T]he mother is looking at the baby and what she looks like [from the baby's point of view] is related to what she sees there" (Winnicott, 1967: p. 112). According to Winnicott, from our first moments, we are constructing our model of intra- and interpersonal reality based on how we are viewed, handled, and responded to by our primary caregivers.

To make this more tangible, imagine the experience of a baby born to a crack-addicted mom. There would be the initial enormous physical pain and discomfort of withdrawal from the prenatal drug that we were on before our own birth. This would make our initial arrival on Planet Earth a painful enterprise. Then there would be the physical experience of being 100 percent dependent, but attended to by someone not consistently able to apprehend or respond to our most basic needs. Then—and this is hard to imagine—but imagine having no language with which to think your way *around* these moments. Added to that, there would be the progressive psychological disappointment of trying to form an attachment bond with someone not able to be *there* on the receiving end of our efforts.

Imagine that the same level of inconsistency persisted hour after hour, day after day, throughout our earliest days and months of development. Now add in that during this formative time, we would be building our right brain's foundational impressions of the emotional and interpersonal world, and actively wiring up our ways of handling that world. We would not have the tools of perspective or logic at our disposal. Those would come much later in our development. We would be likely to form some unworded, but strong hypotheses about the safety of human beings in general and about our own merits, in terms of *meriting* someone's attuned attention.

If these tentative hypotheses were reinforced, unabated, over time, we might progress to what Mary Ainsworth has called an "insecure attachment" style (Ainsworth et al., 1978). She and many other attachment researchers in her wake have observed that as early as the one-year point in infant development, some infants exhibit this "insecure" attachment style, in one of its three subtypes—"avoidant," "ambivalent," or "disorganized"—depending on the elements of nature and nurture. In contrast, a child born to parents who were better able to be attuned to its needs and individuality might form a measurably "secure" attachment by age one. This would be accompanied by different initial (unworded) hypotheses about the safety of human beings in general, and that child's inherent merits; again, in terms of meriting someone's attuned attention.

Theoretical Backlighting

It might help us to give credibility to some of the tenets of Object Relations Theory if we backlight the theory for just a minute here with a couple of things from current attachment and interpersonal neurobiological research.

It is now clearly established that a great deal of *inter-* and *intra-*personal action is going on quietly in the brains and experiences of infants during the first eighteen months of life, before they have developed the language with which to narrate it to themselves or to us (Schore, 2012). While we as observers of these early days cannot directly ask an infant what they are thinking/feeling/constructing about the *other* or the *self*, we *can* observe some of a child's non-verbal adaptations to their interpersonal environment, and ultimately can view the scenery clearly in the rear view mirror.

Infant researchers study carefully what emerges in the behavior and emotional patterns of infants, toddlers, and children from heavily compromised early environments such as the one I just asked us to imagine, or those orphaned by war or parental incarceration or death, or even those raised in chronically mis-attuned, neglectful, or violent environments. We know from such "naturalistic" experiments that there are interpersonal and intrapersonal sequelae strongly associated with certain early emotional deprivations, and that *self* concept (feelings of the worthiness of the self) and *other* concept (basic trust) are quite consistently affected. Such basic aspects of humanness as trust versus distrust; feelings of security and love in relationship versus feelings of suspicion and wariness; feelings of self-appreciation and acceptance versus feelings of self-hatred, these are what is at stake in the earliest days and months of infant development.

We have traced patterns of the *self* and *other* concept (initially measurable at one year of age) across time, and find strong consistencies as children progress up the maturational ladder. Without deliberate intervention, insecurely attached one-year-olds develop into insecurely ("ambivalently," "avoidantly," or "dis-organized(ly)") attached five-year-olds, who become ambivalent, avoidant or disorganized eight-year-olds, who carry these patterns into adolescence, and ultimately exhibit these same relational patterns as adults. These consistencies are strong and well established in the longitudinal studies of attachment researchers (Waters et al., 2000).

Additionally, through current functional MRI technologies, we are now even able to observe certain neurological compromises in the *brains* of children raised in grossly suboptimal relational environments. I find two of these particularly clinically relevant.

The first is that for children in such grossly suboptimal environments, there can be prominent alterations in the frequency of the young child's use of *dissociation* as a self-soothing strategy. These alterations are accompanied by stable *alterations in the neurological pathways governing dissociation*, making that state much more likely to occur and to be prominent in that person in later years (Schore, 2009).

The second is that we can observe compromises of the orbitofrontal mediating centers of *self* and *other* in some children—permanent alterations in the part of our brain whose job it is to make proper integrative sense of our intra- and interpersonal world. These neurological changes can be observed very early on—as early as during the first eighteen months of life (Gerhardt, 2004; Schore, 2009; Siegel, 2012).

I share these examples to give credence to what the theorists in our field observed long before the scientific community developed adequately sensitive measurement instruments. Our brains remain plastic our entire lives, open to re-wiring efforts as long as we are alive. But the foundational tracks—the things we come to know *in our bones* about self and other—are laid down early in our experience, and are much more difficult to re-wire than they would be to wire correctly in the first place.

Back to Object Relations

Object Relations theorists have asserted that we use the inter- and intrapersonal data we accrue from our beginning days and months to construct a set of emotional expectations within ourselves. The advantage of this is that we can then, with some efficiency, predict and prepare for what is coming in subsequent human interactions. Our accrued expectations make us more efficient. We don't have to reinvent the interpersonal and intrapersonal wheel again and again, and we don't have to suffer surprise or disappointment if we already know what the world is like. We are already braced for (or open to) the experience.

This is completely congruent, if we think about it, with our more general tendency to learn as humans. Our prior exposures help us to predict and prepare for the new, whether it's in tackling long division or in assessing the interpersonal landscape. The difference is that the things we learn really early (implicitly, with our affectively-wired right brains), we learn really really well, and they are much less subject to revision or modification than things we learn in school. We "know" long division, but we "know in our bones" whom and what to distrust.

Practice Makes Perfect

Now, let me take us one step further in Object Relations Theory. We've already said that we construct a kind of internal reference bank for ourselves, one that includes impressions of the other and impressions of the self. Writers in Object Relations assert further that as time goes on, these impressions begin to have more and more intra- and interpersonal specificity to them. We get interpersonally smart over time, in terms of handling our particular childhood environment.

What does this mean? It means that we develop the emotional tools to handle the particular people we happen to land with as our caretakers, and whatever else is in the family configuration. It's a little like developing the muscles for a particular sport. We train and train and train for that sport. We become stronger and more sophisticated at it. If we try an unrelated sport, we have neither the muscle nor the technique at first. We might be excellent on the tennis court, but a relative klutz on the soccer field.

So if a child lands in an emotionally challenging environment, she or he devotes mental and emotional resources to learning whatever will be the optimum strategy for managing that environment, given his or her natural endowments. Suppose, for instance, that a child grows up in a family where dad is alcoholic and mom is unable to set effective limits with him. If dad is dangerous when he drinks, a developing child's task might be to learn how to maneuver when dad is over his limit—whatever is available to that child—whether that means reading the signs of it early, being compliant, becoming invisible, or taking care of the other children; whatever works and is possible. Likewise, if mom is fragile and inept when dad is drunk and dangerous, the child's task is to learn how to manage her, how to calm her fears or to keep her safe, or to salve her emotional or physical wounds in the aftermath—again, whatever is possible. Additionally, of course, that child also very likely has feelings within him or herself in the midst of all of this discord, which might include feelings of being terrified, covered over by feelings of being the steady one, and, underneath these, as is often the thought process of a child, having somehow (magically) caused it all.

Now, changing the metaphors from tennis to academics, when that child grows up, he has a Ph.D. in managing drinking-dangerous dad and fragile-inept mom. The theorists assert that he will (unconsciously) look for situations that allow him to exercise his hard-won knowledge and skills. He will scan for the familiar, and when he finds it, he'll know exactly how to handle it. Some of us find ourselves doing that in our professional lives; some repeat the trauma in our personal lives.

You may know of a child who grew up in an explosive or violent home, wishing his or her whole childhood for something more normal, only to find him/ herself creating exactly the same kind of environment in his or her adult home. Or the social worker in my own practice who spent her childhood managing an on-and-off psychotic mother, and now interfaces all the time with parents who are too psychologically compromised to keep their children at home. Even the job of being psychotherapist often involves putting to use skills that we learned as children: reading the nuances of the emotional environment as children, and listening to the emotional world of our own parents. It makes sense.

Pause and Collect

So, increasing time in some adverse emotional environments confers specialized skills in children. They become hyper-expert at certain parts of managing the interpersonal environment around them as little ones. They grow up with these skills and often find places and ways to exercise them as they move onward in life. Sometimes, such application of hard-won skills is redemptive; sometimes, it is tragic.

But here's an important thing to note. Anytime a child has to spend time and energy managing emotional adversity in his family of origin, there is something that child is *not* doing. They are *not* investing that emotional energy in the normal, essential tasks of being a child. *Something* is sacrificed. Some parts of who that child was meant to develop into and *be* get sacrificed in the bargain. This damage is invisible. It's hard to know what was truly meant to be if it never got space to emerge. (This is one of the exciting parts of doing psychodynamic psychotherapy— the parts we sometimes get to see emerge).

Gathering it up. We've said that we have filters through which we view others. We've said that we have ways we learn to perceive ourselves. We've said that we have our particular spin in relationships to help us customize relationships into what we're comfortable with. We drilled down more specifically on the acquisition process. We've said that we experience the various parts of our caregivers and learn how to manage them. We've also said that we carry this experiential reference bank within us to help us evaluate and navigate our subsequent relational world. We've said that we unconsciously look for the familiar—even when it is difficult—in order to operate in known territory.

Why is all of this important for us to study and think about and ponder? The answer is simple. Because it helps people make sense to us, and it helps us help them make sense to themselves. If that can happen, sometimes it enables something new to emerge—new perspectives, new questions, new feelings, new freedoms, new choices, new pieces—something other than what has always, always been.

One More Step: Internal Objects and Internalizations

Now we're going to take one more step in Object Relations Theory. This is clinically helpful, but hard to get one's mind around at first. So I'll take it slowly and provide examples along the way.

First some vocabulary. We have within us what the theorists refer to as "*internal objects.*" *External* objects are the *real* parents, caregivers, and others in the family environment who related to us as we grew up. (External objects can also refer to real people in our current lives). These people—these *real* objects—are highly influential in our formation of self-perceptions and other perceptions, as we have said.

Internal objects, in contrast, refer to our early *conceptions* of these external objects. As children (primarily during years zero-to-five), we build a set of images or constructs within us that *represent* various aspects of our external objects to us. We might have within ourselves an image of the mom who rocked us when we were distressed, the one who did our hair, the one who yelled at us when we were fighting with our siblings, the one who would cry when she was overwhelmed. We might have an image of the dad who played with us, or read to us, or sang to us, or scared us when he got angry. We install a vast array of these images within ourselves as little people—in essence, fractionated pieces of our parents and significant caregivers, as we experienced them back then. Once installed, they remain permanently inside us as part of our psyche, subtly influencing the ways we think, feel, and behave within ourselves all the way through our adult years. We call them *internal objects*.

It is theorized that on an unconscious level, these fractionated pieces of parental interactions—these *internal objects*—can and do remain dynamic within us, continuing to relate to *us* and to *others in our lives* in much the same ways that our external objects acted toward us when we were young. So in times of distress, for example, we might (not usually consciously) draw on an *internal object* mom who used to calm us down and take care of us. We might feel that care, and be able to calm ourselves as she would. In times when we make a mistake, we might feel the disapprobation of our (*internal object*) parent from within ourselves. If we had a neglectful parent, we might treat ourselves with neglect at times in terms of basic needs for food and sleep. If we had a dangerous, violent father, we might have a part of ourselves that may be psychically dangerous and violent toward *ourselves*. We might assault ourselves mercilessly for a vast array of perceived crimes, perhaps even using the exact words and tone that he might have used.

I saw a micro example of this yesterday at a family Thanksgiving gathering. My brother-in-law was serving pie and dumped a piece of it in his lap. He said, "I'm so stupid!" I replied, "My fault. You were just trying to get me a small enough piece." He replied, "I'm clumsy. My dad used to yell at me for that all the time." I said, "All children are clumsy. They don't have their full coordination yet." He responded, "My father thought that children should be perfect." "Then he shouldn't have had children!" I volleyed back. But more to the point, I thought that I often observe him being harshly self-critical, and that in these moments I'm probably indirectly visiting scenes from his childhood with his frequently harsh father.

Multifaceted Identifications

Now, here's another important thing about this internalization process—again, a little hard to understand. We store *both sides* of the early interpersonal/emotional interactions with our caregivers inside us: the child's side *and* the parent's side. We internalize *all* of the following: (1) what it felt like to be on the receiving end of our parent in micro moments (soothed, contained, frightened, missed, etc.); (2) the interpersonal strategies we launched in order to manage our parent, if such management was necessary (calming, supportive, mature, invisible, etc.); (3) what it felt like to *be* our parent in these moments (out of control, violent, depressed, anxious, etc.). Yes! We internalize *both sides* of the emotional interaction in a way we don't really do as adults. We store these things in our implicit, emotional memory banks as children. They become part of who we are, how we think, how we feel, and how we function.

For instance, if we had a fragile, inept mother—whom we took care of emotionally—we are likely to have not only a caretaker part, but also a part of ourselves, that, given the right mix of circumstances, itself collapses into emotional fragility and ineptitude, making us not able to manage ourselves in certain times and moments in the ways we would normally function. If we had a parent who was psychologically dead or depressed inside, we might carry and struggle with that same deadness within. If our parent was violent, we might find that violent streak inside ourselves. If our parent never asked for help with the ordinary tasks of life, we might find that exact trait in ourselves. We internalize our parents' characteristics, and then (sometimes inscrutably to us) enact them. This is an important thing for us as therapists to understand. Such identifications preserve people's psychic linkages to their original parental objects. (This makes them highly resistant to change).

Externalizing the Internal

Then one more thing. Our internalizations—our internal objects—can also influence our treatment of *others* in our lives. We see many examples of this all the time. The child who was the victim of violence grows up to have the abuser within; to be abusive toward their own children.

Why would this be? Why would we have parts of our minds or psyches that behave toward ourselves or toward others in our lives the way our parents behaved toward us, especially if those ways were hurtful? Perhaps the why of this is hard to answer, but the how is not.

It's important to realize that we learn differently as developing children than we do as adults. As little people, we *absorb* experience rather than studying it. For the first eighteen months of life, we *absorb* emotionally formative experiences with our right brains (the emotional side of our minds), without having the services of our left brains at all to weigh and evaluate what is happening to us. We simply absorb. During our second eighteen months when we are acquiring language, we don't study language in order to learn it; we *absorb* it.

Young children *absorb* the experiences that they participate in. Emotionally, children are perfectly cross-trained within. They master not only their own role in childhood scenes, but the other person's role as well. They take into themselves what it feels like to be *themselves* as little children—to be on the receiving end of dad's violence and rage, and what it is to be the *other*—to be in *dad's* role in those moments—violent and rageful. We learn—"internalize"; we "internalize," or take in, whole cloth, entire experiences as young people.

Here's another thing about this internalization process. We seem to do it across the vast array of emotional elements in our interpersonal environment as youngsters. We absorb not only mom's fragility and ineptitude when dad is dangerous, but her gentleness, her strength, her self-doubt, her sense of deprivation as well, across the full range of her traits and states. We absorb not only dad's dangerousness in drunken moments, but his obsessiveness, his imperiousness, his sense of humor, his judgmental nature as well. Then, depending on their prominence in our interpersonal environment, we might take in parts of older brother, or grandmother, or nanny. We take these parts and pieces into ourselves from the interpersonal environment of our raising. We do this subjectively—with the subjectivity of a little child—with no particular demand for emotional balance or truth in the process. Two children in the same family can absorb different degrees or valences of these features, depending on such factors as their own temperament and needs, their particular perspective, their resilience, differential parental projections, real-life external pressures, etc.

Net-net, our reference bank of internal objects is, in essence, alive within us, and has an unconscious life of its own, ever ready to exert its influence.

Regathering

So let's count pieces of Object Relations glass thus far for our kaleidoscope. We have the self, we have the external objects that were actually there in our original interpersonal world (mommy, daddy, brothers, sisters, perhaps a nanny or grandmother). We have the *internalized* objects, the mommy inside, that is our early, emotionally and perceptually-biased experience of our mommy; the daddy inside, etc. As an elaboration of these internalized objects, we have the fractionated emotional parts of these others across their various moods and states of being. We have these in two forms: they are internalized as parts of the self and they stand within the self, acting on it, internally. Then we have the real everyday external others (external objects) that we encounter as we go forward in life: teachers, peers, coworkers, ultimately loved ones, partners, children, perhaps even a therapist. (Yes, these are also called objects—yes, confusing!). Then we have what we make of these external others inside us. In other words, the world of Object Relations is a well-populated world. It is a lot to take in, theoretically.

But let's take a step back and think about this together. That we misperceive our interpersonal reality is hardly disputable. We all do this. It comes with the territory of being a human. That we all have a source (more properly, sources) of commentary on ourselves inside is also indisputable; sometimes voices of approbation, sometimes of derogation. That we experience ourselves as different across different emotional contexts and moods is likewise beyond argument. Sometimes we are reasonable and open; sometimes immature and irascible (in ways strangely like our own mother, which we hated as a child). That we seem to have parts and pieces of our parents installed inside us, not just their genes, but their emotional attitudes and motivations; this, too, is the lot of mankind. Object Relations Theory gathers up these scraps and pieces of the experience of being interpersonally and intrapersonally human, and attempts to weave an explanatory netting around them.

As individuals, this theory helps us look at and understand our own emotional parts, pieces, neuroticisms, and inconsistencies. It helps us to see what William Faulkner (1950) wrote in *Requiem for a Nun*, that interpersonally and intrapersonally, "The past is never dead. It's not even past."

Clinically, the perspectives of Object Relations are an invaluable aid in making our way through the often confusing and counterintuitive morass of the *other*. It helps us to understand, for instance, why, on the heels of a step forward, a certain patient will consistently suffer self-defeat and self-sabotage. Or why someone else is so viciously harsh with themselves or with us. Or why someone with a full palette of life skills will act in critical moments as though they cannot solve the simplest of daily challenges. Or why some find it so abysmally hard to trust: us and others.

Perhaps a clinical example or two will help pull these concepts into sharper focus. It's difficult to choose, because Object Relations Theory provides such a powerful viewing lens that I might choose any of the people I see or have seen (or myself, or my "others"). I'll briefly sketch a woman named Jackie I saw several times a week for about six years. Jackie was in her early 50s, divorced, with two adult daughters. She worked in visual production in a large corporate firm, and came initially to deal with overall feelings of depression and ennui.

Jackie was well above average in intelligence, but found herself unable to accomplish the simplest of life tasks. For example, she could not load her own camera, she could not learn the elements of computer programs that were critical to her job. She could not use the information provided in a community college catalogue to figure out how to register for a class.

She was good at getting people to do things for her. This was her interpersonal "spin," so to speak. She related to me that she had special access to her physician, and need not make appointments to see him. She'd drop by, he would see her and send her out loaded with a bag full of free pharmaceuticals. She had a special stool behind the counter where she would sit and visit with her pharmacist. She was a member of a church of 2,000 people, but had a standing one-hour a week appointment with the head pastor of the church. She had a "prayer team" at church who would specifically target her weekly as their special, ongoing object of concern. When I inquired as to how this came about, she said, "Oh, you know—I did my wet kitten routine and they sort of adopted me as their project." Of course, she angled me into treating her "specially" at first, negotiating a 1½ hour session twice a week because she found the 50-minute hour not enough for her.

Her "spin" had a well-developed Object Relational root system. She was thought to be the last of three children in a family that would, after a five-year gap, ultimately include several more children. But as she was thought to be her mother's last, her mother had treated her as though she needed special help for a full range of ordinary tasks and responsibilities. For instance, the mom acquired the books for first grade in advance of Jackie's attendance, so that she could tutor her in advance. When Jackie began to attend school, the mom asked the older two children to find their sister in the playground at the end of each recess, and to alert her to come back to the classroom when the bell had rung.

This special infantile place was abruptly discontinued with the arrival of the next set of children. My patient never got over the interpersonal loss, and orchestrated her life and the lives of those she interacted with to re-sample the feelings of specialness she had enjoyed from her mom's (illegitimate) need to still have a baby. Through the filter of Object Relations Theory, I could make sense of her "spin" with me, and of my own feelings of being used by her (as she was by her mom). Ultimately, we were able to regularize our meeting times, to notice her bids with me for infantile specialness, and the terrible costs of that spin to her over time (in the loss of her marriage, her job, and the disrespect of her daughters).

Another brief example comes from a patient who was the first daughter of two daughters (and a son) of a woman whose life was predicated on her own beauty. The first daughter was thoughtful and intelligent; the second had the mother's beauty, and was the mother's favored one. When the first daughter became seriously involved in an adult relationship, she found herself inconsolably jealous with any mention of her live-in boyfriend's ex-relationships. She found her own reaction crazy and disturbing. But her internal object world had been so scarred by the chronic unfavorable comparison with her sibling that she found the psychic threat of comparison implied by her boyfriend's (abortive) stories searingly intolerable. She carried within her internal object world what it felt like to be on the receiving end of her mother's unequal love, and (despite its apparent groundlessness to her) could not tolerate having the feeling activated again in the present.

Closing Comments

In this chapter, I've presented the broad strokes of Object Relations Theory. Given this schematic view, you may perhaps be able more easily to parse authors who write with a finer-grained approach, which is well worth the effort. In the next chapter we will look at the special case of Object Relations Theory applied to the relationship between the patient and the therapist. This next pile of kaleidoscopic glass will take us together into the multifaceted world of "transference" in the therapeutic relationship—a fascinating part of the journey.

10

TRANSFERENCE

Now we're going to gather another pile of colored glass for our kaleidoscope. The "transference" pile. Transference is insider language. We have to say it correctly. It's "trans'ference," not "transfer'ence." We sometimes get to say "*the* transference," or in clinically mature company, "transference-countertransference." The word "transference" is like a secret handshake in the psychodynamic world; a signifier of membership.

I'm being a little irreverent here, because transference is hard to write about. It's hard to explain. It's hard perhaps in part because it's uncomfortable to think that we as humans are involved in relationships built as much on our own fabrications as on the brick-and-mortar of things. It's hard because if we're honest, all of us have had a whole host of transferential relationships over time. So let me move out of irreverence and head into the conversational headwinds. Let's stalk this word together, "trans'ference," and what is its crucial contribution to the *art of understanding* in psychodynamic psychotherapy.

First Experience

I remember clearly the first time someone talked to me about the transference. It was my clinical supervisor at the V.A. twenty-five years ago. There had been nothing of this in my previous therapies up to that point. Perhaps four months into our working together, my supervisor said out of the blue to me one day in a session, "How do you think it's going in our relationship?" A straightforward enough question, but I remember feeling completely stunned by it, and somehow not able to find my verbal footing. It was strangely anxious territory.

The fact was that I had come to like, respect, idealize, study, and want to emulate this person, and that I felt seen, tolerated, understood, and made room for. But I also felt in a way slow to develop, so somehow anxious about that as well. I don't remember my answer in the moment. I probably said that I thought it was going well, but that wasn't the whole truth of it. The truth of it was bigger than my capacity to put into words in the moment. I know I didn't do a good job of it at all.

I do remember writing a piece after that session where I described feeling like an armadillo in a ballet school, and that somehow it was my supervisor's job to help me evolve from one state of being to another. The written piece allowed me to share with her the range of feelings I'd experienced in having her be my supervisor, and so, what the relationship felt like to me. But oh, the *threat* of talking about the relationship. It's not as though I'd never talked to anyone about a relationship. But this was somehow different, and was my introduction to talking about *the therapeutic relationship—the transference*—with a supervisor or therapist. It was awkward and weird and foreign, and certainly has stayed in my memory since.

Transference: A Relationship

I start with this personal story because it's important to ground any conversation about transference first in two things: *transference* refers to a *relationship*, one which often has an amazing amount of feeling in it; and secondly, it is not an easy relationship to talk about. Talking about it is often fraught with *anxiety* from both sides of the exchange. But it is really a central piece to the *art of understanding* in psychodynamic therapy, so let's wade together into these uneasy waters.

The first thing to understand about the transference is that it refers to a *relationship*. Our patients have a *relationship* with us. It's true. We may not talk about that relationship, or think about it, or think it exists, but it is there, nonetheless. Years ago in working with a male (rather schizoid) patient, I made a reference to our relationship. "No, no," he interrupted me, "we don't have a *relationship*. We have an *arrangement*. I have an arrangement with my mechanic. I have an arrangement with my accountant. I have an arrangement with *you*." "Fair enough," I said, "I've noticed something in our arrangement." This was to be the patient who several years later said to me out of the silence of a morning session, "I have come to have the most intimate relationship with you that I've ever had with anyone in my life, and I know almost nothing about you." He then added, "and I don't *want* to know anything about you. You've been my mother, my wife, my lover, my sister—I can make you all these things."

An Imaginary Relationship

Simply put, transference is the *imaginary* relationship a patient has with us as therapist. Or, from the other side of the matter, it's the imaginary relationship we have with our therapist (or clinical supervisor, as in the earlier story). It is, in addition, the imaginary relationship we somehow fabricate with respect to other figures in our lives, but most prominently, those who are in some authority position over us.

Imaginary, meaning that it is built at least in part on the basis of our imagination. Sometimes it is built more on imagination than it is built on the basis of who that person *actually* is, the position they *actually* hold in our lives, or how that person *actually* treats us. Transference is a "fill in the blank" phenomenon—something we do as humans all the time. Sort of like what happens as we watch movies. Movies don't actually move. They are a successive series of still shots. But perceptually, we connect them in our minds to create the movement. Interpersonally, we do this even more. We see pieces of the picture of the other and then create the rest. When patients do this filling in of the blanks about us as therapists, we call it transference. How they fill in those blanks tells us a great deal about their pre-existing internal object world, but we'll get to that part.

An Invisible Relationship

Transference can be invisible. It's at first really hard to see. Have you ever looked carefully at a water drop and been able suddenly to see some of the living critters that are swimming around within it? They're there all the time in shockingly abundant supply. But they occupy an invisible world. Until you look for them deliberately, with the right light and focus, they are not there.

Transference, when you're new as a therapist (and sometimes when you're not), is that invisible a world. Even though you may approach your sessions knowing to look for it, it won't be there at first. You won't see it.

Part of the reason for this is that it just takes time in the chair as a therapist to get beyond the anxieties of being the therapist so that you can see other things. For a while, we have to struggle with the internal war between our task of listening—never mind listening deeply—and whatever anxieties we carry inside about our own competence as therapists. It takes time—lots of time—before the world beyond our own anxieties can emerge into view.

But just beyond and to the other side of *our* anxieties (about being a good enough therapist, setting the right tone, picking up on the right things, etc.) are the *patient's* anxieties. The patient comes initially to therapy with a roster of concerns that have *nothing* to do with us as therapist. *Nothing*. But from the first moments of our first phone contact, the patient has begun to have impressions of us, reactions to us, positive and negative feelings about us, and is silently filling in the blanks about us. Whether or not we are tuned into this, they are, from the first moments, silently trying to manage their interpersonal anxieties with us: what we think of them, whether we're judging them, whether they are doing it right, whether they feel comfortable enough to talk to us, and so on. From the first moment of the therapy, a patient is silently efforting to manage their anxieties with us so that they don't show, and so that they don't get in the way of their narrative about the things they have come to talk about. But why the anxiety? What is its source?

An Asymmetrical Relationship

Therapy takes place in an interpersonal matrix. From the beginning, it represents an asymmetrical relationship: one person seeking help, one person providing that help. Because of these elements, it puts the relationship with *us*—the comforts *and* the anxieties of that relationship—somewhere on the patient's screen. In most therapies, patient and therapist (perhaps unconsciously) work really hard to keep the anxiety part out of mind (or at least, out of view) in the course of a therapy. Many theories of psychotherapy suggest that therapists should work actively to obliterate the inherent threat posed by the asymmetry of the relationship—should actively work to equalize the playing field. After all, the focus should not be about *us*, the therapist. It's about what our patient came in with. We'll get back to this inherent asymmetry part in a few minutes.

A Replicative Relationship

But here's the thing. What they came in with, usually, is a set of concerns about how they function and are treated within their interpersonal world. In one way or another, given enough time, this will replicate itself in their relationship with us (or "arrangement," should I say?). The therapeutic relationship becomes, almost from the beginning, a fractal of the relationships the patient has come to therapy to fix.

Let me say this another way. The issues that a patient brings to the therapy room to talk about are most often things interpersonal and intrapersonal. Patients talk about their relationships—with their bosses, their partners, their coworkers, their relatives, with themselves. They talk about their perceptions of others; their reactions to others. They talk about how others treat them, how others make them feel, how they make themselves feel, and how they handle those feelings. But all the while, as they are talking about others, they are talking *to* us, and, in that context, are gradually forming a relationship with *us*. And here's the crucial thing about the relationship between patient and therapist: it eventually brings the patient's inter- and intrapersonal object relational world right smack into the room with us, where we can see it, experience it, put our hands on it, interact with it—*live*.

What's powerful for the therapy in all of that is that we do not have to conduct the entire surgery remotely. We don't have to operate exclusively on relationships we can't see or feel or touch. We have the body right there in front of us, so to speak. Freud (1912: p. 108) said it this way:

> It is on the field [of transference] that the victory must be won—the victory whose expression is the permanent cure of the neurosis… For when all is said and done, it is impossible to destroy anyone in absentia or in effigie.

This is not to say for a minute that a patient's external concerns are insignificant. They are crucial in their lives. It *is* to say that sometimes the most powerful way to work with these external concerns is to catch them going on in the therapeutic relationship.

You may be thinking that ours is a circumscribed relationship with our patient, so it may not be representative of the kinds of problems they talk about in their external lives. This is true to some extent. But a couple of other things are true as well. One is that no matter what else they bring, they bring *themselves* into the room with us. Over time, inevitably, especially if we set up the context for this correctly, they will bring at least some of the same range of feelings that they experience in their relationships outside of the therapy into their relationship with us.

The second is the "fill-in-the-blank" part. Over time, they will come to perceive us in certain ways. Some of these will be directly reflective of the object relational "filters" they use to refract interpersonal reality in general. Once again, we will be able to catch this—alive and in action.

Options

We can choose to query this set of feelings and this set of perceptions, or not. This choice—to use the therapeutic relationship as a point of observation and intervention—is one of the defining features of psychodynamic psychotherapy. It is a powerful point of observation and intervention.

But if we choose to make our relationship one of the focal points of the therapy, there are certain looming challenges to be faced. For instance, in order to query a patient's feelings about or perceptions of us and the relationship, we have to *assume* they're having such feelings and perceptions. This is an uncertain leap of faith, at least the first few times we do it as a therapist. It takes a certain prior belief on our part—that we are significant enough in our patient's life that they have some feelings about and perceptions of us.

But let yourself think about this for a minute. Is there anyone you talk to with regularity that you *don't* have feelings and assumptions about, or perceptions of? Our minds are constantly, quietly working inside to make interpersonal sense of the other, all the time. Safe? Unsafe? Makes me want to engage? Makes me want to stay back. Is attractive to me? Is not? Makes me want to play? Does not? Makes me want to take care of them? Makes me angry? Makes me open to feeling cared for? Makes me feel sad or distressed if they are unavailable? These are brainstem level goings-on. They are never not going on.

Exercising the Option

So, next step. Suppose you decide you're game for this part, and would like to let the relationship in the room become part of what you talk about with your patient. We'll talk about how to do this, and what it might yield, but a word of preamble. Talking about the relationship is almost always fraught with anxiety, for *both* the therapist and the patient, certainly in the initial conversations about it anyway, and it is almost *always* entirely the therapist's job to introduce it. In my work, the people who have come to me for therapy have rarely initiated this discourse. They are more than happy to make the focus of our work their external-life concerns. Their relationship with me as their therapist is something, almost invariably, I need to introduce into the mix.

The "Transference" Part

To get a better understanding of the transference, let's go backwards a minute. We spent time together in the last chapter painting the Object Relational landscape. We considered that as developing little ones, we were busy putting together our interpersonal and intrapersonal sense of things. We were doing this with all the wisdom and experience of a 6-month-old, a 1-year-old, a 2-year-old, a 6-year-old, a 12-year-old, and so on. We were in a *dependent* relationship with our guardians at the time. Our guardians, for the most part, were doing the best they could; the best that circumstances would allow.

So as little people, we were efforting with all the neuronal power at our disposal (including during the first eighteen months, with our pre-linguistic right brains) to put together a model of the interpersonal world that would best equip us to cope with and respond to whatever were our circumstances. We continued to do this over time. But the 6-month, the 12-month, and the 18-month-old got *first dibs* on perspectives. The 6-month-old in essence coaches the 6-year-old and the 12-year-old (and often the 42-year-old) as to what to think, or should I say *feel* about it all.

Here's an important note. In psychologically healthy environments, earlier perspectives are seasoned and revised by later ones, with flexibility and relationship-appropriateness. In pathology (and we all have some measure of this), the infantile and young child feelings determine and *fix* much more of how we view and respond to the others around us, and to ourselves.

So, our Object Relational history affects our present perceptions of and relationship with our therapists. OK now, here's where the *asymmetry* of the therapeutic relationship comes in. As much as some may chafe against the inherent hierarchy represented by the therapist-patient relationship, if we squint for a minute, that relationship looks for all the world like one person coming in need to another person whose role it is to respond to that need. This is where it gets interesting. That *very* set of asymmetrical roles—given that it replicates structurally the arrangement we had as little people with our parents—makes the therapy relationship ripe for a replay of relationships past, so to speak.

Here's how it goes. We as infants/children were in dependent interaction with an "other." That other could only approximately get that infant/child, so there were inevitable misses that occurred. In "good enough" homes, the misses were tolerable (but left their mark); in some homes, the misses were egregious and chronic. These inevitable misses cause a range of anxieties in the infant/child, moment to moment (which we'll discuss in Chapter 12). With the transition into language roughly around 18 months, these anxieties, attached as they are to the handling by the other, are pushed into unconsciousness. As we move into subsequent relationships (particularly dependent or authority relationships), we superimpose the familiar relatedness *plus* the familiar anxieties generated within that original relatedness. It's what we have come to know (in our bones).

Slowing Down

Let me slow us down here to be sure that part registered. We have carry-over expectations and anxieties within us that we don't really understand. They come from a time we cannot remember. They were initially experienced in the context of our dependent relationship with our parents. But every subsequent relationship that replicates aspects of that authority or dependency role for us—be it our relationship with our spouses or partners or bosses or therapists—each of those relationships can trigger relational patterns and anxieties that were deposited into us from our earlier days, before we had choice in the matter.

To take it a step further, we become active players in re-creating our early relational scene. We exert pressure on the other to act/treat us in ways consonant with our experience of our original other(s). We don't know we're doing all this because we are just "being ourselves," but "ourselves" includes this unconscious set of maneuvers we developed to respond to our caregiving environment and to manage our early anxieties.

We're also somewhat indiscriminate in this process, in that we do this across the range of our relationships, but in particular, we do it with those whose responsibility it is to respond to our needs, again, because that replicates the parent-child arrangement. Thus, we do this with our therapists. "Transfer"-ence. We "transfer" forward the interpersonally familiar onto our therapists.

Tracking the Transference

Now, as someone comes to us for therapy, we as therapists, if we're paying attention, are going to be getting a core sample of this patient's anxiety-management mechanisms, predicated as they are on how this person felt related to *back then*, in some measure, and how they attempted to manage the anxieties inherent. It will walk in the door as the "transference."

How do we see it? What do we look for? The answer is, we try to observe and feel their anxiety in the room. Is it nervous? Is it slick? Does the patient laugh a lot? Are they deferential? Are they hidden? Are they prickly? Are they trying to obliterate the divide between us? Do they see us as irritated? Distant? Judgmental? We try to feel the feel of it. If we, as therapists, are too nervous in the first session, we pay attention in the second session, or in the third, or whenever we finally can. We try to describe to ourselves what this person's energy is like. What does it feel like to be on the receiving end of them? What assumptions are they making and perhaps trying to work around from the beginning? How does my body feel in their presence? What does my body know that I don't know yet about the feel of things? How do *I* act in *their* presence? In other words, what is my countertransference like? (We'll take up the countertransference pile of kaleidoscopic glass in the next chapter.)

Quadraphonics

Thankfully, we get some help in all of this wondering about how this person is attempting to relate to us. As therapists, it's as though we were listening to a quadraphonic sound source: we have four distinct tracks available to us to listen to.

First, we have what's going on in their relationship to us: the transference. Second, the patient is going to give us narratives about how they relate and are related to in *their present* by others in their life. These stories will include some of the same thematic undertones that are present in the relationship with us, perhaps more subtly at first, but they will be there. Third, we're also eventually going to hear their rendition of their interactions with significant caregiver figures from their *past*. These will often carry the melody clearly for us, that is, unless the patient has not yet gotten over their "perfect family of origin" narrative. (If that's the case, we may have to wait a while for that information source to open up to us). Last, with some patients, we're hearing their *dreams*, which paint at times unambiguous inter/intrapersonal pictures.

These four sources—their relationship with us, their relationship with current significant others, their past relationships with parents, caregivers, siblings, etc., and their relational dream-life—will all tend to line up like lights on an airstrip, meaning that the patient's position in and response to these interpersonal experiences will tend to be congruent or consistent with one another.

Of the four sources, however, the most powerful (because it's the most accessible) is the relationship they have with us. We can see it, feel it, taste it, query it, help the patient put words on it, moment to moment. In essence we can say to our patients (slowly, over time, and not in these words, exactly), "Who am I to you? Which parent or early significant other? In which stance? With what darksides? Given that, how do you position yourself and try to position me to manage all of it? Then, in the context of all of that emotional sizing up and maneuvering, what have you always assumed, and as a result always foreclosed for yourself? Or, more fundamentally, in all of this, how have you sacrificed something about being more fully human? And here's the most powerful part—how might it come to be different in here with me?"

Very important paragraph. Read it again.

Delicate Surgery

Let me say here that this pursuit is our job and our privilege, but that it is delicate surgery. Neurosurgery, if you will. It can't be rushed; it can't be overplayed; it isn't our brain that is laying splayed open on the surgery table. There must be a profound respect for what the child who grew up to be this person had to manage in their interpersonal (and therefore intrapersonal) environment while they were young and dependent. They are carrying forward into the transference relationship a set of assumptions that at some level saved their emotional lives. We must have the knowledge that however safe and attuned and containing we as therapist may feel ourselves to be, we are inviting our patient to disarm in territory that has been (and continues to be perceived as) a war zone for them, fraught with real psychic and sometimes even physical dangers.

Given all this, how do we operate as therapists in the territory of the transference? What do we *do* with a patient's transference, when we finally see it?

The role of the therapist with respect to the transference is twofold: first, to recognize the territory of the transference in this particular patient (often first experiencing it through our own countertransference—(see Chapter 11)); second, (and this part is timing-critical) to *name* it: to put words and pictures to it; to symbolize it; to name the assumptions and anxieties that underlie it—attached as they are to the handling by their original others. It's also important to name what is *sacrificed* to avoid experiencing that original anxiety, and to understand what keeps the anxiety away (the defense). All the while, in the process, we attempt to offer the patient a more attuned, fluid "other".

Working in the transference involves talking with the patient about their experience of the relationship with us. That's what we attempt to put into words. An aside here: notice I *didn't* say talking about our experience of *them*. This is a little counterintuitive, but very important. In doing the work of therapy, we want, as much as possible, to help the patient elaborate *their* experience of *us*. Our experience of them, as beautiful and lovely as it may be, is not mutative, because it is *our* experience, not *theirs*. We have no power to influence their earliest internalizations by merely asserting what *we* see as true of them. We can't change someone who feels unlovable by saying, "But *I* love you." We can't change someone who feels empty and uninteresting by saying to them, as much as we might like to, "But *I* find you reflective and interesting."

These are off-point because *our* experience of *them* isn't the point. Our job in working with the transference is to help the patient to word *their* experience of *themselves* in relationship to *us*, and to explore that. This work, repeated over time, will cause them to consider the basis of their assumptions about us, and the ways in which they unconsciously effort to maintain those assumptions, despite accruing evidence to the contrary. This is how the slow work of deep change goes. It is slow work, indeed. There is no pitocin to help the baby come out sooner. We must, in Winnicott's (1960) words, be prepared to wait a long time.

Difficult Work

Now, how hard is all this? Being human ourselves, let me acknowledge at this point that talking to *anyone*—friend, lover, parent, sibling, patient, therapist—about "the relationship" is a strangely anxious thing to do. If we're riding along with someone doing just the ordinary things of life that two people do together, and they say to us,

"I'd like to talk with you about our relationship," what happens? Our heart rates rise, our breathing becomes more shallow, our muscles tense, our arteries constrict. We physiologically read the entire event as a potential threat of some sort. So let's acknowledge that. Talking about the relationship in therapy is an anxiety-ridden act. It's magnitudes more threatening to the patient and to us as *therapists* than is our listening to the patient talk about their significant others in their outside life.

It is, of course, possible to conduct an entire therapy without the slightest mention of the relationship in the room. Many, perhaps most therapies go without this. So why do it? Because sometimes it's the only way to get to certain aspects of who this person is, and *not* to do it in some ways robs them of what they've come to fix. That's why. But that doesn't make it easy. Let's be clear.

From There to Here

Given its importance, how does one introduce the topic of "us" to someone who is talking about the people and scenes of their own life? How do we get from *there* to *us*? Ogden (1989) writes of this in an article entitled "The Initial Analytic Meeting." He says that he tries as much as possible to introduce something of the way the patient is relating to him in the first session. He observes that the first session always contains anxieties that can be spoken about. Let me show you briefly how this might look in a clinical example from a case consultation several years ago.

A 29-year-old female in middle management (in charge of recruiters) presented for her first session to a female therapist. She seemed energetic in a rather "charged up" way, and set a tone in the session that struck the therapist as more like an interview than a therapy session. For instance, she strode across the room with big strides to shake the therapist's hand in the waiting room. She spoke with a loud voice. She asked the therapist a series of questions. She used a number of words and phrases that were clichéd, and seemed to get in the way of a true attempt to express something of her experience. She talked about being in distress regarding the end of a two-year relationship. She wanted to discover why she gets into bad relationships. But it felt to the therapist in a strange way as though she were being interviewed for a job opening.

The consultation group observed that there was anxiety evident from the first seconds, that the anxiety was reflected in her big welcome. They suggested that the therapist stop the new patient after a few minutes, and simply ask, "I wonder whether you can share with me what it feels like being here today?" After the answer, "How was that connected to the way you greeted me?" Then, "Why does it seem important to make this relationship just another professional relationship?" Or, "What is it that you're perhaps minimizing that's distinctive about this relationship compared with everything else?" If the patient were to follow with some response about not knowing how else to be, the therapist could comment on the elusiveness of achieving a quality of realness, and that in its place, the performance is all she's able to generate. But can she say where she is in this performance?

It's possible and desirable to start the conversation about the transference really from the first session. Now, clearly, this is part of the acquired art, and takes some time to develop, some real skill and real guts. After all, it's the first session, and not only is the patient anxious, but we, as therapists, are anxious. Over time and with practice, however, we can come to contain our own anxieties about starting up with a new patient. When that maturing occurs, we start to become available for different kinds of pursuits, even at the beginning of a therapy.

First Moments

From the first moments of a therapy, we in essence want to communicate—in our words, in our tone of voice, in our feeling of calm authority—that this is a place where we can speak the emotional truth of things. So from the beginning, we want the patient to know that they are with someone who knows how difficult starting therapy is, and we are not wanting to fake it. Up front, little things matter a lot. Staying away from questions such as "Did you have any trouble finding the office today?" or "How was the parking out there?" (which function like verbal benzodiazepines for both parties), and saving yourself for such questions as "What does it feel like to be here?" "To meet me?" "What were your anticipations: yesterday, last night, today?" "There seemed to be a great deal of feeling in our greeting. I wanted to know if you could tell me what the experience was like for you?". This is how we mark out the therapy office as a place where we will speak the emotional truth of things between *us*. These are the kinds of queries that begin to introduce the patient-therapist relationship as part of what we'll talk about in the therapy.

In my own practice, if I have not managed to come up with a way to address the interpersonal anxiety during the first session (because I can't find my way), I hold a question in reserve for the end of it. I'll use some version of, "We're in the last few minutes of our time today, but before we end, I'd like to ask if you can put into words what it was like for you to be here today, and to try to talk to *me* about the things you talked about today? How did you experience it? Yourself? Me?" This is an important moment. It's important if it's at all possible to find a way to address the anxiety the patient walks in with up front because it sets the tone for what we'll be doing together in the entire rest of the therapy. We'll be trying to get at the emotional and interpersonal truth of things, as hard as that is. The truth is, first sessions are anxious for everyone.

Beyond First Moments

Beyond first sessions are second sessions and third sessions and fortieth sessions, and so on. As time goes on, the relationship builds. Things accrue. Good sessions happen. Bad sessions happen. We talk about a full range of things: relationships past and present, feelings, dreams—the full gamut. Our job in all of it is to try as much as possible to keep our finger on the pulse of the relationship, again, because it's our most powerful point of entry. Now, to be sure, all of this is clearer in the writing than it is in the living.

Remember the swirl? The swirl is most of it. Moments of meeting come along the way—hopefully just enough to keep hope alive (for therapist and patient). Moments of precipitation are those moments when we see what's been happening in the transference, and what's been happening in the countertransference (next chapter). And most certainly, the transformative work of becoming more fully human is not done via the brute force of our therapeutic brilliance. It is lived together, little by little, in human ways.

So how does this go? What do these moments of decoding and talking about the transference look like? Since pictures outweigh words by a thousand to one, let me take you now to several moments in several therapies where I attempted to explore and understand the transference. Sometimes it's smooth. Sometimes it's awkward. Always it's a little scary. But scary is often required to get to places we otherwise would never get to.

Trevor

I had had a patient for a number of years, and was beginning to notice (think *precipitation* here) that I somehow didn't talk to him about our relationship. This seemed odd to me, and odd that I hadn't noticed it sooner. So I tried, and failed. And tried. And failed. And noticed. And tried again. And failed again. I made some attempts. They fell flat. Finally, one week, he was speaking about a woman he was newly dating, and the fact that she seemed quite present to him, at least initially. I used his attempt to describe her presence as the entrée to my question about our relationship. I asked him how he experienced the quality of *my* presence with him.

What happened in the wake of that question was stunning, meaning that the patient was stunned by my question. He said he didn't want to answer it. He didn't want to think about it. It was somehow foreign, he said, not what we do in here. I asked him if it struck him as too intimate; too date-like? He saw it in part as a bid for a compliment, and he didn't want to be forced into a compliment.

He looked somewhat angry, and wanted to know what had prompted me to ask him this question. I told him that I had been thinking about how unworded our relationship had become, and that things that can't be spoken can have tremendous unconscious power. He wanted to know if others spoke to me about the relationship they have with me, and could I share examples of what people say. I told him that yes, this is part of the dialogue I have with others, and shared what I could in the moment: that someone found me cold and withholding, that another commented on my presence as extremely present, that another once said that he had the most intimate relationship he had ever had with anyone with me.

My patient began a series of de-centered and unsettled reflections that included the idea that if something positive found its way into words, it could be pillaged in his family of origin. He said that speaking the negative was far less risky for him. He wondered out loud about how he spoke to others significant to him. He said that he didn't want to risk making the relationship with me of less value to him. He reflected that his now girlfriend had shared that it had taken her five years to get over the loss of her last significant relationship, and that he was aware that he doesn't let anyone matter that much to him.

As the session moved toward its close, I observed to him that the reflections he had engaged in on the heels of my question were perhaps more valuable than the answer to the question I had posed. We ended the session with my observation that today was about talking about talking about. In the next session, we revisited this tender and to him dangerous territory, with more insight and less swirl from both of us. We have begun to traverse the territory of his interpersonal anxieties and the unconscious ways he has kept us from talking about them. This will be ongoing.

Tamara

Here's another scene from a more negatively transferential therapy several years ago. I had 90 minutes between patients this day, and decided to do a 40-minute round-trip errand. I planned plenty of time around the errand, knowing that my 1:00 patient was particularly sensitive to time. As it happened, there was heavy construction on the freeway access on my way back, and I got held up in the traffic, which stressed me a great deal. I arrived on the street of my building 9 minutes late, only to see my patient's car turning the corner on the way out to the cross street. I thought she must have seen my car, but kept going.

I quickly made my way upstairs and phoned her cell phone, which she never turns off but had turned off. I left her a message as to what had happened, that I was now there, but should she not get the message in time, we had an appointment two days later.

In this next session, I opened with a reference to the breach that had happened between us, and asked about her experience of the incident. She shared with me that there was only one explanation: that I had dropped her from my mind, that I had failed to think about her and had left her stranded, that if she had been important to me, I would never have let such a time lapse happen. I explored with her what it felt like to be with me, given her feeling that I had dropped her. She wasn't sure, but at least I wasn't defending myself. This led to associations of her having been left waiting repeatedly as a child, sometimes for long and frightening periods of time, sometimes into the darkness after sunset. This represented a hole in the therapeutic container to her. For those moments, I was that parent in the transference, but at least we were talking about it, which for her was different (and better).

Jenny

Another patient whom I have seen twice a week for two years presented a dream in which she described an apartment with many more rooms than she had thought were there at first. Many were expansive and exciting to her, but several were dangerous, and to be avoided. In the dangerous rooms were figures from historically past time periods: in one room, a Victorian woman; in another, a legion of soldiers. The danger was that were she to open the door to either room, the figures would either invade her space or pull her irretrievably into the room.

As we considered the dream together, we noticed that thematically, the rooms might be thought to represent the dual themes of sex and aggression. I decided to pursue the aggression part in our relationship, and asked her if there were times when the youngest parts of her wanted to aggress against me or to yell at me, perhaps to stop something I'm doing or to protest something in our relationship.

She answered that for the vast majority of the time, we were in sync, but that when she talks about leaving her longterm live-in boyfriend, she senses my dispermission, and feels like I won't let her leave him. She said that she feels penned-in in those moments. We explored how she was getting this message from me, and the courage it took to tell me this. We explored her lack of protest in those times when she feels penned-in by me. Passivity as defense. Given the fact that there was no room whatsoever for her protests or her aggression in her family of origin, this registration of her displeasure with me represented a step in the pathway forward.

Alethea

Then recently I had a patient who wondered how much my relationship with her was driven by my interest in her as a person—my liking of her—compared with my obligation to listen to her because of our therapist-patient arrangement. I asked her how she might be able to discern the difference; what would be the "tells," in essence. She reflected on her own mother, and how at some points she would exhibit outright disinterest; at others, bare tolerance of her daughter's questions and stories. I asked if she could pick up anything in my eyes or my tone of voice to help her to know. She wasn't sure.

Summing It Up For Now

Transference. There, like weeds in a garden. There in some measure in all of our therapeutic relationships. There as a powerful key to past anxieties, and to the patterns and defenses that grew up around them. There as a pathway for catching the anxieties and patterns and defenses developed to ward them off *in vivo*. There and present in the therapeutic relationship. There, and, handled with honesty and courage in the therapy, offering a different way of being. Scary. Powerful. Ultimately healing.

Working in the transference is scary business. It makes us as therapist step up into the moment, and into the relationship. It makes us have to be relationally real, and to bear the brunt of others' perceptions of us, as wrong as they sometimes may be. It smokes us out of our caves, and calls us to be as human as the patients we're working with. A high challenge. A privilege, and an acquired art.

There are thousands of pages to be written about transference. I've written a few. Perhaps I've piqued your interest such that you might explore this trail in your reading and consultation. It is a rich treasure trove, and leads to powerful therapeutic change. But for now, we'll leave it and move on.

In this chapter, we've gathered up another pile of colored glass for our kaleidoscope. But there's one right next to it, really intermixed with it, although it's easier at first to keep them separate. So now, let's take a look together at the bits and pieces we call "countertransference." This will help us immensely in the swirl of the transference, so here we go.

11

COUNTERTRANSFERENCE

Transference and countertransference fit together like interlocking pieces of a puzzle. They give form and context to one another, and allow more of the full picture of what's happening in the therapy to emerge into view. In this way, together, they contribute mightily to the art of understanding, and belong, really, intermixed in the same pile of kaleidoscopic glass.

This may seem an oddly positive way to introduce the topic of countertransference. Students are taught from the beginning of things to look out for their own countertransference as they begin their work with people. Countertransference is the dreaded intrusion of your "stuff" into the therapeutic matrix. It colors what you see and how you feel and respond, and is the enemy of good and decent therapy. Right? Well, let me confuse the matter a bit.

Countertransference(s)

Countertransference has two lives. It's almost like someone who has been relocated in a witness protection program. Although it hasn't changed names—is still called countertransference—it is now thought of as having a different identity. Now, it's become a sort of GPS device in the therapeutic journey—very useful in helping you to navigate in the therapy, especially when you've lost your way. But this "relocated" version of "countertransference" is not to be confused with the original version (still called "countertransference"), which was thought to be an impediment to therapeutic progress. So which is which? And how do you tell the difference? And why on earth do they have the same name?

Countertransference 1.0

All right. I again apologize for the name thing. But let's do some history. Freud (who seems to be standing close to ground zero almost every time there are conceptually important things being discussed in psychodynamic theory and practice) felt that therapists (analysts) should be thoroughly analyzed before doing the work of therapy. That way, the analysts' perceptions of the patient would be unclouded and realistic, and their responses to the patient's transferences would be completely therapeutically appropriate.

This was the ideal. But in practice, Freud soon recognized that occasionally, something less than pristine would occur. Some unanalyzed, unconscious part of the analyst would break onto the scene and produce inappropriate or misdirected responses. This breakthrough of unconscious derivatives in the therapist he called "countertransference." This was, of course, an unwelcome intrusion, and Freud felt that the therapist should by all means rid himself of this impediment to the therapy through self-analysis, consultation, or re-entry into formal analysis.

This is the iteration of countertransference that is often spoken about in introductory counseling classes and beginning supervision sessions. Students wonder with a great deal of apprehension when the fog of countertransference will roll in and overtake them unaware, silently shrouding out the light of day, rendering them useless in their role as therapist. It's a little like how it is during a serious flu season—knowing the germs are everywhere, and knowing that you might be struck anytime by the dreaded gambu. Such is the specter of "countertransference," especially to the newest practitioners in the field.

But, back to the history. Blessedly, history continued. After several decades of pursuing the ideal of the countertransference-free analyst, there began to grow up in the field the recognition that this ideal was unattainable, and that countertransference was, in Michael Kahn's (2002: p. 198) words, both "inevitable and continuous." In the 1950s, it came increasingly to be entertained as perhaps even *useful*. And by the 1960s, it had been upgraded to "indispensable."

This transformation of countertransference, from dreaded, unwanted visitor to welcomed, if sometimes inscrutable friend is extraordinary, if we think about it. Freud, of course, was not entirely wrong in his initial concerns. It is possible to have a patient so step on the scars of one's own issues that doing therapy becomes nearly impossible. This is part of why we in the field have to have a goodly amount of our own therapy. If we haven't identified the territory of our own object relations, found out where our scars are, and where the various bodies are buried, we won't know our own unique vulnerabilities, reactivities, and neuroses.

Certainly, it is possible that a patient so completely re-instantiates in us the feelings we had when we were terrified by a parent, or vilified by a sibling, or molested by a relative, that doing therapy with *that* person would be just too fraught with our own "stuff" for us to be helpful to them. Or there is also the possibility that a loss for us is just too fresh to allow us to be with another's feelings about a similar loss. These are legitimate instances where our "countertransference" would compromise the therapy. But these countertransferential assaults on the therapy tend not to sneak up on us from behind. They walk in the front door, armed and unmasked. It's not all that hard to feel when it's time to get out of there.

Countertransference 2.0

Let's consider carefully together what "helpful" countertransference might look like. Back to the history. Led by such thinkers as Klein, Bion, and Sandler, analysts gradually gave up the notion that they could consistently distinguish between reality—what was really happening with a patient, and distortion—what might in some way be contributed to by the therapist's own emotions or perceptual biases.

The looming questions were these: what if objectivity were not even *possible*? (Think Heisenberg principle here.) What if the subjectivity of the therapist might *always* be present, affecting what he was seeing and experiencing? Then "pure" observation would not be possible, *ever*. Everything might be affected to one degree or another by the therapist's own psychic reality.

Then, what if, in addition, there were unconscious processes at play that allowed the patient to induce or heighten certain emotional states in the therapist? A patient might (without conscious intention) stir up certain feelings within the therapist that were more about the patient's internal world than about the therapist's. What then? Where would such emotional stirrings begin and countertransference end?

All of these thought currents began to come into the active discourse of psychoanalysis just before and during the second half of the twentieth century. Notions of intersubjectivity began to eclipse former notions of objectivity in psychoanalysis. There came to be a recognition of two subjectivities in the therapeutic relationship, not just one. And countertransference came to be viewed much more broadly, not as the therapist's illegitimate, idiosyncratic reactions to the patient, but instead as the *totality* of feelings, thoughts, and perceptions the therapist has about the patient.

This perspective, of course, would move the full gamut of the therapist's feelings about and reactions to the patient out from underneath the veil of shame, and into the open, where they could be owned, valued, and considered. Countertransference not as impediment, but as tool. Revolutionary. Freeing.

So the field came almost full circle. Countertransference, first as anathema to the therapy, then as unwanted intruder to be driven out by the therapist's own therapy, then as rather ever-present, if uninvited visitor, often hard to tolerate, but hard to get rid of, and finally as welcomed, perspicacious guest, who might drop in anytime, unannounced. All this in the course of fifty years.

We'll speak in just a little while about what this guest looks like, and how you can tell him apart from a dangerous intruder, but for now, let's find our way back to our starting point: that transference and countertransference fit together like interlocking pieces of a puzzle. Let's take a closer look at that together.

Transference-Countertransference

When a therapist and a patient come together to work in the psychologically intense ways that characterize psychodynamic psychotherapy, their two psyches gradually make contact and intermingle. Their respective feelings, thoughts, perceptions, bodily experiences, histories, hopes, dreams, motivations, and internal object relational worlds are all there in the silence of the space between them. They mix—remember this word—*asymmetrically*. They make soup. They co-create an analytic third. The "electron particles" from the one enter the emotional subjective field of the other, and have their impact.

This is always going on in a therapy—every minute. Sometimes, as the therapist receives the electrons, the impact is ordinary, as would be the impact of hearing stories from a friend or a student or a colleague. The therapist may feel empathy, or sadness, or joy or anger or fear, but all within amplitudes that seem commensurate with the story. These would all now correctly be called countertransference reactions: thoughts, feelings, experiences of the therapist in response to who the patient is, and what he is talking about.

We as therapists may at times or in moments also experience our patient's transference, consciously or unconsciously—their seeing us through their pre-existing filters (as they always are)—transferring forward onto us characteristics that are really not true of us, which is never really comfortable, even when it's positive, but particularly when it is not positive. Our detection of and reactions to our patients' filters on us are also now called our countertransference. These first two variants of countertransference happen routinely in the course of things. This transference-countertransference matrix comprises the moment-by-moment warp and woof of therapy.

Then, there are the times when we experience the "old" kind of counter-transference—moments when we surge with some kind of feeling or reaction that seems as though it's identifiably our stuff, just big enough to notice but not big enough to compromise the work. I have a patient who seems to get every possible holiday off. I find myself envious when she announces another upcoming 3-day weekend. This is something for me to notice and be curious about. Our job as these things come up is to take this into our own therapy or consultation and talk about it, so that we don't subtly communicate our reactivity to our patient or act out in some kind of way.

These are all ordinary and daily kinds of experiences we have as therapists. And, at some level, they all make sense to us. OK. And then there is another variant of countertransference. In this variant, the impact of the electron particle exchange on the therapist is *decidedly unordinary*, more like an undertow or a tsunami; like the sensation of losing one's footing or of feeling certain things with great intensity, and not knowing why. In these times—in the swirl—we find ourselves, or should I say *lose* ourselves, in the transference-countertransference matrix.

Projective Identification

What I am about to write may be something you've never read about or heard about or experienced, at least consciously before. So get ready for something new. Here we go.

Remember the internal object relations worlds within, comprised of such linked elements as dangerous dad and frightened young person? So one or the other of these linked roles can be *externalized* by the patient, can be unconsciously "projected" into a present-day other, in this case, the therapist. This *is* a decidedly unordinary event, and we're likely not to have encountered it (or at least *recognized* it) in non-therapy contexts.

In such times, we, as therapists, may be inducted (without being asked directly) into playing some role in an object relationship from the patient's internal world— say, for example, the frightened part of the dangerous dad–frightened child pairing. A patient can "extrude" part of his internal object relational world onto us, and the therapist, through his voluntary psychic openness/responsiveness, can find himself occupying that extruded role—feeling certain ways, thinking certain thoughts, drawn toward certain behaviors that aren't entirely congruent or commensurate with the conscious exchange going on in the therapy sessions. *This*, too, is countertransference. And this is definitely the *swirl*.

This particular kind of countertransference, which bears the name "projective identification," can go on—sometimes unrecognized—for a long time, even months and months; sometimes longer. Transference and countertransference. The puzzle pieces click together, sometimes exactly, and simply don't make sense without one another. I'll give you an example or two from my own clinical practice in a minute. But first, let's explore this a little more.

Thanks to Klein and Bion and Ogden, we have a specific name for this particular kind of transference-countertransference, the mysterious induction process I just spoke of. We call it "projective identification." "Projective," because it involves the extrusion of a feeling or a set of feelings that are part of the unconscious psychic world of a patient. "Identification," because as the therapist, we "catch" the extrusion, and feel it as though it were coming from within us. We "identify" with it. It's good we have a name to describe this process. It makes us able to talk about it and make sense of it to ourselves and to others.

Drilling Down

We'll drill down on this just a bit, because it's not uncommon in the therapeutic mix, but easy to miss, or to dismiss. Projective identification is a subset of the world of countertransference, which, as mentioned above, has come to mean the universe of feelings we feel in the presence of and about a given patient. Projective identification is a particularly "swirl-y" aspect of doing psychotherapy.

This projective identification subset of countertransference has fundamentally three parts. First, a patient projects a feeling or set of feelings out from himself, *unconsciously.* (Just as a mental picture, think for a minute of how a baby deposits feelings into his caregivers; feelings that are too big for the baby to bear by himself.) This may serve to lighten the patient's psychic load, to get rid of something he experiences as toxic, or to safeguard a good feeling that he feels might be obliterated within himself. The projected feeling can be any of the vast array of human feelings, positive or negative. The feelings I've received (experienced) from my various patients include fear, suffocation, helplessness, self-consciousness, love, admiration, hopelessness, longing, and deadness, to name just a few.

Second, we as therapists become the unwitting receiver of this projection, and experience the extruded feeling *as though coming from within our own feeling world.* We experience it as though it were our *own* feeling, and don't initially think of it as coming from outside ourselves. In order for this to happen, the feeling(s) being extruded have to find an emotional resonance in us—have to be something we can identify with or have experienced in our own emotional repertoire. To help this along, the "extrusion" comes with a particular "undertow" or gravitational pull that pulls us to align with it as if it were actually a part of ourselves.

Third (and if there were not a third point in the sequence, this would not be clinically useful), we, as therapist, live with the feeling inside—sometimes for a long time (sometimes for months; even years; a *long* time). We feel it without knowing its source. It feels so "us" to us that it may not occur to us to even wonder about it.

At some point (in the swirl of it), we may awaken to the intensity and perhaps oddness of the feeling, or the lack of context for it (this would qualify as a moment of *precipitation*). For me, these awakenings have happened in consultation with a colleague, in reading a particular case study, or in comparing how I feel with this patient versus how I feel with the other people in my current and past practice.

Upon so "awakening," we can begin to feel curious about what the feeling or feelings represent about the psychic world of the patient, given the patient's history and experience. We gradually come to understand our experience more and more fully as an extrusion of their feeling world, and we may even be able to put it together with parts of their narrative that we've heard, but not fully understood. In other words, through this "swirly" process we can come to know something of the experiential world of our patient to a depth and specificity that we could not have known any other way.

Meanwhile, all this time, the patient, having given us something intimate, guarded, and precious to them (if also toxic), feels especially linked to us. We've become the repository of something of their psyche; they therefore will work to keep us psychically close so as not to lose part of themselves.

As we come to feel and understand these projective "extrusions," in terms of their history and their psychic load on the patient, we come gradually to be able to move them into pictures and words for ourselves, and ultimately, to symbolize and represent them to the patient.

As the process comes full circle, then, the patient has the experience of being deeply understood, and of having an intolerable part of themselves "lived with" by the therapist. This process serves, in measured degrees, to de-toxify the extrusion to the patient such that over time he can reclaim this part and own it more consciously and more fully.

That, in a nutshell, is projective identification, the most baffling, befuddling, beclouding, confounding, disequilibrating, muddling, perplexing, mystifying, and unsettling kind of countertransference.

Disclaimer

Now I want to undo something I made an explicit point of a minute ago. This process is less rare than I've suggested. It actually occurs to some extent in almost all intimate relationships and a lot in other relationships as well. It occurs between friends and at work. We might wish it only happened in the therapy office, but we have a better chance of making good use of it in that setting.

Gathering Up

That's a lot to take in, so let me now step back and simplify for a minute. Transference is the totality of feelings a patient has toward us. It will be a mix of past and present, distorted and undistorted, conscious and unconscious. It will have a certain measure of interpersonal anxiety in it. Countertransference is the totality of feelings we have toward, and in the presence of that patient. It will likewise be a mix of past and present, distorted and undistorted, conscious and unconscious. It, too, may carry some interpersonal anxiety. But in this way it is different from the transference: it will be our psyche's *response* to the patient's way of relating to us—to their transference.

What we feel in the presence of a particular patient winds up being very important data in the therapy. To be fair, it must be said that what we feel in and with a certain patient may be just what we happen to be feeling that day. We all have days when we're overly-tired, don't feel well, or are preoccupied with our concerns about ourselves or a loved one.

But in and around our "me" feelings, there are other feelings. The "me" feelings, even when prominent, are likely to have a different character and to be experienced differently across the different patients in a day. In other words, the impact of a particular patient's psychic particles affects even our "me" feelings. But aside from those occasional times when our own concerns preoccupy us prominently, we have a constant stream of experience in the presence of each of our patients. We have, as it is now called, our "countertransference." A welcomed friend. Welcomed, because what we experience in the presence of a particular patient is likely to be meaningfully attached, in some way, to that patient's internal emotional world.

The Intersect

Now, having said all that, *here's something really pivotal*. We, as therapists, have the potential to do our most important work at the *intersect* of these two elements—at the intersect of the transference and the countertransference—because (and this is Freud's insight (1915c)) *that place*—*that* matrix—that *relationship*—will pull toward itself the patient's most important psychological issues.

Why? Because how they relate to us will be a reflection or refraction of how they relate to themselves, how their parents related to them, how they relate to their partners and their children and their co-workers, how they relate to their world. In psychodynamic psychotherapy, *that* place (in the universe of all possible places to be, mentally and emotionally), *that intersect* is where we try intentionally to locate ourselves as therapists. It all gets gathered up right there in their relationship with us.

So what we feel, think, experience in our bodies, have enter our minds as reveries; what we wish we didn't feel, but feel nonetheless; the whole of our "countertransference" helps us to understand what is the most important thing emerging in the therapy in the moment. *Because*—and this is a big because— transference and countertransference are linked as would be two adjoining puzzle pieces—pieces that are imbedded in the larger puzzle of this patient's object relational world. That makes countertransference an incredible guide to us as therapists: our personal GPS.

Whether our patient is talking about the upcoming weekend, the issues with his wife, the tax forms that he has failed to prepare, again, this year—whatever and wherever the patient goes, conversationally, if we keep an eye on what it feels like to be with this patient in this moment, and what it is like to be the patient in relationship with us in this moment, we're tracking on the most important thing we could possibly be tracking on.

Do What?

The next question is always right there, so I'll go right for it. What do we *do* with this information? Once we've registered something of what we're feeling in the presence of a patient in a given moment, and what they may be feeling related to us, what do we do? There are two answers because the question has two levels. There are the *this-session* feelings and the *across-session* feelings.

In *this session*, we listen. The patient talks about the full range of concerns that is his life's panoply. We listen deeply, using our bodies, our right brain's image-making capacities, our left brain's verbal symbol-making facilities. Some sessions are entirely about this process of resonating with the patient's story. But when we detect *anxieties*, session-by-session, in the therapeutic relationship, we try to speak to the patient about what we think is going on between us. Ogden (2001: p. 42) puts it this way:

> From the beginning to the end of every analytic session, I am attempting to locate myself and the patient in relation to two overlapping aspects of experience: (1) my sense of what it feels like being with the patient at a given moment, and (2) my sense of the leading anxiety in the transference-countertransference at that moment.

Within any given session, we give preferential treatment to the tensions, anxieties, discomforts that seem to be there in the therapeutic relationship. If there are no real relational discomforts in the moment, we're free to go with the content stream of what the patient is talking about. But if there *are* relational anxieties, either in this session or left over from the last one, it becomes our job to go there, because whatever is in the way relationally will choke the life out of the other things the patient is trying to tell us.

If we think about it, this makes complete sense. It's true in our everyday relationships. If there is something in the way in the relational field, our attempts to relate about the other ordinary stuff of life are stilted and flat. They're held hostage by the interpersonal muck of things in the relationship.

OK. So how do we know what's going on, relationally, in any given moment? Simple. We pay attention to what we're feeling in the presence of this patient. This is a really hard thing to get, because it's just so counterintuitive, certainly for new therapists. We're trained to attend to the *other*; not to ourselves. And yet, because what is happening in the relationship may not be entirely conscious to us as therapists (often isn't), it's important that we use the tools at our disposal to track the trail of it. We get some of our cues from our trained intuitions, but a lot of our clues, as in the case example in Chapter 8, come from the back-channel reveries that are washing across our psyche. These can be feelings in our bodies, images in our minds, songs or poems or dream fragments—a whole variety of subliminal experiences—that help us know what it feels like to be with the patient in these moments.

Once we have a sense of what it feels like to be in this patient's presence, (attached, as it is, to what it may feel like to them to be in our presence), what are the specific ways we speak to the patient about the immediate or the accrued interpersonal anxieties in the transference-countertransference matrix?

This is the stuff of the acquired art of psychodyanamic psychotherapy. It takes study, supervision, and practice, as would any acquired art. But here's a basic to start with. We use our own experience in the soup of the analytic third as a guide to help us get a sense of things, then try to use language that is *drawn from, but not directly descriptive of,* what our reveries have generated within us, to talk to the patient about what he might be experiencing in our presence. This means that if we're sitting with someone and we have the visual image come to our mind of a young child eating an ice cream cone, we *don't* say, "I see a young child eating an ice cream cone in my mind's eye, I wonder what that means to you?" We sit with it, and wonder about it internally.

Perhaps, if we've been able to make any sense of it, we finally offer a transformation of it to the patient. This is entirely contextualized by who the patient is, and what has been going on in the therapy. We might, in the context of this particular patient on this particular day, say to them (in response to the ice cream cone image), "It seems today as though all you really want in here is the innocent pleasure of having something all yours, not to be shared. Is that how it seems to you?" This harvesting of the reverie picture would need to make sense to you in terms of how you might be experiencing the patient that day; otherwise, reveries are better left in the soup pot. This is only one example, but hopefully, it gives you some idea. At the end of the chapter, I'll direct you to further reading about this.

Now, here's something else about the *how* of speaking to the patient about the relational currents extant. We try, as much as possible, to put words on the *patient's* experience of *us*, rather than *our* experience of *them*. Again I will use Ogden's (2001: pp. 42–43) words for clarity:

> What is of value to the patient is not an account of what the analytic relationship … feels like to me [as therapist], but an account of what the relationship and its attendant anxiety feels like to him, and how that experience relates to other experiences (both real and imagined) that he has had with me and with other people in the course of his life.

This is subtle, but crucial. Putting into words what *I* feel about a patient in the transference-countertransference will typically not move the therapy or the patient along. This is hard to really get and to really believe as therapists, because it's easy to overvalue the power of our own words to try to convince a patient that they should feel or behave a certain way. What *will* move them along is our putting into symbols and words what *they* feel in the relationship. This will sometimes deliver into language what Bollas (1987) has called the "unthought known," the thing that has always been there as a "given" to the patient (in their bones), but has never been recognized or "cognitized."

In special moments, what will move them along even more critically in the therapy is *their* putting into symbols and words what *they* feel in the relationship. Why? Because what they feel has been, in many ways, predicated on a child's view of relationship. Breathing this view into their own words allows a new examination of these feelings—a new examination of the basis for the feelings, the anachronistic nature of the feelings, and perhaps the inherent handicaps freighted by these feelings. Lacan (1953) points out that we construct ourselves in language, and that in the process of therapy we can deconstruct and reconstruct ourselves in language in ways that better fit past and current interpersonal reality. Our role as therapists is to provide the kind of relationship that allows and facilitates such internal self-revision.

Across Sessions

OK, one final step. So far, I've spoken about making sense of and speaking to the relational currents within a given session. But what about the across-session feelings, often experienced as projective identification. How do we handle and ultimately speak about these feelings as therapists, which are sometimes large, mystifying, ego-dystonic, and uncomfortable?

One of our most difficult jobs as therapist is to allow these feelings to arise in us, and to contain them over time (as best we can, in non-acting out ways). Our job is to let them be there in the swirl, session by session. Our job is, at some point, to begin to notice and observe ourselves having those feelings, to wonder about them, to allow ourselves to have reveries about them, often to consult about them. Our job is to allow our experience to accrue to a level or to a point where something precipitates in our own psyche to help us to understand where these feelings have come from in the context of the patient's internal world.

Eventually, our job is to be able to speak to the patient from the basis of all that countertransferential work within ourselves; to be able to speak with insider knowledge of what we have come to know of the patient's internal experience. To be able to speak about it, because at some level, we have *lived* it from the inside, ourselves. This can be a long, emotionally difficult process, but therapeutically, a crucial process.

Working in the Matrix

OK. Let's step back again for a minute together. The kaleidoscopic world of the transference-countertransference matrix. A complex, multicolored, ever-changing world. A world with powerful potentials for intra- and interpersonal change in our patients. But all of this, of course, presupposes our willingness to let ourselves as therapists be used emotionally in these ways. To get into the transference-countertransference mud of things. To do the work of it. A colleague of mine used the metaphor of lending her psyche to the patient as a jungle gym, which they could climb all over in any way they needed to be able to build or rebuild themselves. It often feels like that.

My own personal metaphor is that I picture my emotional world as a full piano keyboard, on which have been played the various emotional songs of my own life. Sometimes one song or another comes to the fore as I work with a patient. As patients develop in their work in the therapy, they may at times even reach over and play *their* songs on my emotional keyboard. That may be the only way it would be safe enough for them to hear and feel the music.

Particularly in the process of projective identification, I experience it within *as though* it were my own emotional music—it's being played on my keyboard, after all. But as I listen over time to what is playing inside me, as therapist I come (often after much struggle and swirl) to moments of precipitation—where I recognize the song as my patient's rather than my own. Then I listen more, to the nuance of it and the feeling of it. Finally, because I have come to know the tune from the inside out, I can begin to talk the music with my patient, and in return, they with me. It is, perhaps, a song they haven't let themselves know all their lives, but which has been playing in the background, directing their rhythms. This is work. It's psychic work. The rewards are deep and life-changing, but there's no getting around the psychic work of it.

What does this countertransference stuff look and feel like in a real therapy, particularly this projective identification stuff? As therapy-pictures are often more powerful than theory-words (although they too fit together like puzzle pieces), let me now see if I can give you some examples of the kinds of transference-countertransference experiences I've been describing here. I'll take you to three patients, all in one way or another evoking countertransferential experiences in me as therapist. The first will be a long example; the second two, shorter.

Grace

Several years ago I had a patient, a strikingly beautiful, strikingly confident and competent female in her mid-40s who was referred by a psychiatrist for her intermittent depression. She came in weekly, and as the therapy developed, I felt shifted from my normal therapeutically steady stance, to a place of feeling more and more incompetent. I wasn't sure why, but I began to anticipate each session as our last, and felt braced for a barrage from her about how useless the therapy was, and how incompetent I was as therapist. She was well able to eviscerate people, from her own accounts of life outside the therapy office, so I figured my fears were well founded. The longer she came, the more fearful of her I became. This lasted for months (and months). I was quietly tortured within, but tried to be valiant and go forward with whatever therapeutic bravado I could muster.

Now, of course, within each of us are fears of our own incompetence, so it didn't even cross my mind to wonder why I felt such fear—after all, it does have a place in the repertoire of my own songbook. But one day, I found myself talking about this case with a much older analyst colleague of mine. She proposed to me that this fear—so big—might be coming from some aspect of my patient's psychic experience, rather than from merely my own, and that I might think about that a bit. So incredibly helpful. The thought hadn't crossed my mind. My patient was so confident; so competent.

In the aftermath of that consultation, I lived more with the fear, and began to stalk its particularities. I began to realize that it had a peculiar hair-trigger-like feel to it—as though it might come out of nowhere and erupt with the force of violence. I let myself think about what I knew of my patient's history: that she had been the peculiar target of her mother's physical rage, and that it would erupt hard and fast, that she did everything to pretend it didn't affect her, but that there was no warding it off. The more I filled in the blanks for myself, the more the feeling of my fear and intimidation seemed to fit her history more than our *present*. I considered that I might have become the unconscious repository for long-held feelings of fear within her; the kind of fear that a child would have around just such a mother. This allowed the fear to lessen just a bit in me—just enough to allow the following exchange.

She came in this particular day speaking about "Cruella," the name she had for the angry, rageful part of herself. She had generated an email to her affair-lover. It had been a brutal evisceration. She relayed to me that she loved the powerful feeling of that anger. She asked me, "Is that bad?" and confided to me that she wished, just once, that he would go "toe to toe" with Cruella.

Using the power (and shelter) of metaphor (harvested from my reverie), I said to her, "It's rather like a tornado. It feels good if you're the tornado, but can be devastating to everything around." I referenced the movie, "Tornado," and she laughed about the movie, given her Midwest roots.

In speaking to her, I noticed less of a sense of fear in me. I felt at this juncture that it was time to take the chance to talk to her about my response to this part of her, and what it might mean.

I asked her, "I wonder what you would imagine would happen if *I* were to go 'toe to toe' with Cruella?" She responded with a gesture of her hand in the air, "Pheuuuuuw, you'd *dust* her—no contest!" she laughed. (I, of course, having harbored intense fear for many months, was nothing short of hugely surprised and relieved to hear her say this.)

In Yoda-like demeanor, I nodded, and ventured forward, "It's because I understand Cruella. The fearful side of Cruella." "What do you mean?" she asked back. I said, with borrowed steadiness, "It's because I understand that *fear* is the birthing-place of Cruella, and the context that makes her emerge." She took this in thoughtfully, and responded, "But she doesn't *feel* afraid." "No," I said (having lived with this fear a long time by now, and known it from the inside out). "No, but she knows fear well. It's the part she's trying not to feel." "Oh, that," she laughed, "yah." This "yah" contained a world of recognition, and served as the sign to me that she could begin to recognize this song as a part of her own disowned repertoire. In subsequent sessions, this exchange was to be followed by further explorations of her fear of her own mom, and how she had hidden it so well from herself, instilling it into others, over time. We also talked about the dangerous parts of her mom, which she had also internalized, and used liberally toward others. The Cruella session was to begin the diminution of my fear, and her progressive owning of hers.

By projecting her fear outward—into others in her life and ultimately into me as therapist—my patient had become less-fully human, less vulnerable, less approachable, less contactable. What she *gained* in this deal was protection for herself and a feeling of strength she could not have as a child. What she *lost* was access to an important, albeit painful part of herself.

My job in the countertransference was the psychic containing of her projected fear, first by my experiencing it, then, by my understanding it, and finally by my helping her to understand and feel it. This long and arduous process was the pathway to her being able to reclaim that part of herself, and to begin to lay claim to the humanness she had sacrificed in the (completely understandable) bargain. This was to have impact across the relationships in her life, especially the one with her husband, in which she softened, and he came forward. A powerful experience, I dare say, for both of us.

I will give two more examples, just to give you a couple more samples of countertransference in action, both a bit briefer.

Bryan

Another patient, whom I will call Bryan, had been coming for once-a-week therapy for a number of years. He was a nice-looking man, ten years my senior, whom I had enjoyed seeing, although I was somewhat puzzled by the spareness of his life. At some point, something in me began to shift. I began to feel a change in my feelings toward him, in the direction, at first, of a subtle sense of having to fortify myself before my time with him. I would be sure to have a snack before he came in. There was just the slightest undertow. I began to tire of how we talked together, of his batting away of my least obtrusive observations and interventions, of his narcissism, I thought to myself. I began to notice that my feelings in anticipation of our sessions were different. He would come at the beginning of my week. I was already tired. The things that failed him were everywhere: girlfriends, job, parents, siblings, peers. The only thing he never named was himself. I wanted him to own something—*anything*—of his own role in the things he complained about. He was in a relationship with a woman who seemed good for him. She was right in every way except her height: she was slightly taller than he. That was a deal-killer for him. I found myself deeply offended on behalf of womankind. I had begun to want to be aggressive with him. I wanted to tell him that he was not perfect.

The feeling snuck up on me. There was nothing either big or all of a sudden about it. But one evening at the end of my therapy day, as I reflected on the patients I'd seen, I realized that I had come to hold him in some kind of—what was it? Impatience? Dislike? Disdain? (A moment of realization, if not yet precipitation.) I didn't like the feeling. I didn't like seeing it in me. I began to stalk my own disdain.

Here it was. Countertransference. But now that I could own it, it was out in the open, so I could wonder about it. What of his history and his inner object world might I be experiencing? Hmmmmmmm. There was all that aggression in his family of origin, especially in the siblings. All that narcissism in his dad. The needing to be perfect in order not to be attacked. Even the lack of food available in the house. I began to see myself as having taken on, psychically, several pieces of that action. I had joined forces with the retaliatory siblings in attack of one another out of the frustration of not being seen, noticed, or cared for—(he barely noticed my moments of intervention)—out of the frustration of watching the guise of perfection in the family cover the hypocrisy of shame and disconnection. I had been handed a subtle script by my patient—assigned a familiar role that would allow him to play the counter-role.

All of this contertransferential swirl allowed a certain re-positioning in me inside. Sometimes, the action in the therapy is non-verbal. Sometimes, it's in the "particle exchange," as it was this time. As I became aware of these feelings in me, and began to make sense of them—with more compassion—an odd thing happened in the therapy. My patient began to own and verbalize the struggle within himself— to be perfect—and the awareness of his falling so abysmally short of his own standards. He began to verbalize a sense of shame, and of warding off these feelings by finding fault in others. This began an entirely new chapter in the therapy, and in the patient, which unfolded slowly and carefully over time. The feelings in me of liking and valuing the patient returned, with a certain added respect. The exchange between us became, over time, less one-sided; more related.

Sara

Then there is the patient, described in Chapter 8, in whose presence I often feel intense feelings: longing, confusion, ineffectualness, sadness, fear, discouragement. These are all feelings that are part of being me. They pre-existed this patient in my own experiential world. They are keys on my own emotional keyboard. But when I am with this patient, I am awash with these feelings. They are strong, and often unrelated to what we're talking about. It's as though somehow, she is reaching into my psychic world and playing these keys. My feelings in her presence are my countertransference, but the kind of intersubjective countertransference that we've been talking about. They are linked to the patient's object relational world in ways that have become clearer over time.

In one session, I asked her to describe to me her experience of the silences in our sessions. She responded (eventually) that the silences were sometimes peaceful; sometimes filled with self-derogation. When I asked her if she could share with me what the self-derogations sounded like, she responded that there's an internal chorus that describes her to herself. The self-derogations are (she said the list slowly):

"Empty."
"Not smart."
"Not able to have an effect."
"Not interesting."
"Needy."

The tenor of the list matched my countertransference feelings exactly: longing, sad, ineffectual. My feelings in her presence were an induction in me of feelings she used to feel in her highly misattuned relationship with her own parents. I was receiving, through the feelings induced in me, a core sample of the patient's inner emotional world. She was sharing that world with me in the fullest way she possibly could. Through countertransference.

Final Comment

Just a brief comment before we close. The countertransference we experience as therapists is very, very likely not the only venue in which the dynamic *we're* feeling is happening. It's quite likely to have occurred and to be occurring across many of their relationships. It may be deeply unconscious, so not something they talk about or know about themselves. But because the therapeutic relationship, from the asymmetrical side of therapist, is non-dependent, we have more degrees of freedom than might be there in a spouse or a family member or a friend. Because our training and experience helps us to recognize certain patterns, anxieties and defenses, we may be able to see a bit farther or deeper than would a partner or relative. Our unique position as therapists allows us to be a different kind of receiver of these electron particles. We at first experience (the swirl), then study, and then perhaps come to understand (the precipitation), and finally hopefully communicate about this way of being in some way to our patient. All of this while we maintain the stance of empathic (or at least, non-retaliatory) other.

Countertransference—a crucial element in the art of understanding. So, equipped with these ways of seeing and being, we wander out into the human synapse of all of it. We use what we have, and hope for the courage to meet what may come. This is the challenge of it. This is the aliveness of it. This is the heart of it. This calls forth from us the human blend of grace, truth, and sheer persistence that are our necessary companions in the kaleidoscopic swirl of the transference-countertransference.

12

DEFENSES AND ANXIETIES

We have yet one more pile of colored glass to gather up for our kaleidoscope. Defenses and anxieties, and just what they add to the art of understanding in psychodynamic psychotherapy. I teach masters students at both ends of their journey en route to licensing as Marriage and Family Therapists, and so have the opportunity to interact with those brand new to the field in one of the introductory courses.

Usually, around the sixth week of the quarter, I ask them to tell me about defenses. "Yes!" they say. "We know about defenses!" "So talk to me," I say. "Well," they say, "defenses are when we are defensive." "Good start!" I say. "Tell me more. What are we defending?" "The ego," they answer, with due pride. "What's that?" I ask. "Our *selves*," they say proudly. "Good. And why do we need to defend ourselves?" "Because we feel threatened." "Yes! And what is the threat?" Now the chorus begins to thin out. "What's the threat? Hmmmmm. Something feels like it is going to damage the self," someone offers. "Yes! The self might suffer damage! And what would that feel like or look like, if the self were to suffer damage?" "Uhhhhhhh" (more slowly)…"Disorienting," one person might say; "fragmenting," another might offer; "annihilating," someone else might say with conviction.

Now we're into it. Into the world of defenses—and the anxieties that lie underneath them. It's always struck me that some working concepts are more or less taken for granted in our field as therapists. Defenses seem in my mind to top the list, because while everyone knows the word, and has some intuitive sense of what it means and what defenses might look like, few really understand their ontogeny, their linked anxieties, and what that means in the experiential world of our patients. These are all essential if we are to understand the relational world of our patients, and if we are to understand the full measure of courage required to engage in the process of psychodynamic psychotherapy.

Before I go any further, I want to fasten this discussion to what we've explored so far in the art of understanding. So here we go. We have Object Relations: the set of internalized relationships between self and caregivers, with all of their associated, serpentine anxieties. We have transference: the externalization of aspects of these internalized relationships (including their anxieties), especially relevant within the therapy relationship. We have countertransference: the set of responses and reactions we have as therapists in the relational matrix with our patients, along with the anxieties that get evoked in us in the soup of it. These are the elements already loaded into our kaleidoscope.

Then last (but probably first) we have defenses and the anxieties they defend, which reach backwards and derive from our original relationships, connecting with the inevitable misses we experienced at the hands of caregivers, and the psychic pain they evoked within us. Anxiety (in its most general, non-DSM sense) is a feeling of impending danger or psychic pain. Defenses are simply what we do to stay away from the feelings of anxiety that we once felt (or might feel in the present), because if we were to feel their full magnitude, our selves might suffer damage, and could even shatter. So defenses are the visible part—rather easy to see. Anxieties are the invisible part, hidden in the background, trying to stay out of sight. Defenses and the anxieties they defend. Together they comprise our last pile of colored glass.

Backstory

So let's start *before* the beginning, with a conversation about the self. Because the self is what defenses defend. What is the self? How does the self get going? Why do we have automatic mechanisms that rise up to protect it, without our conscious assistance?

OK. The self. The self is one of the basic structures of the personality identified by Freud (here's Freud again!). He named those structures id, ego and superego. Actually, in Freud's (1923) writings in German, he named them "nicht ich," "ich," and "uber ich" ("not I," "I," and "above, or in charge of, I"). These are much more meaning-filled than they became through Strachey's translation of them into English ("id," "ego," "superego"). So as we talk about defenses, we're talking about defending the "I" part of us—what we think of as the self of us.

So, how do we get an "I," and how does that "I" develop? And where do defenses come in? We have to go backwards to get this. There is simply no other way to truly understand the territory. So, follow me, if you would, into this set of caves—this labyrinth. I promise that we'll emerge on the other side into the light of day, and be clearer for it in the conversation about defenses.

Developing a Self

So first, development. We are born into life as a vortex of potential. We have surging DNA and an irrepressible phalanx of need, pushing forward ahead of us, clearing the way for us. Part of our DNA is that we have an incipient self— a definition of ourselves that awaits our experience; that awaits our being met, in an interpersonal way, by our environment. The "I" genes, if you will, are "experience-dependent." They require certain conditions from their environment in order to be fully expressed. Current neuroscience has studied and named this, but we have known it from human observation for a long time. "Experience-dependent." Our language system, for instance, is "experience-dependent." Children whose hearing is compromised from birth may have their DNA loaded up for normal speech, but since speech is experience-dependent, their spoken language may be grossly affected by the absence of crucial auditory experience.

So we're packaged with experience-dependent "I" DNA. And then we engage in the random lottery of parent assignment, and find ourselves, one way or another, in an interpersonal matrix. We arrive on planet Earth, and are (usually) given into the arms of a mothering person or persons (gender-neutral term). We carry certain genetic information that will govern our activity level, temperament, appearance, talents and disabilities from the get go, but the expression and development of our "nature" is experience-dependent on our "nurture." The "I" awaits interactivity with the human nurturing environment in order to reach toward its pre-loaded expression. (In fact, 70% of our cerebral cortex develops post-natally, most of it (90%) in the first three years of life) (Lipari, 2000).

Upon our Earth-arrival, and fixed within the medium of that mothering person/s, we begin the task of cobbling together sensory and psychic experience—registering sensory experience, recognizing patterns, sorting them into "OK," "not OK," "safe," "not safe," "pleasurable," "painful;" sorting them further as time goes on. The mothering person/s is all the time providing an environment, serving to cushion the developing infant from the forces and blows that would end his struggle to be alive and to move along his/her developmental trajectory.

This, of course, is an impossible task, and every parent fails at it repeatedly. The number of misattunements—"misses"—an infant suffers in the context of ordinary development is staggering. We know from studies in attachment research that even in babies who later (at one year) will be classified as "securely" attached, there is a parental misattunement every eighteen seconds, on average (Biringen et al., 1997; Nelson, 2012; Stern, 1985; Tronick, 2007; Tronick & Cohn, 1989). These misses, as routine as they are, cause real stresses and anxieties in the developing infant.

To a baby, stress is anything that disrupts attunement with its caregiver and pulls it into a negative emotional state. This includes everything from short, unwanted breaks in the mothering person's attuned attention, to maternal misreads, to unwanted intrusions into the baby's moments of contented quiescence, to physical discomforts, to separations from the mother, to extremes of sickness, accident or abuse. Because babies lack the ability to regulate their own physical and emotional states, they rely on the relationship with the mothering person/s to put them into a re-regulated state after momentary distresses and misattunements.

Pre-Loaded Defenses

Thankfully, the human package carries some pre-loaded defensive equipment/ operations. We need only observe human infants in distress to see this/these in action. Ordinary misses are signaled by the baby and quickly corrected by "good-enough" ("attuned") parents, and the infant moves forward. Such signals as the baby's disquieted facial expressions or bodily tensions, squirmings, and archings are the initial signals. These are quickly followed by the baby's cry if intervention isn't forthcoming. Continued distress, however, will progress to screaming, and increases in the infant's heart rate, blood pressure, and respiration rate. These all build to a hypermetabolic cascade in the infant's brain, causing surges in levels of major stress hormones, and elevating the brain's levels of adrenaline, noradrenaline, and dopamine. Such hypermetabolic states in the developing brain are in essence toxic to the baby, and temporarily interrupt the laying down of DNA-driven neuronal tracts, particularly in the infant's right (relational) brain (Brown, 1982).

Misses that are too intense, too chronic; misses that are too prolonged and are allowed to continue, un-intervened upon, for too long a time, move to another level in the infant. The fail-safe defense for infant distress is the phenomenon of dissociation. Moved beyond all tolerable limits, the child has the capacity to disengage from the external world's stimuli and retreat to an internal world. This reaction involves numbing, avoidance, and lack of reaction. The searing documentary film footage of René Spitz (1945) captures the unmistakable look of vacancy in the faces of chronically dissociative, orphaned children in foundling-home settings. In such a state, pain-numbing endogenous opiates and behavior-inhibiting stress hormones such as cortisol are elevated. Blood pressure decreases, as does heart rate, despite the still-circulating adrenaline. In biological and evolutionary terms, this is the same process that allows an opossum to "play dead," or a mammal to retreat from overwhelming situations to heal wounds and fill depleted resources. However, as a response to misattunement in infants and developing children, it is devastating. The effects of even short periods of dissociation to brain development are profound, altering the size and function of such basic relational and emotion-regulating brain structures as the orbital frontal cortex and the limbic system. Furthermore, in the infant, because "states become traits," the repeated effects of such early relational traumas become part of the structure of the forming personality (Perry et al., 1995).

Implicit Memory

So, as much as we would wish otherwise, misses leave their mark, and, as might be surmised, larger or more chronic misses leave larger and more chronic marks. The marks are left both on brain structures and in our early memory system. We learn rapidly and well as infants and toddlers, keeping a kind of tacit, unworded record of our experience, including the patterns of misses—what we needed, how it felt, what the response was, what arose within our minds and bodies as a response. These are not recorded in "explicit" memory, as we would normally think of memory—the way, say, events such as the first day of kindergarten might be. No. They are recorded, instead, in "implicit" memory: a somatic, emotional, behavioral etching of things that happen to us before (and apart from) the dawn of expressive language (Siegel, 2012). Implicit memory, while not experienced as "memory," is not lost. It forms an un-worded background of understanding and prediction. It can come forward into the present at times—unbidden—not as bits of memory, but as the re-experiencing of feelings, sensory impressions, and behaviors— "anxieties"—torn completely away from their original context and seamed into the now. Something in us records the feeling of misses, and can be reminded of (or catapulted into) those feelings, given the right stimuli.

We would rather this not be true, and on a cultural level, "defend" against such knowings. Caricatures of the trackless and trivial excavations of psychoanalysts are common in our culture. There is even the widespread naïve belief that early trauma doesn't matter because it isn't remembered—because children will forget. But the unbridled truth of it is that experience-dependent experience *matters*; that it is indeed formative (Gerhardt, 2004; Siegel, 2012). Over time, our early-acquired "knowings" become layered with experiences that may either reinforce or modify them. But at the bottom of it, these "knowings" remain what we learned earliest and best. They are the silent background that makes parts and pieces of our experience that seem not to make sense, make sense.

So let's recap. We come pre-loaded as infants with self-protective ("I"-protective) mechanisms. These are our initial "*defenses*". They are there from the beginning, to function on behalf of our consummately dependent selves. The defenses function at first consciously to alert the caregiver of misses, then to up-the-ante in all-out panic states, and when all else fails, to mobilize the cascade of endogenous opiates to numb the pain of existence. These are our initial defenses against what may feel to us like (and may well be, in some cases) threats to our survival. These threats—*anxieties*—are experienced as psychic pain, panic, uncontained fears of dying, of dissolving, of falling into endless space, of being annihilated by the other, or of being left by the other. Importantly, these anxieties are, at their root, *reality-based*. Theorists have argued this over time (for example, Klein versus Winnicott), but we now have the neuroscience to understand this more clearly. Unabated stress *does* in fact damage the incipient self, as it reaches toward its genetic expressions.

Field Soldiers

Despite their reputation, then, defenses have an important and noble job: they are tasked with the preservation and protection of the self. They are field soldiers. They mobilize—they take up arms—when anxieties alert them that something potentially damaging to the self is happening. Anxieties are the experience—or the anticipation of the experience—of pain, disconnection, over-stimulation, under-stimulation, abuse, separation from the caregiver, etc. Defenses are our front and rear guard against experiencing these things. The anxieties and defenses are thought by some theorists to exist in the unconscious parts of us from the beginning of life; by others, to develop with experience. Either way, they ultimately come to function for us automatically, unconsciously, out of our awareness—silently performing their safety patrols on a constant basis.

So if defenses have a legitimate pedigree, why are they held in such disfavor or disdain (at least when we see them in others)? I recently had a patient who was plagued by her own paranoia. It often paralyzed her. For instance, she once received an unopened notice in the mail from her insurance company, and proceeded in her mind and emotions down the long trail of assumptions to the endpoint of being uninsurable, having to leave her home, her animals, her gardens, all that gave her security. Then there was the inevitable collateral damage because she would freeze in fear in response to such paranoid assumptions.

As we together began to notice and study this hair-triggered response, we were eventually able to link it meaningfully to a familiar set of feelings in her—feelings that had *always* been there—of mounting and imminent disaster in the midst of her mother's lapses into psychoticism. Her early defense was the kind of hypervigilance expressed by her paranoia. It kept her aware and primed for the potential cascade of calamity lurking a hair's breadth away.

Interestingly, as she put more and more words on this stance over time, she began slowly to be able to lessen her vigilance, and to be less plagued by her own forecasts of doom. One day she came into the office and announced with a fair amount of conviction that we needed to shift how we'd been talking about her paranoia. As life-interrupting as it had been to her over time, she wanted us to recognize that it once had a profoundly legitimate place in her young existence: it had been looking out for her the whole time as a young person as she managed her mom's mental illness. She wanted it not to have to retire in dishonor or disrespect. It was a war hero. It had kept her alive. She wanted it decorated, held in honor, and given a new, non-combat assignment. We truly had some fun thinking together about new and adaptive uses for this well-developed part of her. It struck me in these moments that this was the best description of the biography of a defense that I'd ever seen or read.

The Point of a Defense

Typically, from the outside, when what we encounter is the defense, we don't have access to the underlying psychic pain/anxiety that the defense has been tasked with managing, minimizing, or staying completely away from. From the outside (and often from the inside), defenses look unnecessary—even gratuitous—if we don't understand why they're there. They have a feel; they affect us as audience. They can be as annoying as narcissism or as frustrating as black-and-white thinking. They can feel impenetrable, as when someone bores themselves and us with endless verbal minutia. They can even feel seductively playful, like the use of humor to stay away from the thoughts and feelings it may be meant to cover for. Therapists in training are often taught to look for and identify defenses, but—and this is important—identifying them *to the patient* puts the cart before the horse most times. *The point of a defense is the anxiety it is paired with.* If someone is fleeing the scene of a disaster, it's off-point to observe and describe to them their running style. We want to find out what they're fleeing, how they've been hurt, and what happened to them at the scene of the disaster.

Defenses Have Their Effect

OK. So why this conversation about defenses and anxieties positioned in the kaleidoscope along with the other piles of colored glass? Because defenses and anxieties show up in relationships. And they will show up in the therapeutic relationship—in the transference. They will be there in the assumptive framework of the patient. They will silently steer the therapy toward this (safe) topic, and away from this (dangerous) one; toward this (safe) feeling and away from this (dangerous) one. They will color how we as therapists are seen, and how our interventions and missteps are experienced, interpreted, and reacted to.

I talked to a patient yesterday about a series of images that emerged between us to describe our relationship in its first twelve months. In her initial image/reverie, she was a young refugee child, alone, in a cave, crouched in front of a fire. No humans around. Where was I in the picture? Nowhere. Not in the picture. This was her defense, self-sufficiency, the absence of dependence on anything human.

What anxiety did it keep her from feeling? The soul-ripping disappointment of chronic neglect as a young person; chronic misattunement. She used to call it "benign neglect." Humans were around to be related to, but in a one-off sort of way. It had a certain feel. As therapist, my job was to notice the self-sufficiency, and to wonder about it (to myself).

I was of course impacted by it. It didn't feel at all good to have spent multiple hours a week efforting to attune to this patient, only to find out I was nowhere near the cave for her. But my job was to try to come to know the anxiety *underneath* the self-sufficiency; for us to co-explore that, in whatever slow-motion ways we needed to. Trying to operate on the defense (the visible part)—her self-sufficiency—without understanding its *raison d'etre*, the "benign neglect" she had suffered, would have been an exercise in therapeutic futility, and might even have been experienced by the patient as an attack or a criticism.

It's easy to get this wrong as therapists and as people. We are often affected by people's defenses. They are frustrating, irritating, off-putting, perhaps even hurtful. They seem unnecessary when viewed from the outside. Our job is not to judge or attack the defense, but to seek to understand the anxiety that underlies it.

Many therapists are trained to notice the defense. This is a fundamentally flawed strategy. Defenses defend themselves. Understanding and speaking to the anxiety underneath the defense softens the defense, allows the anxiety to come out of the shadows, allows it to be experienced and known—sometimes for the first time, consciously—and makes the patient feel profoundly seen and understood.

As an aside, it's worth noting that as the therapy described above proceeded, the cave image came in a number of times, introduced each time by the patient. With each successive telling she re-positioned me: not in the cave at all; in the shadows, with only my eyes visible; out of the shadows but still at a safe distance; nearer the fire circle but far enough away to watch; next to her near the fire, silently stirring the coals.

Defenses of Early Development

There are three general categories of (pre-oedipal) anxieties and defenses described within psychoanalytic literature. These are profoundly helpful to us as therapists. Why? Because while defenses are often visible—and often frustrating to interact with—their underlying anxieties are far less obvious. Melanie Klein contributed mightily to our understanding of anxieties and defenses by describing two "positions"—paranoid-schizoid and depressive—predicated upon early developmental experience. Tom Ogden added a third and most primitive—autistic-contiguous—to the mix. Together, these two authors provide us with a unique window into the earliest and most unworded anxieties we experience in the course of our development as human beings. I'm going to give a brief sketch of these, just to alert you to their existence. You'll need further reading and supervision, of course, to really make use of this brief schematic.

The Autistic-Contiguous Position

I'll take us first to Ogden's "autistic-contiguous" position (Ogden, 1989). Ogden posits that among our first tasks as developing infants is that of establishing a sense of location, a sense of occupying a particular space with its particular sensory boundedness—its starting and stopping points. We seek as infants to know what it feels like to occupy our own skin boundary—to know that we have a being that *is*—that will not leak out into endless space, that will not wash down the drain with the bathwater, that will not dissipate like the fog of the morning. Our experiences of being swaddled, held, and handled in our beginning days help to contribute to this feeling of substantiation, but all of us have unremembered anxieties related to this early developmental space. A baby in the first few days of life suffers the unshelling of itself with each diaper change, the invasions at its surface—of cold and wet and handlings and pokings, of light and sound and gravity; the contrast of the first days of life with all that came before.

Most of us have a sense of what it feels like to have our physical boundaries breached in some way, or to feel what it feels like not to occupy our familiar space—to be displaced. But the specter of losing our fundamental spatial definition—of disintegration into nothingness—is more than we can let ourselves imagine. A most disturbing illustration of this is the bombing of the World Trade Center in 2001. It is unthinkably haunting to us to have there be no physical trace of the *us* that once was. This is perhaps the most primitive anxiety we face as infants: the acquiring of and threats to our sheer physical definition.

Second Skin

Although this is a universally human anxiety, and it can come up in different forms in all of us, some are particularly plagued with this anxiety. I think in particular of patients who suffered initial medical crises, or were not held and handled in the ways they needed to be as infants. Their overriding (unconscious) psychic concern becomes that of knitting a "second skin" for themselves, to cover for the psychic skin that was never adequately helped to develop (Bick, 1968). This second skin is what, from the outside, we encounter as a defense. This can take many, many forms. People can "wrap" themselves in words, in substances, in routine, in compulsive rituals, in exercise, in rhythmic movements—even in their own body fat. The distinctive piece to be aware of as clinicians is that someone who uses autistic-contiguous defenses is doing so to gather themselves up in one place. Given the preeminence and priority of this unconscious concern, they do not have much bandwidth leftover for the job of relating to someone else. So there is a peculiarly non-related feel to someone whose primary anxiety is autistic-contiguous—almost an autistic feel, as the name implies.

I had, for instance, a patient who used to come into session and launch (before sitting down) into a verbal gusher. There was no stopping her. She was animated, anxious, and emphatic, and she fixed her eyes onto mine with the power of magnets (which I felt entrapped by). I had the sense while I was with her that I was, all the time, utterly interchangeable; that there was nothing about my particularity that she was relating to. Given the degree of her anxiety, she needed *someone* to gusher into, but anyone would have done for the job. I found myself swept along by her outpourings during the session, and couldn't at the end of it remember much of anything she had said. It was as though she and I were both absent at some level for the entire meeting time. There could be no real meeting, because for that, she would have to have had an "I" gathered up in one place. This is exactly what she did not have, so her efforts in the session were in the service of preventing her own dissipation rather than relating to me as a separate and real other.

Now, why is understanding her anxiety as a fight for her own primitive self-definition (and against the terrors of dissipation) so important? Because it sets the parameters for my job as therapist, and allows me to meet (or at least, be with) that patient on the ground most crucial to her. If the therapeutic task is to *be* the chrysalis that houses a patient's process of primitive self-definition, then I had best settle down to that task, and not try for something different from that—not insight, not connection, not process. No. For someone in the grip of this autistic-contiguous set of anxieties, my job is to provide a *place*, by my regular presence, my attention, my therapeutic frame, and my willingness to be used, for as long as it takes, for the self-knitting of a more supple skin. My job is to contain a process that requires my presence, but occurs largely without my worded intervention. As humbling as this may be, that's the job, and knowing the nature of the underlying anxiety helps me know my job.

I frequently meet with interns new to the field. Many of the patients in their agency-based settings are in this exact developmental place. The interns try out all their skills of empathy and reflective listening, and wind up wondering what they're doing wrong, because none of their interventions seem to matter, or even to be taken in. The simple truth is that the patients they're working with are in autistic-contiguous territory.

This knowledge is relieving to the fledgling therapists (when they can really take this in). It restricts the range of their therapeutic interventions down to showing up for the session, and on rare occasion putting words on such unconscious anxieties as dissipation, disappearance, evaporation, falling endlessly, slipping through the holes in the floor, etc. Really *getting* this allows the therapists-in-training to content themselves with the goal of witnessing another's process, rather than trying actively to midwife that process. These, and other issues related to the clinical applications of autistic-contiguous, paranoid-schizoid, and depressive positions are taken up in much greater depth and detail by Ogden in his books entitled *Primitive Edge of Experience* (1989) and *The Matrix of the Mind* (1986)—must-reads for any aspiring (or mature) psychodynamic therapist.

Interlude

OK. So defenses and the invisible anxieties they defend. Three broad categories: autistic-contiguous, paranoid-schizoid, depressive. As observed above, some of our deepest and most unconscious anxieties are spawned during our earliest times. These become protected over time, as the irritation of a piece of sand would gradually become protected by the nacre within an oyster's shell. From the outside, we don't see the grain of sand in the middle. We see the cover. But if we can know what's there at the heart of things, then we can intervene on the right part of the arrangement. We can explore, expand, bring words and thoughts to what has been previously un-nameable, but always there at the center of it nonetheless.

The Paranoid-Schizoid Position

So, I'll now take us to the next step in this developmental sequence, Klein's paranoid-schizoid position (Klein, 1946). A note before we continue: these positions are both developmentally sequential *and* ongoing. So once in place, we don't ever completely outgrow them. They form a silent experiential background within our psyche, and, developed with proper support and in the right balance, bring life to our being as humans.

OK. So the paranoid-schizoid position. Klein felt that each of us is born with instincts that pull us toward life and toward death, *both*. She felt that, congruent with these instincts, an infant was pre-programmed to experience the interpersonal world alternatively as good or bad; as life-preserving or life-threatening. She also posited that infants anticipated and elaborated their interface with the real world through a host of internal phantasies—expressions of their bodily experience, but shaped by these life and death instincts.

Whether or not we subscribe to Klein's life/death and phantasy-based metapsychology, we can observe with her that infants operate in an intensely interpersonal world, tied completely to the ministrations of an *other* for sheer physical survival. We can further observe that the world of an infant is a *binary* world, with the infant experiencing contentment or distress, pleasure or pain, safety or threat, often in rapid succession.

Good and Bad

Klein felt that among our primary psychic tasks as developing infants is that of sorting good from bad experience—of figuring out distinctly which is which. She believed that the physical and psychic fragilities of earliest development (for Klein, the first three months) makes this sorting process itself quite fragile, and requires, for the sake of clarity and simplicity, clear demarcations between good and bad. Things simultaneously good and bad could become neither; or worse, good things could at any moment be invaded and contaminated by the bad, which would leave the infant in an all-bad universe—an unimaginably frightening state in the pre-verbal, completely helpless infant. So keeping good and bad experience far apart and separate from one another becomes an absolute infantile imperative. As a part of this, there need also to be clear attributions about the human beings involved in mediating our good or bad experience. In other words, moment-by-moment, an infant needs to be clear about *who* is good and *who* is bad.

For Klein, this bifurcation of experience—good experience, bad experience; good *purveyor* of good experience, bad *purveyor* of bad experience—describes a psychological "position" that all infants occupy as they are coming into their psychological being. Through this lens of *good* or *bad* all early infantile experience is refracted—their experience of the world, of the other, and ultimately (through instinct, inference and internalization) of the infant's self. Of course, one and the same mothering-person is associated with good and bad experiences, so this primitive organization, according to Klein, includes the bifurcation of primary caregivers into "good mother" and "bad mother," held separate and distinct from one another in the infant's developing mind. Should good and bad, loving and hating aspects of the *other* collide with one another, the good and loving aspects of existence could be completely destroyed, and the self with it. So the ever-present psychic threat of this position is the fear that one's self would be *torn apart, fragmented, annihilated* by the interpersonal forces of evil contained within the hated caregiver and in the hating aspects of the self.

Defensive Equipment: Splitting

It's a fragile and treacherous psychic world to have to traverse when the people we depend on can, and might in fact, do us in. But again, thankfully, we come pre-loaded with the defensive equipment for the job. The defense of "splitting"— the process of locating the good and bad in separate psychic locations—is something for which the infantile brain is well equipped. It's easier for a just-developing brain to sort things into two bins rather than into two thousand. Splitting makes the world become a predictable place where meanings are clear. As the children's rhyme goes, "When you are good you are very, very good"—

your intentions are good, your ministrations are good, and I can relax and take you in. I *need* to be able to relax and take in what you offer me as a developing infant, unencumbered by fear. "But when you are bad, you are horrid"—you are powerfully against me, you are not to be trusted or believed in any way. I use whatever capacities I have to distance myself from you. I cry uncontrollably. I resist your attempts to soothe me. I maybe dissociate. I hate you in those moments, and can get along fine without you. Go away! This state allows me to treat you from the hateful and aggressive parts of myself, intentionally and justifiably, with no brakes on. This is the defense of splitting, a cardinal (and necessary) feature of the paranoid-schizoid position.

Why necessary? The best way I've come up with to think of this is using metaphor. Suppose, for a minute, that you were in a room that was beginning to fill with poison gas. Suppose that there were two rooms connected to one another: the one filling with the poison and the adjoining one. Best strategy? Get yourself over into the adjoining, non-poisoned room, and *seal it off.* Don't let the atmospheres intermix. If, perchance, you need to enter the poisoned room, hold your breath and seal the door behind you. This would allow you to survive. Not to do this would lead to your annihilation. This is a picture of splitting. The underlying fear (anxiety) is the certainty of annihilation if you don't keep the rooms—the one with the good air and the one with the bad—separate from one other.

OK. That's splitting, as desperately necessary, psychically, for adults in that paranoid-schizoid position as it is for infants. I'll give you an example of splitting in a session in a few minutes, but first, there's one more piece of defensive equipment at the infant's disposal in this paranoid-schizoid world that we need to consider. It is related to, but not the same as splitting. It is the phenomenon of projection and its cousin, projective identification.

Projective Processes

"Projection" is the capacity to relocate one's psychic experience somewhere else within the interpersonal field—the capacity to evacuate or "project" parts of the self-experience onto or into an other. Infants are masters at such relocation of experience. Their cry is a concrete example of this relocation capacity. Infant-upset very quickly becomes the upset of the adults around that little one. The adults are, in effect, handed parts and pieces of the infant's emotional world to carry around inside.

Projection is a lot easier to point to experientially than to describe theoretically. But it models something quite real that happens in and outside of therapy. Sometimes, in the presence of some people, there is a palpable experience of their psychic particles. We feel *different* in their presence, somehow. Maybe we feel less safe, like we're having to walk on eggshells; maybe we feel intimidated and less able to find our center; maybe we feel superior. There are a million maybes. But, if you scan your experience, there are no doubt some people in whose presence you feel a strong psychic undertow. Sometimes this is your stuff—your transference of early relational filters onto them. Sometimes, it is their particle field, extruded out, seeping into and affecting yours. So let's think about this business of projection for a minute, especially in its infancy.

The world of "I" is rather fluid in its formative stages, in the beginning stages of life—sort of like the yolk of a not-yet-cooked egg. Given the not-yet fully-formed state of the infant's "I," it is highly permeable, and can easily lose its integrity; its shape.

The infant's "I" can also easily take in emotional experience from outside itself. It takes in emotional experience whole, as we have said. And it can also offload emotional experience easily. Without words, it can make the people around feel quiescent or tortured.

The infant's "I" can merge psychically with that of another in her interpersonal space. She can introject the experience of the other; she can seamlessly "project" pieces of herself outward—in phantasy, relocating parts of herself into the other—for safe keeping, or to protect the infant self from her own (hateful) influence. This permeability allows the infant to deposit into an other what is too difficult, toxic, or unsafe for her developing self to house; to "project" it outside of herself.

This two-way permeability is extremely adaptive in the caregiver-infant relationship. In that relationship, it opens the door to the process of projective identification (discussed in Chapter 11), allowing a mother to feel and "contain" the psychic emanations of her developing infant, and thereby to attune more closely to the infant's experience. It also opens the door to the process of internalization, allowing the infant to internalize parts and pieces of the mother's psyche—for instance, over time, to internalize a mom's soothing functions so as to have them inside, eventually enabling the developing child to self-soothe.

Projection is an important feature of the paranoid-schizoid position— important for us to understand as therapists, because in the role of therapist we are sometimes the unwitting recipients of parts and pieces of the psychic world of our patients. At times of regression in some patients, or in the course of what is normal with other patients, we can be caught up in the swirl of their projected psychic particles.

Theory can be very helpful. It is extremely helpful for us as therapists to have a really good understanding of the anxieties and defenses inherent in the paranoid-schizoid position for two reasons: that human beings all have aspects of these ways of being still within, even as mature adults; and that some of our patients live predominantly in this world, or retreat into it in times of psychological stress or injury. The world of borderline and narcissistic defenses is a paranoid-schizoid world—as are often the worlds of divorce and all other declarations of war.

To illustrate this paranoid-schizoid position, I'll take you straight to a brief example from my practice, one I've already given in Chapter 10, but which, viewed from this lens, nicely illustrates the world of paranoid-schizoid defenses, and the anxieties underneath them.

Tamara, Revisited

After having been in twice-a-week therapy for a number of years, one of my patients had the experience of my being late for our session by nine minutes. She left, and made herself unreachable by cell phone.

When we met for the next session, she shared with me that there was only one reason I would be late for the session: I had dropped her from my mind. She was angry and impenetrable. She was not the least bit interested in hearing an alternative explanation. I had dropped her. That was that.

Here's what was happening in terms of paranoid-schizoid defenses and anxieties. The normally good and consistent therapist was transferred in her mind to the category of "bad therapist." No accumulated record of on-timeness or attunement was available to her. She had had a bad experience; I had been the purveyor of the bad experience. The underlying anxiety? If good and bad are allowed to co-exist in the same "other," then she might suffer psychic annihilation—an internal feeling of being destroyed by me—of having the bad so overtake the good without and within, that the universe would turn uncontrollably frightening. So in these moments, it feels to her as though she's fighting for her life, and will bring all the power of her own hatefulness inside to the battle.

This is incredibly important to understand from the inside—the anxiety side—out. Otherwise, I might have been tempted to use the powers of rationality, logic and history to try to talk her out of her psychic pain, which would have been worse than useless; it would have been further wounding. My understanding of the paranoid-schizoid position was also helpful to me in those moments because there were powerful projective riptides going on between us. For me, the riptides were the feeling of being scared, almost immobilized by fear.

So what are we to do as therapists? Fight to find our psychic footing, and speak to the *anxiety*, rather than to the defense. Here's how it went:

"It must feel as though you've been completely dropped by me."

"*Yes.*"

"And like there's no shred of goodness left between us."

"*Yes.*"

"It's an awful experience for you to be left waiting, knowing that if I had had you in my mind, this would never have happened. You thought of not coming today—of not coming anymore to therapy."

"*Yes.*"

"It feels desperately important that I know how you've been hurt by me."

"*Yes.*" (Softening)

"What's it like to have me know your experience of our non-meeting earlier this week?"

"*Well, at least you're not making up some story to defend yourself.*" (More softening)

"I wonder what it will be like, trying to go forward together with this breach between us?"

"*Yah.*" (More softening)

"How is it feeling in here for you right now?"

"*A little better.*"

"Yah. Why do you think?"

"*It feels like you're getting it.*"

"OK, I wonder what more you might need from me on this?"

"*I don't know. I used to get left so much by my mom. I'd wait for hours, sometimes into the darkness.*" (More softening)

"Yah. Frightening."

"*Yah.*" (I've now been silently relocated back into the good therapist bin, someone she can trust to hold the pain of her experience.) Full circle.

It may be obvious, but perhaps important to note that we all have paranoid-schizoid defenses within. In the times when we decide that someone is "a jerk," or "useless," or *any* one way, we're engaging in an infantile process that collapses and simplifies reality so that we can bear it more easily.

Once again, why is this identification of a patient's psychological position helpful? Because it puts us as therapists in touch with the real psychological anxieties that are being experienced by the patient underneath their defense, and therefore the real agenda that's going to play out in the moment. In the example of Tamara, if I had thought that my most effective intervention would have been to get my patient to understand the innocent set of circumstances—road construction leading to my getting lost on the way back to the office—that had occurred between us, I would inadvertently have escalated her anxiety, and driven myself and the therapy further into badness.

The anxieties at stake are not obvious on the face of things. That's why theory is helpful. It tells us what would otherwise elude our intuitions, and gives us empathy for forces and threats otherwise invisible to us. When someone is in the paranoid-schizoid position, it is an emotionally infantile place, and requires a containing of the anxiety rather than a challenging of the defense. Again, for further reading on the paranoid-schizoid position, see the previously-referenced clinical works, especially *The Matrix of the Mind*.

The Depressive Position

OK. We have one more step to take. A less complex one, or maybe, at least, a little easier to understand. Let me now take us forward to the final step in this developmental sequence, Klein's "depressive" position (Klein, 1935). Klein placed our capacity to begin to conceptualize the "otherness" of the other at the age of three months. To my mind (and to many), this seems too early, but the precise carbon-dating of this process does not matter so much as does the substance of this newly emerging capacity.

The depressive position, as Klein named it, is characterized by a large developmental step forward. The developing child begins to take in, psychically, that the person providing for him/her all the time exists as a separate person—actually has an existence and a set of concerns that go beyond care for that child.

Little by little (for several years) the child confronts the reality that the mothering person has a separate psyche, motivational system, way of thinking, set of desires— all different from the child's. With this dawning and *daunting* knowledge comes the realization that the other experiences pain just as the child does; that it's as real to the other as the child's pain is to him/her. And along with this comes the dawning of another rather ponderous reality: that the child can be the *source* of pain for the mother. If so, combined with the mother's separateness of volition and motivation, it could be that the child would so injure the mothering person that she/he would decide to leave the child. The child could suffer the loss of the desperately loved and required mother. Now, this would be an insufferable loss, and *depressing* knowledge.

All the "givens" in a child's life *shift* around this knowledge. I can cause pain to the other, and can no longer magically whisk it away by simply wishing myself and their experience into an "all good" bin. The experience of the other matters. Experience is remembered. History matters. I must treat the other with care. I must take responsibility for the pain I cause the other, and seek to repair the damages I cause. The obliteration of history is no longer possible, as it was in the rather magic-driven time of the paranoid-schizoid position, so magical reparation is no longer an option.

Related to this is another implication of the depressive position: that I no longer function in a perfect universe. I can no longer claim to myself to be all good (or all bad), or you to be all good or all bad, or reality to be all good or bad. I am some amalgam of good and bad, as are you—as is life. No amount of wishing it were not so makes it not so. This knowledge, while potentially disappointing, brings with it an entirely different orientation to one's own human condition, and that of others. It takes the pressure off the illusory goal of perfection, and moves it toward the more attainable goal of truth. The self and the other can be looked at as some combination of good and bad, and these valences can be held simultaneously, "ambi-valently." This attainment within the depressive position is called the achievement of "ambivalence."

Additionally, and subtly: if your thoughts, feelings, and desires are separate from mine, then my reality is no longer the only reality. There are multiple realities, depending on whom they belong to. This sophisticated psychological step allows the according of subjectivity to ourselves and to others. In the full bloom of this psychological position, then, we are no longer merely the passive or hapless recipients of our experience. We are the interpreters of our experience. Things are not fixed in their meanings. We make meaning of things. One interprets one's reality, so can filter it through a multiplicity of lenses. Thoughts and feelings, then, become one's own psychic creations; they can be explored, understood, and changed.

The apprehending of subjectivity—in ourselves and in others—is the hallmark of the depressive position. When this position is truly in place, our job as therapists becomes one of progressively exploring and unpacking meanings with our patient. Unexamined meanings, infantile meanings, life-determining meanings. And with this unpacking process comes the potential for individuals to stretch out into more and more of their experience-dependent "I." Life no longer merely "happens" to me. I stand as an interpreting subject, assigning meanings to my own experience, and changing how I think about and live my life in response. I accord you the same freedoms. It is a truly different world.

The *anxieties* of the depressive position are real, and represent day-to-day reality: the ever-present potential of loss, and imperfection in ourselves and our objects. These are at some level terrifying, even to fully developed adults. But as children, or in the younger parts of ourselves beyond childhood, how does one *defend* against these potentially paralyzing realities?

Klein has described what she calls the "manic defenses." These are: control, contempt, and triumph over the object. These defenses are borrowed from our own paranoid-schizoid repertoire, but used in the service of keeping at bay the realities of the depressive position. Control: if I exert control over the loved person, then she/he may not feel the freedom to leave me. Contempt: if I lower their status in my own eyes, then my real or potential loss of them hurts me less. Triumph: if I ultimately emerge victorious in my pyrrhic struggle with them (through achievement, wealth, a new relationship, a new status, etc.), then I need not feel their loss at all. These are a range of defensive maneuvers we all use at times to ward of the searing realities of change and impermanence—when to let those realities in would at some level disable our "I."

How do these defenses show up in the therapeutic relationship? Here are a few. Some patients routinely minimize our importance to them. They exhibit uncommon flexibility to changes in schedule. They hardly react to our vacation absences. They report glowing advances in our absence. They avoid or derail talking about their relationship with us. They try not to let us matter too much. These things can be there in the therapeutic relationship. They are there in people who otherwise appear to occupy the depressive position for the most part, and despite evidence that the therapy has become valuable to them. Our job with these patients is to notice *the anxiety underneath the defense*; the risk of valuing, balanced against the potential price of losing.

I have a number of patients for whom this set of anxieties and defenses are at play not only in their relationship with me but also in their relationships in their outside worlds. It's a quite delicate task for someone to open fully to the realities of impermanence and imperfection. None of us ever does this completely, toward ourselves or those whom we love. But a fuller opening of that aperture allows a much more truthful and fulsome embrace of the *now* of relationships—of the realities of who that person is, and who I am, and who we are to one another. It is my job as therapist, over time, to help my patients look at the anxieties underneath the defenses in *our* relationship, so that they may expand the limitations of their own humanness which they have imposed on themselves and others in their life-space.

Summary

This brief sketch of the anxieties and defenses described in the context of these three psychological positions—autistic-contiguous, paranoid-schizoid, depressive— is in no way meant to offer extensive clinical guidance. Others have taken on that mission, and done it thoughtfully and well. Nor it is meant to be exhaustive of the defenses or anxieties available to us in our human repertoire. We are infinitely creative in how we draw hospital curtains across our internal psychic space. In this chapter I have focused on the anxieties and defenses associated with early development. There are other anxieties associated with the oedipal passage which I have not taken up explicitly.

This rendering is simply meant to position anxieties and defenses in general in their proper place with respect to one another, and also to alert you to the enormous clinical value of the Kleinian and Ogdenian positions. They serve as incredibly helpful directional lights to us as therapists. If we pay attention to their signals, they orient us. They determine the routes available and those closed to us—which pathways would advance the therapy and which turns would be flat-out dangerous.

Back to Our Kaleidoscope

It's a shame if any child grows up having not been able to look down the barrel of a kaleidoscope. We've now loaded up the kaleidoscope—Object Relations, transference, countertransference, defenses, anxieties—the basic pieces of glass that color the therapeutic relationship. In the room, they mix together, and the neat world of exactitude gives way to the swirling world of patterns and colors and ever-changing shapes we've never seen before. Sometimes magical, sometimes beautiful, always fascinating, and ultimately beyond our capacities to dream up in advance. This is the world of psychodynamic psychotherapy. This is the art of it; this is the privilege of it. This is what keeps us studying and pondering it as long as we have eyes to see and minds to wonder.

13

ENDGAME

Now it's my job to begin to put this all together for you. *Essential Psychodynamic Psychotherapy: An Acquired Art.* In this final chapter I will attempt to address the bigger question: what are we doing when we meet with someone in this deliberate medium of psychoanalytic psychotherapy? What exactly are we up to, and why would it move someone along toward a more mature and satisfying way of being in the world?

I've entitled this chapter "Endgame." I give credit for this chapter title to one of my consultees, Janet, who, along with a group of us, was reading along through the early drafts of these chapters. Moving to the end of the last chapter she asked with eagerness one morning, "Now do we get to talk about the endgame?" Now we do.

I've allowed this chapter to emerge from my right brain—really, my better brain. So it has the whole picture in mind, the whole way. And, given its nature, it's less tightly rendered—more stream of consciousness—than what has preceded it. But it wanted to speak, and in the end, I wanted to hear what it had to say. Come with me now, on this, our final lap, for now.

So how do we gather it all up? How does this all knit itself together? This multi-faceted process of listening, of listening deeply, of listening with the entire satellite dish of our bodies, our minds, our spirits. How do we gather up this business of creating space for the sacredness of the other, and of waiting in that space for the new to be birthed? How do we make practical sense of and integrate these daunting technicalities of object relations, transference, countertransference, anxieties, defenses—all of it? And what, to quote Janet, is the endgame of all of this? What is it we're driving toward? And how do we know when we've arrived at that place?

Why Am I Here?

Everyone who comes to our office for the first appointment asks himself or herself this question at some level: "Why have I come?" The answer is vague at first. Something is not right. Something isn't working. I can't do *this*. I *do* do *that*. I'm not like who I want to be. I'm in my own way, somehow. Being *me* doesn't work for me or for the people I love. Or simply, I'm profoundly wrong, and always have been.

So is *that* the answer? Is that the endgame—that something's not right and it's our job to find and fix it? Is the answer in the "not right" part of the question? Or is it buried in the "right" part of it—that some way, somehow, in some form there *is* a right? That there's a right buried deep within—perhaps so far down that it's never really seen the light of day. There's a what's truest, most robust, most clear, most outrageous, most impassioned, most tender, most flexible, most able to love. That there's a right somewhere buried beneath the wrong.

Perhaps this is what we do that's unique to psychodynamic psychotherapy. We do the *wrong*. We sit with the trackless, hopeless, immovable, unspeakable, unutterable wrong. We sit in and with the anguish of it, the barrenness of it, the ickiness of it, the tragedy of it. We sit with sometimes a lifetime's full of discouragement and defeat. We sit with it and in it. And we sit there for a *long time*—as long as we need to. We refuse to abandon our vigil. That's our job. It's our call.

But in it, in the longest, darkest, scariest, least promising times of it, we keep an eye on the right. We keep the hope, even when we're the only one holding the hope. We move with someone all the way through the labyrinth of the wrong—with no short circuits, no manic fixes, no novocaine. But at the same time we hold somewhere within us a space—a place—for the right. A sense of the right. I've put it in simple language. But *that* is the endgame. *The right* is the endgame.

The Right

The other night in our group psychotherapy for women who have used food chronically in their lives—*all their lives*—a woman in the group wanted to share something. She had been to Macy's, and needed to get something new to wear. She went to her normal place to shop—way way back on the bottom floor of the store, back beyond the juniors displays and the lingerie department, to a section with cement floors where they keep the women's plus-size section. Well, she told the group, to her surprise, she could not find anything to fit her there.

She told us that she then found herself wandering around the store trying to find the "regular" women's department. She had not shopped in the "regular" section in several decades. She quietly told the group that she had noticed her body getting smaller (oh, and that by the way, she was off blood pressure meds and her lipid levels were now in the normal range), but that wasn't the point of interest for her, really. What she really was noticing was that *she* had become different. In so many ways. She no longer "uses" food, she told the group simply. And she has become an exerciser. Not a religious one, she assured us. But she now has that piece integrated with her self-definition. She said these things as statements of fact, not as goals she was somehow pursuing.

She turned to a woman relatively new to the group and said, "This has been five years in the making. That my body is getting smaller is simply the endpoint in a chain of so, so many profound changes that have gone on inside me in the last five years." In that time, she had finished off a divorce that had been ten years in the making, transitioned from being an unpublished author to having published seven books (yes, seven!), cleaned out the basement relics from her 25-year marriage, claimed the once-shared house she now lives in by herself with new paint and a new sense of ownership.

In that time also she had moved from a certain emotional stolidness to having a kind of permeability and openness to her own process and to that of the others in the group. She was absolutely telling the truth of it that this thing she came for that was *wrong*—this downsizing of her body, with the legion of physical and emotional problems it brought with it—that the thing that was "wrong" wasn't at this point nearly so important to her as the things that were becoming *right* in and for her. Stunning.

Many theorists have tried to put words and concepts on the endgame of psychotherapy—of *why* we do what we do, with what end-states in mind. The field of clinical psychology in general carries on a somewhat fractious debate about what is or ought to be the focus of our work. American psychology in general has now moved toward short-term, symptom-focused interventions, manualized treatments, outcome measures. There is a push in the research community for more precise defining of evidence-based practices—the most effective way to treat this symptom or that.

But in the midst of this discourse, the mission of psychodynamic psychotherapists has remained broader in scope, less defined by symptoms and more by the much harder-to-define task of human optimization; of getting down to the underneath of things and resetting the bones of it.

To Be Alive

This broader mission presents us with the gnarly problem of knowing how to talk to ourselves about what exactly we're doing from moment to moment in this ineffable space. Are we attempting to focus on the unconscious? On the transference? On emotion? On defenses? On anxieties? And what about presenting symptoms? What do we do with that part? How do we gather it up into words that are clear to us? Clear enough to keep us oriented in the long and often dimly-lit trek we engage in as psychodynamic psychotherapists. We are, after all, in the daily business of gathering up the unspoken and unspeakable into *words*…

As usual, I am deeply benefited by the reflections of psychoanalyst Tom Ogden on the topic of what we think we're doing as psychodynamic

. psychotherapists—on what is our endgame. In *Reverie and Interpretation* (1997), he uses Goethe's character Faust to describe Faust's earnest desire to be merely human: "to experience a full range of the 'joys and griefs, the heights and depths' of human emotion" (p. 17). Ogden frames this as the ultimate goal of psychotherapy—the expansion and enhancement of our capacity *to be alive to our own human experience*. Our capacity to be *alive*. Let's stop here for just a second and think about what this means.

We, each of us, seem to walk our lives in patterns that are the parameters of the familiar for us. The routines we find ourselves in; the kinds of relationships we inhabit; the things we do daily that keep us on track, that manage our anxiety inside, that allow us to survive this day; this time.

For the woman I described earlier, one of the constants in her life was her relationship with food. Food was her go-to for moments of distress, boredom, excitement, celebration. It kept her emotionally contained. Now, why? Why food, with all of the obvious costs involved to her? Why would she need to turn to food as a container of her emotions? She has begun to understand the answer to this lifelong question. It is that it was the one way she knew she could contain what was inside her. She had a limitation to what she could bear of her own human experience—a limitation acquired in the early matrix of family stress and tragedy for her—a limitation that caused her to reach toward the tried and true—the thing she knew would momentarily deliver her, or anaesthetize her, from what might otherwise overwhelm her about the experience of being alive to her own human experience.

Let's be clear. We all do this. We all reach to the familiar to keep ourselves on track. I'm having coffee this morning as I sit with my laptop and feel the December sunshine flooding into the upstairs room where I go to write. I always write in the morning. Always in the same place. I never write without my first cup of coffee. I'm held by these routines in the anxiety of wandering into the next part of the next thought; wondering if there will be a next thought; feeling my way all the way to the end of this sentence.

Ogden (1997) observes that we all make (largely unconscious) deals with ourselves that truncate our capacity to experience our own aliveness. We deaden ourselves to our capacity to be alive. We swap the counterfeit for the real. He says that we do this (reflexively) because "the prospect of being more fully alive as a human being is felt to involve a form of psychic pain that we are afraid we cannot endure."

This is our inherent limitation as humans, and can take many forms (that may or may not be listed as "diagnoses" in the DSM)—but which choke off our humanness, including such things, in Ogden's (1997) thinking, as

> a constriction of one's range and depth of feeling, thought and bodily sensation, a restriction of one's dream-life and reverie-life, a sense of unrealness in one's relations to oneself and to other people, or a compromise of one's ability to play, to imagine and to use verbal and non-verbal symbols to create/represent one's experience.
>
> *(pp. 18–19)*

We constrict ourselves, and in so doing, miss the moments of our lives. Miss what it would feel like to be fully, honestly present to the height and the depth of our own experience.

I take this—the constriction of the depth and range of our ability to feel alive in our lives—as my working definition of psychopathology, and its inverse—the capacity to be alive to our own experience—as my working definition of psychological health. This may be as good a way to describe the endgame as any—this (never fully achieved) set of capacities.

So, if the coming alive to and within our own life is the *endgame*, what are the steps and processes that make this coming alive possible? How does the wrong become right? And how do we as therapists know when we/our patients have arrived? We've been talking about these processes the whole way along together, but let's see if we can put the critical pieces together in relation to one another, so that the puzzle can form at least a tentative whole in our minds.

Identifying the Wrong

First, how do we identify the wrong in our patients? Patients come to us with certain elements they've identified as "wrong." But often, they've seized on epiphenomena—byproducts of the thing, rather than the thing itself. "I am too aggressive with my sons." "I am afraid I can't learn the things necessary for me to keep my job." "I can't seem to not use food." These are real concerns. But soon on in the process, we begin to run into our patients' unseen, most often unconscious constrictions. We feel what it's like to be in this person's lifesphere; we feel the subtleties of the interpersonal and intrapersonal pushes and pulls. We pick up in our bodies (with our satellite dish) something of the constrictedness of *being* that person—the seemingly un-self-imposed constrictions on their capacity to feel alive. This is what we feel when we sit with them (countertransference). It begins to take shape and form in the myriad subtleties of their relationship with us (transference). We witness their behaviors in and outside of the sessions (defenses). We feel their dis-ease within ourselves (anxieties)—often very, very difficult to word.

These pushes, pulls, dis-eases all exert a certain psychological strain on us—a strain that's different with each patient. It's often a strain, though, that exhibits itself in their life external to our sessions, and that has emerged from the circumstances of, and as a response to their at first external, but ultimately internalized, object relational world. When we sit with our patients, we experience them—both what it's like to be on the receiving end of them, and even, at some level, what it's like to be within them. We get to know the wrong. Intimately. Slowly. Painfully.

Yesterday I wrote a poem, as I often do, in my attempt to put into words for myself something of what it is like to be in interaction with a particular patient. The patient addressed in this poem has said out loud that she feels dead in her own life. This was my attempt to word some of the subtleties—the strain, the flavor, the wrong—of being with this person. I called the poem "Leftovers":

I absorb so much of the risk between us
I can feel it
It's the thing you need me to absorb
I'm sure of it
It's in the leftovers.

Leftovers—
Maybe that's why I use that word so much
With you
It's in the leftovers
of how you used to feel
And now
You pass it forward
That unconscious feeling
Of uncertainty and risk
Of never quite knowing
If the next move
Will be the wrong one
The move that drives you
Somewhere beyond reach
For reasons I'll ponder
and wonder about
and second guess
in the aftermath.

Meanwhile,
You keep one foot out the door
(just in case)

These are the terms
Of endearment
Right?
These are your terms.
Because to plant that foot
Would mean to feel the weight of the risk
Yourself.
Something you felt
Way too early
And found way too devastating.
So for now
You've given it to me
The heavier part
The riskier part
The feel of it
In the leftovers …

What do I word for myself in this poem? I attempt to capture for myself the strain—part of the strain—of what it is to be in relationship to this person. The constriction that has made its way into her lifestream. The constriction that absolves her of the burden of risk in relationship—that prevents her from ever really being entirely present, interpersonally, which is both protective and deadening. Of course, this was her only play as a youngster—a brilliant strategy for surviving the relational sparsities of her growing up environment. But the safety of that constriction for this patient comes with a high cost. To never really show up for the risk of things is to never really enjoy the loveliness of feeling real in relationship to another. It's to never really feel the entirety of another's presence, another's love; to never really feel one's aliveness in the risk of it, in the reward of it, in the loss of it.

All right. So with each patient, there are constrictions. We're on the receiving end of them. And, we "sit with" that, meaning we try to be present to the feeling of what it is to be the "other" in relation to them. This can be for a long time—for years. The constrictions are years in the forming, and years in the living. They don't let go quickly.

Closer to the Right

And so, what if we're able to be in the transference-countertransference world of our patient, to experience it, to feel the strain of it, and to word it to ourselves, progressively, over time; what does that do to move them out of constriction and closer to the right inside themselves? Ahhhh. This is the nub of the question. Several pieces assemble themselves around this question. Let's see if we can walk around and look at them together.

Attunement

First, and perhaps foremost, is the business of attunement. This is the focus of much current neurobiological research. So often, the damage in a person is a set of adaptations they've done over time in response to the misses they experienced as very young children—encoded in the experience-dependent and emerging structures of the right brain (Schore, 2012). Someone whose job it was to tune in to the subtle emotional world of the patient missed part of that of the assignment, in any of the ways one human can miss another, for any of the reasons. Winnicott (1954) believes that when we offer consistent attunement as psychotherapists, a patient will regress with us to the point where the original misattunements began to cause contortion and constriction within. Our simple, unflashy, day-to-day tuning into the emotional truth of what's there in the room—the moods, the anxieties, the playfulnesses, the darknesses—reaches into the points of damage and begins to touch them.

I have recently had the experience of having a series of treatments on the soft tissue in my lower back. The physical therapist I'm seeing is working on a point of injury that happened a dozen years ago. The work is slow, painful, and decidedly unflashy. But in each session, as he works simply on the tightnesses he can palpate, something progressively lets go into the more underlying parts of the injury. It's more painful each time, but each time I leave with a slightly greater range of motion, and a sense that we are getting to the bottom of things. This is the way therapeutic attunement works. It responds to what's there in the moment, and opens the way to deeper and deeper attunements, closer and closer to the root of things, over time. This is why listening deeply with the whole satellite dish available to us is of such enormous importance. It takes us to the bedrock of the thing.

Hope

There's another part to this, I think best expressed in a piece by Loewald written in 1960. In Loewald's language, it is about holding a vision for who this person is beyond the damage; beyond the constrictions. He observes that it is the privileged call of a parent to imagine who a particular child will become; how they will develop and stretch into themselves over time. It is not the parent's job to impose an identity on a child, but to hold a place inside for who they might become, and to give room for that to emerge.

We do this as therapists. This piece of the process is critical, even if completely (and necessarily) unstated. We hold the hope. We see the potential. We make room for that within us, and in that process, often necessarily quietly, we confer hope. The simple act of believing in another human being is a powerful act. Seeing and believing in another with accuracy is a powerful intervention.

Years ago when I did a rotation at the brain and spinal cord injury unit at Valley Medical Center, I was outside a set of glass double doors leading into the central lobby of the place. I saw a youngish man begin slowly and unsteadily to try to negotiate opening the door to get in. As I had learned to do on that rotation, I asked him simply, "Would you like some help with that?" "No thanks, ma'am," he answered. "It's taken me five years to be able to open this door myself." That was it. But it's stuck with me ever since. Someone looked at this young man in the early days and months of his injury and held a vision for what he could reclaim one day. Who he could be. It gave him the courage to struggle when all there was for him was the struggle.

We do this. It's a necessary part of things. Freud (1906) called psychoanalysis "a cure through love." It's not that our love is curative. It's more that it's positional. It puts us in our place. It enables us to see and hold who this person might become, and it enables us to stay with it through the long and often painful process of the becoming.

Constructions

This is linked to a notion that I have, over time, come to see as pivotal to the process of psychodynamic work. I used the phrase "grace and truth" a few chapters ago. I want to drill down on this a bit.

Lacan (1953) felt that we construct ourselves in language, meaning that over time, we build a narrative of ourselves to ourselves—what we think we are like, what we think are our capacities, our limitations, our necessities, our passions. This narrative is prominently reflective of early experience, immature perspectives, family myths, cultural constrictions, primitive thinking, defenses that keep parts of the picture out of our awareness. We build this "self" image in language, whether or not we speak it explicitly to ourselves. Lacan felt that one of the cornerstones of the therapy process is the progressive *deconstruction* of this early fabrication of ourselves, and the subsequent *reconstruction* of ourselves, once again, in language. Dan Siegel (2010) and current interpersonal neurobiologists have termed this process constructing a "coherent narrative."

This is tidy wording, but it refers to a decidedly untidy process. Messy because the language we settle on as our self-definition satisfies many simultaneous linear/emotional equations within. To disturb any part of this psychological edifice means ultimately to de-stabilize the whole of it.

Emotional Truth

But here's the other piece. We humans are truth-seeking beings. Something always remains disturbed within us when the story we are telling ourselves about who we are is not quite true, or not quite complete.

The task of telling ourselves the emotional truth is part of being alive to our own experience (I don't think we talk about this nearly enough in our field). It's what we're attempting to achieve every step of the way in psychotherapy: the capacity to tell ourselves and to tell the other the truth of things. If we think about it, every defense is an assault on emotional truth. Denial, displacement, repression—just gradations and variations on the theme of hiding the emotional truth from ourselves. We leave out the pieces of the story we feel and know that we can't presently bear; that would destabilize the whole.

Emotional truth. How is this related to the endgame? What is the function of emotional truth? Why do we need this in order to take up our rightful place as humans? The answer is simple, really. It is our premise. It's the thing upon which the rest of us is built. If we have *this* wrong, nothing else can be right. If the emotional truth at the bottom of things is compromised, we have to erect a whole series of compensations, each of which is a compromise of who or what we were meant to be, how we were meant to stand, how much of us we are truly able to put into play. And, like a house with a compromised foundation, the compensations are necessary to keep the structure intact, but signal and reflect that we are less steady; require more maintenance; provide a less secure shelter; and, in moments, may threaten total collapse.

We seem as humans to know this about ourselves, and to be restless inside about the compromises of truth we've done or have had to do along the way. The compromises constrict us; restrict our range of motion in ways that become more and more evident to us over time.

The only way out is through the emotional truth of things. But—and we know this intuitively as well—this truth is searing, like debriding a wound. It's painful. Necessary. Difficult. Requires the decision to go forward at every point. Seems not worth it sometimes. And we somehow know that if we undertake this deconstruction task recklessly, or without proper support, it might leave us in worse shape than if we were just to leave the thing alone.

I'll give you a brief example. As I described earlier, one of my patients had captioned the environment of her growing up with the term "benign neglect." With this rather compacted phrase, she had gathered up a whole array of experiences she had had growing up, and had downsized the truth of things to herself. As a child, for instance, she would often go to school without food, perhaps having nothing to eat until dinnertime. She was a bed-wetter until adolescence, eliciting no apparent curiosity about what might be happening from her caregivers. She began drug and alcohol use in middle school (again without parental intervention). Her passions for singing and dance were completely unattended. She was an invisible presence in an environment marked by maternal absence and paternal rage. She withdrew into herself.

The story she had told herself—that the neglect was "benign"—had left out the personal impact of these moments of her experience. It had also protected and preserved her view of the adults in the house—let them off the hook. She compensated as a youngster by developing an avoidant attachment style, not really feeling the need for anything emotionally sustaining from humans. She had suffered progressively as an adult from a sense of internal alienation and depression. Her narrative had made the absences in her young life less painful for her, but had had the unintended consequence of freezing the familiar internal pieces in place for her.

Her adult relationships provided her with little real support or intimacy. She kept replaying the early drama over and over again in her life, like a musical recording stuck in one spot. Her unrevised narrative preserved the familiar for her, and kept a feeling of stability for her, but at the cost of her being unable fully to inhabit the present—her sense of giving or receiving interpersonal aliveness in her experience.

The truth of things has so many dimensions. It tells us how to think and feel about ourselves and others, our relationship to those others, our expectation of ourselves and others, our expectations of life. It tells us about our history; our root system. It tells us what our capacities and limits are; what we might even attempt as humans, and how we feel about ourselves in those attempts. It determines what we think about, dream about, even feel in our bodies. It is our bedrock.

"With"

Recently, a patient came to my office and handed me a multi-colored rock about the size of a small peach. "How would you describe this?" she asked. Knowing that part of our connection has been made over our shared love of words, I quickly culled through my mind and came up with "variegated." "Actually," she responded, "it's brecciated." "A new word!" I exclaimed. "Tell me what it means!" She said, "Well, you see that the rock has different colored veins in it?" "Yes," I responded, examining the gray-green and yellow sample more closely. "The original rock was jasper," she continued. "See the greenish parts? Those are jasper. But the forces of nature acted on the jasper to cause fissures in it, and to break it into fragments. Do you see the yellow part?" "Yes," I said, now intrigued. "The yellow part is a different material entirely. At some point the yellow substance poured into the fissures of fractured jasper and in essence became geological glue, melding with the jasper and cementing its pieces back together. With the passage of time, the rock re-solidified, and became the rock I just handed to you. It is no longer jasper alone, it has melded with the yellow material and become a *brecciated* rock." With a spark of aliveness, she continued, "If we were to polish the brecciated rock, it would be stronger and more beautiful than the original jasper."

Then, she made this stunning observation: "See the yellow? The yellow is the 'us' part. It's a perfect picture of what we have done in here. It's all about being *together* in it. In this thing we are doing 'together' is where I heal. It's not just me knowing and feeling and understanding. It is doing these things *with you* that is what fills the gaps between my fragmented pieces of self. That is what has led from my being crushed into disconnected pieces into a 'brecciated' whole. See, you and me together—it's that 'we' that makes up the filler between the parts of my formerly fragmented self."

My patient was expressing intuitively what modern neuroscience has begun to demonstrate: that there is a re-regulation of the emotional brain that occurs in the mix between therapist and patient; that there is a world of potency in the intersubjective mix that characterizes the attuned therapeutic relationship over time.

So this *together* thing is where we as therapists begin to fit in, in the deconstruction and reconstruction process. We provide several things at once. For one thing, we become a companion in the truth-journey with our patients. Somehow as humans, in the moments when we're most scared, most hurt, most hopeless in our lives, the presence of an*other* seems to help. The presence of the other settles us. It makes the overwhelming less paralyzing.

As therapists, we do this "being present" with and for our patients. One patient expressed it to me this way: "We explore the unlit caves together. You are right there, right behind me. You hold the flashlight so I can see just enough ahead. It gives me the courage to keep looking. Sometimes, you say, 'hmmm—let's look over there.'"

In many ways, these are the kinds of explorations that perhaps their primary caretakers were absent for. If we can stay emotionally present, it reaches deeply into the psyche of our patients and provides both courage and relief. These things are needed. The pain of the journey has been a lifetime in the avoiding. We become companions (and sometimes guides) in the truth-journey.

A More Benign Superego

So, companions in the journey. In the midst of the journey, we offer what Rogers (1989) labeled as unconditional positive regard, but what Strachey (1934) described, perhaps more precisely, as providing a more benign superego. We pry back the ordinary voices of disapprobation (that are part of the glue that holds the rickety compensatory structures in place), and allow the truth to emerge without the usual self-attack—without a child's self-blame, or distortion of responsibility. So much of a child's coping strategy in adverse environments is to take upon him or herself the responsibility for what is going wrong (Herman, 1992). And oddly, so much of an adult's coping strategy is to step away from responsibility for what is going wrong.

From the stance of therapist, both of these misalignments can be observed without the shame and blame that is their ordinary alloy, and that tend to block them from consciousness. Over time, a patient can begin to benefit from such binocular vision (Bion, 1965)—can begin to see their role both from within their experience and from without it—and they can begin to incorporate the therapist's point of view as well. This affords the patient a new freedom to explore formerly shame-filled territory with less hesitation; with more truth.

A Clinical Moment

I'll give you a rather poignant example of this process. A young male computer programmer whom I saw for several years was becoming progressively aware of being out of touch with moments of his experience. This was, as we explored it, secondary to having been completely left on his own as an infant—*literally* not having ever been picked up and held as a baby in times of distress; orphaned at age three months—this, during the time when his right brain relational structures should have been being brought alive by attuned caretaking.

He had spent his life feeling out of touch with himself and others. He had a strangely stilted manner with me, and was someone whom I experienced for a long time as not really inhabiting his physical body. So, as he became more and more able to explore his feelings of disconnection, he came into the office one day for the second of his twice-weekly sessions, and, upon settling into his chair said to me simply, "I think I've remembered something." (I'll never forget this exchange.) He explained to me (and to himself) that he was now understanding, for the first time, that he may have date-raped two women in college. He slowly put the scenes together for himself in my presence. It was a terribly painful set of ego-dystonic moments—and was made possible by my ability to stand both with him and outside of him in these moments, offering that space of non-superego-infused perspective, and allowing him to come to the honest truth about some of the terrible damage his own disconnection had wrought over time.

The Role of Grace

This touches on another crucial element in our work as therapists. When I speak to myself about it, I use the word "grace." Grace and truth—for me, the double helix of the therapeutic process. Rogers called it unconditional positive regard. Existentialist writers call it "therapeutic love." Whatever words we use, it's as though we as therapists, through our holding of the person in a grace-mediated place in our own minds and psyches, are providing the containing medium for the work of truth.

Without the wrapping of myelin sheath, the nerves in the central and peripheral nervous systems don't fire efficiently. They get interrupted in their transmissions because the wiring can't take the load. The way we hold our patients over time, in the medium of love, or grace, or unconditional positive regard—whatever we call it—this is the myelin. This is what allows the work of truth to take place—truth sometimes spoken by us; often known by us but spoken by our patients. Without the myelin, the truth would be/has been too searing. With it, truth can go about its task of setting things aright inside—of finding its way into the deepest reaches of a human's experience, and correcting (the neuro literature now tell us, literally re-wiring) the unconscious half-truths and compromises along the way.

So is it necessary to like, even love, the people we work with in therapy? What about objectivity? Clinical distance? Not letting the work get to us. I hear this as a concern from beginning students all the time. How do you keep it from getting to you, emotionally? After class one night some quarters ago, after a long in-class conversation about this topic, a student lingered to talk for a while. She was in tears as she began to speak. That afternoon she had been with a family who had just that day lost their teenage son to a gang-related shooting. She wanted to tell me about her trying to contain this with them, and that the talking we had done in class that night about the real emotional impact that is part of doing the work with presence and authenticity—that our conversation made her feel not crazy. She had been deeply, deeply affected. She wanted to know that this was not wrong to feel.

It seems in my experience as though my best work takes place in this special medium of emotional openness to the other. I don't always like the people who come to me at first. Don't always feel a connection; sometimes, even, I feel the opposite at first. And often what I feel is congruent with how they've occupied their own interpersonal world; how their interpersonal world has encountered and experienced them. But the slow and steady progression is toward an opening inside, toward and from the other. A touching of spirits and psyches over time. An *us*.

Necessary, But Not Sufficient

It is intimate work we do. We walk around within the most tender and vulnerable parts of another person. We meet those parts with often the most tender and vulnerable parts of ourselves. This opening of ourselves to ourselves and to the other—this is the lovely and ultimately love-mediated part of the work. But—and this is important—our capacity to love isn't the point. It is, as the rule in logic goes, necessary but not sufficient. It provides a medium, but isn't in itself the healing force. The truth part is the healing force; the grace part makes the truth part possible. They work in tandem. One without the other isn't strong enough for the job.

It's feeling work we do. But the feelings generated in us and in our patients are often unanticipated. From our end as therapists, if we bring our own aliveness to the process, it includes feelings of longing and straining, anxiety and hurt, confusion, and yes, even of love and affection. These are there in us, and should be there in us, if we're really showing up in the relationship. And nothing less than showing up will provide the amount of attunement, grace, and truth required for the work to go as deeply as it needs to go.

The Love Part

Truly, we come to love our patients: their courage, their commitment, their particularities, their essence. There is, however, when things are going well, a kind of asymmetry that can develop in the relationship over time—an asymmetry in the direction of love from our patients toward us. This asymmetry is also something we bear as therapists.

I once received the following paragraph from a patient, commenting on this development in our therapy. It was from a patient I didn't know at first if I could enjoy working with. This was seven years into our work. Overcoming much ambivalence, she read this piece out loud to me in the session.

> It's happened. This clichéd thing has happened. I've fallen in love with my therapist. It's what you do. You set it up—make all the conditions right. I step into it. It's clichéd, and yet so very real. I'm with you; I feel an aliveness that I've always been meant to feel, that I've never felt. I think about you; about our times; about what it feels like deep in my soul to be in your presence; to be held in your presence. It's happened. I no longer want to skirt around it. It's here. And I don't know if this thing has to change over time into something else, and I give this what I have with you up to have this with someone else. I don't know what comes next.

She awaited my response. I tried to talk to her with the same measure of emotional honesty that she had offered to me—without using the words, "I love you too," which can be phony and thin, and aren't really the point. I also had Winnicott in the back of my mind: the agreement never to ask whether a transitional object was created or found. Besides, my capacity to hold someone in love inside isn't the point—isn't why she came. It's part of the medium of the therapy, but isn't the point of things. So this is how I talked to her about it.

I said that the word—that word *cliché*—is such an assault to what really goes on in the intimacy and realness of our relationship. I said that it's only clichéd when someone tries to characterize it to people outside of it. That it's a sacred thing, and that I've never seen the media get it right. That it involves love; is born in love; brings forth love. And that the love, once built, stays. It allows a reaching through this love to other loves, without ever losing this one. Like the one-year-old I saw last night. The look in his eyes toward his mama. It will always be there; others will build on top of it. That the important thing is not how I love, but how your love—your capacity to love has been awakened within you—brought real, here. That it's completely sacred, what is, between us.

Finally, of Course, Failure

Let me mention one final piece crucial to the process of moving toward the *right* in our patients. It came up this week in a poignant way with one of my current patients. I was asking about her reticence to share certain things with me—whether her choosing not to share was a product of perceived disinterest or chronic distrust. She said at first that she's capable of perceiving disinterest when it's not there. I pressed in on this response, and she finally shared that she perceives disinterest in me when things she's brought up are "walked around"—not explored, not brought up again, allowed to go quietly by the wayside.

She was telling me in that moment something really very important about how I work with her—and how I fail her in the work. I recognized instantly and with a deep sense of pain inside that she was telling the truth of things to me in this moment. I said a few words in response. Then I remember saying to her simply, "OK, this is really landing inside. I'll need to take some time with it. We'll talk about it more then. Would that be ok?" And we did.

This is an incredibly important piece of what we do. We *fail* our patients— unintentionally, unconsciously, painfully, humanly, but inevitably, we fail our patients. Our capacity to show up in these moments, with honesty, openness, vulnerability—Winnicott (1955) felt that these moments are often the most healing moments in a therapy. Because *this* experience—to tell a parent the truth of how they have hurt us, and to have them take that in and do emotional work with it— this was the very thing that was often woefully missing from their parents' attempts at attuned parenting. If we're real to the work, these are moments when we must show up with honesty, humility, presence.

Endgame?

So, endgame. How do we know when we're there? How do we know that something that was wrong has become right for our patient? That what they didn't know they'd come for—not consciously—is now there. I like how Hanna Levensen (1995) writes about this. Simply put, she says, we feel a shift. Whatever was the strain, the anxiety, the difficulty, the flatness, the deadness, the induced fear in us—whatever was the strain—is no longer there. In its place, there is a sense of aliveness, of comfort, of new intrapersonal and interpersonal vitality; often, of creativity and playfulness; of authenticity that we can enjoy and interact with.

For some, it's expressed in symptomatic changes, like the woman in the overeaters group who is finding that she no longer fits in plus-sized clothing. For some, like the man who did such real interpersonal damage in his disconnectedness, it was expressed in a certain re-inhabiting of his psyche-soma—even his bodily presence. For others, it's a renovation in their capacity to feel and receive love. It is the right.

I received the following note from a patient of mine—a writer—who put what she had experienced in our work into words so much better than I ever could. It was on the eve of the winter solstice, three years ago. This was how she expressed it:

> Tomorrow is the longest night of the year and when the night is over the days will finally begin to lengthen. It is so dark in my house, so dark with only my oil lamp burning and a single stick of incense glowing from a corner. I am thinking of what to give you for Christmas but I do not have what I want. I wanted to take a really good picture of my little geranium, the last flower of the year, but I was not happy with the picture that I took with my new camera. I have the one I took with my old camera, so maybe I'll give you that one, in a nice frame. This is what I want to give you because a true geranium was one of the flowers I brought you. It was the one you said was "painterly." This was a word I did not know. You gave me this new word. I don't know why, but this is important to me.
>
> [words about her own writing, being a writer]
>
> You are helping me become myself, that's it, plain and simple. And for this, I thank you. What we do is such amazing magic, such incredible conjuring. This whole process seems beyond possibility and yet I am living it and so must believe in it. This whole process, this thing that happens between us, this thing that you and my subconscious are doing together as the rest of me tries to keep up is the thing that I most believe in. I thank you for this. I thank you for being who you are. I thank you for all your hard work with me and for your willingness to wait so quietly and patiently while I figure things out. I thank you for the way you seed my subconscious in the same way a desperate farmer might seed stubborn rain clouds so that they finally let loose the sweet water they are hoarding upon parched cracked soil. So, I basically give up trying to figure out what to give you and will settle for the photograph of the little geranium, the one taken with my old camera, because it symbolizes your gift to me of a word, and that gift symbolizes so much of what we do together, the use of words and the silence between them that are making me whole.

This is the endgame. The right is the endgame. This is what we do in this process of psychodynamic psychotherapy. It's an art—an art acquired slowly and yes, fitfully over time. We feel our way along. We create pictures we hadn't known were there within us; pictures we hadn't known were within the other. We put all the conditions in place—the ones we've studied and practiced and been supervised in over time. Then, day after day, hour after hour, we sit with a blank canvas, and wait for what emerges. We are surprised by it, moved by it, expanded by it, and yes, even ourselves, made whole by it. This is the acquired art. This is why we came.

REFERENCES

Ainsworth, M., Blehar, M., Waters, E. & Wall, S. (1978). *Patterns of attachment.* Hillsdale, NJ: Erlbaum.

Atwood, G. & Stolorow, R. (1984). *Structures of subjectivity: Explorations in psychoanalytic phenomenology.* Hillsdale, NJ: Analytic Press.

Bachelard, G. (1969). *The poetics of space.* Boston, MA: Beacon Press.

Bick, E. (1968). The experience of the skin in early object relations. *International Journal of Psychoanalysis, 49,* 484–486.

Bion, W. R. (1952). Group dynamics: A review. *International Journal of Psychoanalysis, 33,* 235–247.

Bion, W. R. (1959). Attacks on linking. *International Journal of Psychoanalysis, 40,* 308–315.

Bion, W. R. (1962a). *Learning from experience.* London: Karnac.

Bion, W. R. (1962b). A theory of thinking. In *Second thoughts* (pp. 110–119). New York: Aronson.

Bion, W. R. (1965). *Transformations.* New York: Basic Books.

Bion, W. R. (1970). *Attention and interpretation.* London: Karnac.

Biringen, Z., Emde, R. & Pipp-Siegel, S. (1997). Dyssynchrony, conflict, and resolution: Positive contributions to infant development. *American Journal of Orthopsychiatry, 67,* 4–19.

Bollas, C. (1987). *The shadow of the object.* New York: Columbia University Press.

Breuer, J. & Freud, S. (1999). Studies on hysteria. In J. Strachey (Ed. and Trans.), *The standard edition of the complete psychological works of Sigmund Freud* (Vol. 2). New York: Vintage Books. (Original work published 1893–1895.)

Brown, M. R. (1982). Corticotropin-releasing factor: Actions on the sympathetic nervous system and metabolism. *Endocrinology, 111,* 928–931.

Cloitre, M. S., Bradley, C., Herman, J. L., van der Kolk, B., Pynoos, R., Wang, J. & Petkova, E. (2009). A developmental approach to complex PTSD: Childhood and adult cumulative trauma as predictors of symptom complexity. *Journal of Traumatic Stress, vol. 22*(5), 399–408.

Damasio, A. (1999). *The feeling of what happens.* Orlando, FL: Harcourt, Inc.

Decety, J. & Cacioppo, J. (Eds.). (2011). *The Oxford handbook of social neuroscience.* New York: Oxford University Press.

Fairbairn, W. R. D. (1952). *An object relations theory of the personality.* New York: Basic Books.

Faulkner, W. (1950). *Requiem for a nun.* New York: Vintage Books.

Feldman, M. (1993). The dynamics of reassurance. *The International Journal of Psychoanalysis, 74*(2), 275–285.

Freud, S. (1906). Letter to Carl Jung (1906), In *Freud and Man's Soul: An important reinterpretation of Freudian theory* (1984) by Bruno Bettelheim, New York: Knopf.

Freud, S. (1915a). *Introductory lectures on psychoanalysis.* London: Penguin Books Ltd.

Freud, S. (1999 [1911]). Formulations on the two principles of mental functioning. In J. Strachey (Ed. and Trans.), *The standard edition of the complete psychological works of Sigmund Freud,* (Vol. 12, pp. 218–226). New York: Vintage Books (Original work published 1911).

Freud, S. (1999 [1912]). The dynamics of transference. In J. Strachey (Ed. and Trans.), *The standard edition of the complete psychological works of Sigmund Freud,* (Vol. 12, pp. 97–108). New York: Vintage Books (Original work published 1912).

Freud, S. (1999 [1914]). On the history of the psychoanalytic movement. In J. Strachey (Ed. and Trans.), *The standard edition of the complete psychological works of Sigmund Freud,* (Vol. 14, pp. 7–66). New York: Vintage Books (Original work published 1914).

Freud, S. (1999 [1915b]). Instincts and their vicissitudes. In J. Strachey (Ed. and Trans.), *The standard edition of the complete psychological works of Sigmund Freud,* (Vol. 14, pp. 111–140). New York: Vintage Books (Original work published 1915).

Freud, S. (1999 [1915c]). The unconscious. In J. Strachey (Ed. and Trans.), *The standard edition of the complete psychological works of Sigmund Freud,* (Vol. 14, pp. 159–204). New York: Vintage Books (Original work published 1915).

Freud, S. (1999 [1923]). The ego and the id. In J. Strachey (Ed. and Trans.), *The standard edition of the complete psychological works of Sigmund Freud,* (Vol. 19, pp. 1–66). New York: Vintage Books (Original work published 1923).

Gerhardt, S. (2004). *Why love matters: How affection shapes a baby's brain.* New York: Routledge.

Greenberg, J. & Mitchell, S. (1983). *Object relations in psychoanalytic theory.* Cambridge, MA: Harvard University Press.

Greenspan, S. I. (1989). *The development of the ego: Implications for personality theory, psychopathology, and the psychotherapeutic process.* Minnesota: International Universities Press.

Herman, J. (1992). *Trauma and recovery.* New York: Basic Books.

Hogan, K. & Stubbs, R. (2003). *Can't get through: Eight barriers to communication.* Grenta, LA: Pelican Publishing Company.

Horner, A. (1984). *Object relations and the developing ego in therapy.* Northvale, NJ: Jason Aronson, Inc.

Iacoboni, M., Molnar-Szakacs, I., Gallese, V., Buccino, G., Mazziotta, J. C. & Rizzolatti, G. (2005). Grasping the intentions of others with one's own mirror neuron system. *Public Library of Science Biology, 3*(3), 1–14.

Ireland, M. S. (2003). *The art of the subject: Necessary illusion and speakable desire in the analytic encounter.* New York: Other Press.

Jung, C. G. (1955). *Modern man in search of a soul.* Boston: Houghton Mifflin Harcourt.

Kahn, M. (2002). *Basic Freud.* New York: Basic Books.

Kardiner, A. (1941). *The traumatic neuroses of war.* New York: Paul B. Hoeber.

Klein, M. (1935). A contribution to the psychogenesis of manic-depressive states. *International Journal of Psychoanalysis, 16,* 145–174.

Klein, M. (1946). Notes on some schizoid mechanisms. *International Journal of Psychoanalysis*, *27*, 99–110.

Lacan, J. (1953). The function and field of speech and language in psychoanalysis. In *Ecrits* (pp. 197–268). New York: W.W. Norton & Company, 1966.

Lacan, J. (2007). The function and field of speech and language in psychoanalysis. In B. Fink (Trans.), *Ecrits: The first complete edition in English*. New York: W.W. Norton & Co. (Original work published 1966).

Lecours, S. & Bouchard, M. (1997). Dimensions of mentalisation: Outlining levels of psychic transformation. *The International Journal of Psychoanalysis*, *78*(5), 855–875.

Levensen, H. (1995). *Time-limited dynamic psychotherapy: A guide to clinical practice*. New York: Basic Books.

Lewis, T., Amini, F. & Lannon, R. (2001). *A general theory of love*. New York: Vintage Books.

Lipari, J. (2000, Aug. 27). First impressions count with your newborn: Early months time for emotional, cognitive development. *Boston Herald*.

Loewald, H. W. (1960). On the therapeutic action of psychoanalysis. *International Journal of Psychoanalysis*, *41*, 16–33.

McDougall, J. (1989) *Theatres of the body: A psychoanalytic approach to psychosomatic illness*. New York: W.W. Norton & Company.

Nelson, J. (2012). *What made Freud laugh: An attachment perspective on laughter*. East Sussex, NY: Routledge.

Ogden, T. (1982). *Projective identification and psychotherapeutic technique*. Northvale, NJ: Jason Aronson, Inc.

Ogden, T. (1986). *The matrix of the mind*. Northvale, NJ: Jason Aronson, Inc.

Ogden, T. (1989). *Primitive edge of experience*. Northvale, NJ: Jason Aronson, Inc.

Ogden, T. (1994). *Subjects of analysis*. Northvale, NJ: Jason Aronson, Inc.

Ogden, T. (1997). *Reverie and interpretation*. Northvale, NJ: Jason Aronson, Inc.

Ogden, T. (2001). *Conversations at the frontier of dreaming*. London: Karnac.

Ogden, T. (2005). *This art of psychoanalysis*. East Sussex, NY: Routledge.

Ogden, T. (2009). *Rediscovering psychoanalysis*. London: Routledge.

Panksepp, J. & Biven, L. (2012). *The archaelogy of mind: Neuroevolutionary origins of human emotions*. New York: W.W. Norton & Co.

Perry, B. D., Pollard, R., Blaicley, T., Baker, W. & Vigilante, D. (1995). Childhood trauma, the neurobiology of adaptation and "use-dependent" development of the brain: How "states" become "traits." *Infant Mental Health Journal*, *16*, 271–291.

Peterson, E. (1980). *A long obedience in the same direction*. Illinois: InterVarsity Press.

Pollak, S. D., Cicchetti, D., Hornung, K. & Reed, A. (2000). Recognizing emotion in faces: Developmental effects of child abuse and neglect. *Developmental Psychology*, *36*, 679–668.

Rizzolatti, D., Fadiga, L., Gallese, V. & Fogassi, L. (1996). Premotor cortex and the recognition of motor actions. *Cognitive Brain Research*, *3*, 131–141.

Rogers, C. (1989). A client-centered/person-centered approach to therapy. In H. Kirschenbaum & V. L. Henderson (Eds.), *The Carl Rogers Reader*. New York: Houghton Mifflin Co.

Saarela, M., Hlushchuk, Y., Williams, A., Schürmann, M., Kalso, E. & Hari, R. (2007). The compassionate brain: Humans detect intensity of pain from another's face. *Cerebral Cortex*, *17*(1), 230–237.

Sandler, J. (1976). Countertransference and role responsiveness. *International Review of Psychoanalysis*, *3*, 43–47.

Sandler, J. & Rosenblatt, B. (1962). The concept of the representational world. In R. Eissler, A. Solnit, A. Freud, & M. Kris (Eds.) *The Psychoanalytic Study of the Child* (Vol 17, pp. 128–145). New Haven, CT: Yale University Press.

Schore, A. N. (2009). Attachment trauma and the developing right brain: Origins of pathological dissociation. In P. F. Dell & J. A. O'Neil (Eds.), *Dissociation and the dissociative disorders: DSM-V and beyond* (pp. 107–141). New York: Routledge.

Schore, A. N. (2012). *The science of the art of psychotherapy*. New York: W.W. Norton & Co.

Siegel, D. J. (2008). *The neurobiology of "we": How relationships, the mind, and the brain interact to shape who we are* [Audio CD]. Sounds True Audio Learning Course.

Siegel, D. J. (2010). *Mindsight: The new science of personal transformation*. New York: Bantam Books.

Siegel, D. J. (2012 [1999]). *The developing mind: How relationships and the brain interact to shape who we are*. New York: Guilford Press.

Spitz, R. A. (1945). Hospitalism: An inquiry into the genesis of psychiatric conditions in early childhood. *Psychoanalytic Study of the Child, 1*, 53–74.

Stern, D. N. (1985). *The interpersonal world of the infant*. New York: Basic Books.

Stern, D. N. (2004). *The present moment in psychotherapy and everyday life*. New York: W.W. Norton & Co.

Strachey, J. (1934). The nature of the therapeutic action of psychoanalysis. *International Journal of Psychoanalysis, 15*, 127–159.

Tronick, E. (2007). *The neurobehavioral and social-emotional development of infants and children*. New York: W.W. Norton & Company.

Tronick, E. & Cohn, J. (1989). Infant-mother face-to-face interaction: Age and gender differences in coordination and the occurrence of miscoordination. *Child Development, 60*, 85–92.

Tronick, E., Adamson, L. B., Als, H. & Brazelton, T. B. (1975, April). Infant emotions in normal and perturbated interactions. Paper presented at the biennial meeting of the Society for Research in Child Development, Denver, CO.

van der Kolk, B. (2006). The body keeps the score. In Figley, C. R. (Ed.), *Mapping trauma and its wake: Autobiographic essays by pioneer trauma scholars* (pp. 211–226). New York: Routledge.

Waters, F., Hamilton, C. & Weinfeld, N. (2000). The stability of attachment security from infancy to adolescence and early adulthood: General introduction. *Child Development, 71*, 678–683.

Wicker, B., Keysers, C., Plailly, J., Royet, J. P., Gallese, V. & Rizzolatti, G. (2003). Both of us disgusted in my insula: The common neural basis of seeing and feeling disgust. *Neuron, 40*, 655–664.

Wilkowski, B. & Robinson, M. (2012). When aggressive individuals see the world more accurately: The case of perceptual sensitivity to subtle facial expressions of anger. *Personality and Social Psychology Bulletin, 38*(4), 540–553.

Winnicott, D. W. (1947). Hate in the countertransference. In *Through paediatrics to psychoanalysis* (pp. 194–203). Levittown, PA: Brunner/Mazel.

Winnicott, D. W. (1949). Mind and its relation to the psyche-soma. In *Through paediatrics to psychoanalysis* (pp. 243–254). Levittown, PA: Brunner/Mazel.

Winnicott, D. W. (1954). Metapsychological and clinical aspects of regression within the psychoanalytical set-up. In *Through paediatrics to psychoanalysis* (pp. 278–294). Levittown, PA: Brunner/Mazel.

Winnicott, D. W. (1955). Clinical varieties of transference. In *Through paediatrics to psychoanalysis* (pp. 295–299). Levittown, PA: Brunner/Mazel.

Winnicott, D. W. (1960). The theory of the parent-infant relationship. In *The maturational processes and the facilitating environment: Studies in the theory of emotional development* (pp. 37–55). London: Hogarth.

Winnicott, D. W. (1962). The aims of psychoanalytical treatment. In *The maturational processes and the facilitating environment: Studies in the theory of emotional development* (pp. 166–170). London: Hogarth.

Winnicott, D. W. (1967). Mirror role of mother and family in child development. In *Playing and reality* (pp. 111–118). Philadelphia: Brunner-Routledge.

Winnicott, D. W. (1968). The use of an object and relating through identifications. In *Playing and reality* (pp. 86–94). Philadelphia: Brunner-Routledge.

INDEX

Note: Page numbers in **bold** are for figures.